MY LIFE AND OTHER GAMES

MY LIFE
and
OTHER GAMES

Ian Messiter

FOURTH ESTATE · LONDON

First published in Great Britain in 1990 by
Fourth Estate Limited
Classic House
113 Westbourne Grove
London W2 4UP

British Library Cataloguing in Publication Data
Messiter, Ian
My life and other games.
1. Great Britain. Radio and Television programmes. Great
Britain. Broadcasting – Biographies
I. Title
791.44092

ISBN 1-872180-61-2

Typeset by York House Typographic Ltd, York Avenue, London W7
Butler & Tanner Ltd, Somerset

Writing this has been fun. It was written for my wife, Enid;
for my daughter, Susan Beaumont, and her three children, James,
Toby and Emily; for my son, Malcolm, and his daughter, Helen.

Note

This book is as accurate as I could make it. As I have never kept diaries except for appointments – and all those before 1969 are lost – I have leaned heavily on memory, both my own and those of friends, for the accuracy of this book.

Where possible, relevant chapters have been sent to those mentioned in them for checking. Those involved were kind and pointed out where my enthusiasm had had the better of truth. Corrections were made accordingly. But many whom I knew in childhood and during the war are dead so cannot be called upon.

Central Independent Television even had to correct the part about 'Steal' which relates to 1990, for which I thank them, as I do Capital Radio, the BBC, friends and others, especially my dear wife Enid who has had to endure reading sections of the book over and over again.

Ian Messiter
London, 1990

Contents

MY LIFE AND OTHER GAMES

1
Miners and snobs

THIS BOOK IS MOSTLY ABOUT a series of embarrassments, and good friends. It is not a story of success, sweetness and sagacity.

I was born on 2 April 1920 in Dudley, the mining and manufacturing town eight miles from Birmingham and six from Wolverhampton. 1920 was the year when Joan of Arc was canonised, when Prohibition started in the USA, the Marconi Company made the first public broadcast at Writtle and the first gramophone record was recorded electrically. It was therefore a most appropriate year for the birth of someone who was later to be closely connected with the world of reproduced sound. In the world of cinema, *The Cabinet of Dr Caligari* with Conrad Veidt was first seen; Welwyn Garden City was founded; in 1920 the decade of airships began; Galsworthy wrote *In Chancery*.

My father, a surgeon and general practitioner who would rather have specialised in the care of children, was obliged to become a partner of his own father, also a surgeon and GP. Father was overworked and underpaid by his father and mother. That medicine was (and is) said to be such a noble profession is some sort of a defence against its being such a poorly paid business, when looked at in relation to the immense knowledge and skills involved in its practice.

Father's mother, my Grandmother Messiter, lived in a huge Victorian monstrosity of a house not far away on the other side of the road; she was chairman of the board of the local hospital, which she ruled with ignorance and iron. She had a domineering personality and thought any display of either humour or sadness as vulgar as raising one's voice. She was seldom heard to laugh. She never lost an argument, but she was invariably wrong, a faculty my sister inherited from her, along with untidiness. This last deficiency is also in my blood, along with many others, and I passed it on to our daughter, Susan, and our son, Malcolm.

Grandmother Messiter owned the house we lived in, having inherited it, via her late husband, from a Messiter, her grandfather-in-law, who had built it during the reign of George IV. The rent we paid to her was heavy and she did nothing in return. When repairs and upkeep demanded money, my father paid.

The house had a very large entrance-hall, round which the front staircase swept; this was guarded by a seemingly endless balustrade down which it was dangerous and forbidden fun to slide – which my sister and I did frequently, often without being caught. When we *were* caught, she was sent to her room. I was first whipped and then sent to my room.

For some mysterious reason, which Father kept to himself but hinted at, boys were improved by beatings; however, girls, if beaten, would develop some undefined sexual warp. This was never explained but, as Father had said it was so, Mother said it must be true; only Mother would never have used the word 'sexual'.

I was also whipped for bed-wetting and told I was doing it on purpose because I was too lazy to get out of bed. It was a form of torture to wake up in the morning in wet sheets and have to wait for what seemed an age for some grown-up to find out. The whole day would be spent in fearful anticipation of Father's return in the evening from his patients or from the hospital, at which time he would whip me with a leather strap. However, I grew out of this habit by the time I was seven.

I could never explain myself, as I had such a terrible stutter; speech was almost impossible, especially since my sister, and sometimes even Mother, could not resist copying me. This always made me worse. Eventually I learned not to speak to either of them because of the dread of being made fun of. It didn't take long to learn that stuttering did not occur when I was singing or talking to my best friend, dog Sago.

On the rare occasions when we were allowed to have friends to tea, it was a wonderful house in which to play a game we called 'Cocky'. This game was only possible because so many rooms had two doors. Starting in the hall, we could run through the dining-room and into the pantry or straight on through the kitchen out into the back hall and either into the patients' waiting-room and so into my father's dispensary or through his consulting-room round into the downstairs hall again or, by diversion, from the back hall into the scullery, or up the back stairs and into odd boxrooms or along the landings past various bedrooms, and then rush headlong down the front stairs and into the hall again.

It was not wise to go from the hall into the drawing-room, because the grown-ups would be there and they would usually be cross or impatient at our entry, since this was still an age in which children 'should be seen and not heard'. In our case, we should not be seen too often either; as the drawing-room was one of the few rooms with only one door, there was no escape in it from whoever had been appointed Cocky. Nor was it wise to go down into the cellars with their various cobwebbed grottoes and slate shelves of wines, clearly dated bottles of port and with rows of coarse, unloved Staffordshire pot of little grace, which had been given to Father by patients either from gratitude or from a dislike of Staffordshire pot – which was why it was all doomed to gloom, cobwebs and damp.

In the hall on the ground floor was a long, high-backed, Cromwellian oak settle, covered with a huge polar-bear skin. On the seat was a green horsehair-stuffed cushion, over eight feet long, made of some thick material which lay on a web of rope. Anyone caught by Cocky would have to sit on this and call out as a warning to the others where he knew (or thought) Cocky to be, until rescued by another player. To be rescued, a player had to touch you; after rescue, the freed player would dash up the front or back stairs until he or she was caught again and put on their honour to return to the settee. The object of the game was for Cocky to catch all the players and dispatch them to the settee.

In those days we children ate lunch with our governess or nanny, apart from our parents except on Saturdays and Sundays. We were brought down to the drawing-room for tea, at which there were always delicious crumpets and toast with Patum Peperium or butter and jam. If she called at teatime, Grandmother never missed an opportunity to remind us: 'When I was a child we were allowed butter or jam. Never both,' in such a way as to make my sister and me feel guilty.

Much later on we were allowed to eat lunch with Mother and Father on weekdays too; however, we were not allowed to speak because, as Mother would say like a record with its needle stuck in the groove, 'Your father is worried.'

Father was always worried; in retrospect, I believe it might have been because he was a man with a conscience, who could not forget a patient. He never distinguished between his rich or titled, paying patients and his 'panel' patients, whom he treated for virtually nothing. I remember waking one night, when I was about nine years old, to see him on the landing outside my half-open door. I put on the light and saw that he was dressed.

'Where are you going?'

'Go to sleep.'

'Where are you going?'

'It's three in the morning. Go to sleep. I have to go down to the hospital to see a woman whose leg I took off this morning. She'll be in pain now and she trusts me implicitly. I have to see how she is. And the fact I'm bothering to turn out in the night will in itself help her.' Those aren't his exact words, but they reflect the tone of his explanation, to which he added, 'When you're a doctor, you'll understand.'

It was always taken for granted that I must, would and could only be a doctor when I grew up. Apart from tradition, someone would have to take the strain from Father when he was old. To that end, Father continuously drummed into me three pieces of advice concerning the medical career I never had. The first was that, if an illness could not be diagnosed or cured, I must never tell the patient it was 'nerves'. The second was that I must never tell a patient he must learn to accept his illness because nothing could be done. The third was that listening to the patient's words was often more revealing than listening to his chest.

In a sense I *am* a doctor, because in my trade I create situations that generate laughter, and laughter is undoubtedly good for us all. A good laugh can do more for your health than a pill.

In 1925 coalminers were discontented with their lot, and for good reason. In Dudley they had to buy their own lamps. If they missed more than a couple of shifts because they had contracted the coaldust disease in their lungs, they were sacked. Many would incur cut or badly bruised heads because there were no helmets. Many would break limbs, especially when they tripped over the underground coal-truck rails or were kicked by the pit ponies.

These men could be seen every morning, trudging up the country lane (as it was then), past our house, lamp in hand, wearing filthy mining clothes. In the evenings, after long hours underground, they would be coming back, too exhausted for laughing or joking. Some, tired as they were, would have stopped at a pub, got drunk and be in need of help from their mates; others lay, paralytic, where they had fallen in the road.

In every society there are drunks; however, such were the conditions of the mines at that time, these men looked upon drunkenness as a way to blessed oblivion from the slave labour and the filth at the coal face.

I went down a coalmine as a child, taking it for granted that the miners tipped their caps to me. Feeling the coal face, I remarked it was very hot. The explanation was that the temperature rose higher, the further down we went. The detail doesn't matter today; but a week later that mine exploded, with great loss of life. There was no proper compensation at that time for widows and families.

The miners' justifiable discontent in 1925 blended naturally into the General Strike in the spring of the following year. In Dudley, gangs went around turning cars over: in those days, a car represented the exception-ally rich and was an object of envy to anyone who was earning a wage of, say, thirty shillings (£1.50) a week and trying to keep a family on it. Of course thirty shillings went a great deal further then than it would now – but, even with a newspaper at only one old penny, apples at four a penny and mild beer at threepence a pint, some people were near starvation. Stones were thrown by strikers at the windows of houses that looked prosperous.

After our dining-room window had been smashed one night, Father decided there might well be danger in our staying on. Our chauffeur, Redfern, was given orders to drive us – me, my mother, my sister and Nanny Bags, whose real name I never found out – down to a small coastal fishing village in Pembrokeshire called Little Haven.

Father said he couldn't come with us because he was needed in the town, as people were getting hurt. The miners must have realised his value too. No miner or other working man ever touched his car or broke any more of our windows. This was almost certainly due to his caring for those who were injured in the scuffles which he said were not really riots.

He never charged anyone who earned wages. But he was no social reformer. He did not believe in education for the masses, partly because he was sure that more education would be worse education, and partly because he thought society would collapse without 'the workers'. Everyone knew what he meant by 'the workers'. He never thought of himself as 'a worker' even though he often worked an eighteen-hour day and he always worked seven days a week.

We were brought up to be a pair of little snobs and were taught to look down on anyone 'in trade' because a clever businessman has the skill of acquiring more than he earns. This is a confusing thought for a child brought up to associate with the rich – but only with the rich whose money had been in their family for three or four generations. People with 'new' money were easily identified by the way they held their knives like pens instead of gripping the handle, by their use of the word 'serviette' instead of 'table napkin', and by a hundred and one other stupid details, none of which relates to real life or real values.

The better-off people were bigger. Mother would use phrases like, 'I must get the little woman round to measure for the chair covers,' or, 'The clock in the hall has gone wrong. I'll ring the little man to come round and mend it.' These statements were true: these people, eating only as much as they could afford, *were* little. Being smaller, they were naturally 'looked down on'.

This snobbery took years to eradicate. I still look back with shame on my attitude in those days. I'm not even sure it's all gone now. Our dustmen are very decent men but, while I enjoy a chat with them in the road, we have never asked any of them to dinner. For that matter, they haven't asked us to their places.

Little Haven in St Brides Bay on the Welsh coast was a little heaven to us during the General Strike. We ran wild since the governess of the time, Miss Smith, did not come with us. Nanny Bags was not so much in charge as in command. She had a large and formidable presence, in her blue frock and white apron with its heavily starched white breast-plate, looking like a galleon in full sail and smelling of disinfectant and peppermints.

My sister Joan and I knew Little Haven inside out, having spent a month of each year there during our summer holidays, so we could outwit Nanny Bags with ease. Once down on the beach we knew all the caves she would not be able to find and all the rocks she could not negotiate. There were many children there of our own age. We were never told not to associate with the village children; although the implication that we mustn't play with them was clear, no one found out how much fun we had with them.

Our stay in Little Haven was over all too soon because the strike lasted from 1 May to the 13th, when we were driven back to Dudley, lessons and loneliness.

Before the Second World War, servants would light the fires in all the rooms, and they would be blazing merrily long before we were up and dressed. They had an enchanting smell because, when Father heard that the Dudley trams were going to be abolished, he asked one of the town councillors what would happen to the wooden blocks that the tram lines were laid on. Each block was about the size of a building brick. On being told that no one had given a thought as to what to do with them, Father said he would give £5 to the local almshouses if he could have them. In those days, £5 was a great deal of money, but in 1926 coal in the Midlands was two pounds a ton. The back yard to the house measured about fifty feet long by thirty feet wide, and the blocks from the tramways filled it to a depth of six feet. That was a very large quantity indeed. In addition to the wood, the blocks were thick with tar: they had been laid on tar, joined by tar and tarred over. They burned beautifully. We were still using them in 1950, twenty-four years after the delivery. However, they did create a problem for the maids, the gardener, the daily and the chauffeur – in fact, for any member of the community who had the misfortune to work for us – because they all had to use the outside lavatory. This was in the most distant corner of the back yard, well away from the house; to reach it, there was much scrambling over the tarred blocks.

Children are very cruel. We would stand in the window and laugh while we watched people struggling and slipping as they climbed over them, especially in winter when there was snow and ice about.

Shortly before Father's death in 1951, he told me of two horrifying courses of action which both he and his father before him had always taken. One was that they both practised euthanasia on those for whom no cure was possible and to whom pain was intolerable. The other was that they swiftly ended the lives of babies who were appallingly deformed. Father assured me that neither of them pursued either of these policies without first consulting with another doctor from another area. They were never caught performing this illegal but humanitarian practice. When I displayed shock at such behaviour and asked him what right he had to play God, in reply he gave me an example of one such case: it was a baby, not three minutes old, which had a totally blank skin where its face should have been; there was one hole for a nostril and its eye was in the centre of its forehead. It was a cyclops, of whom it was impossible to determine the sex.

As I was not considered to be old enough to go to school until I reached the age of nine and anyway, according to my parents, there were no decent schools in Dudley, we had a series of governesses (who did not have to brave the outside lavatory). My sister and I were constantly warned to do better, otherwise I would end up at the Dudley Boys' Grammar School and my sister at the Dudley Girls' High School, which overlooked our garden. Both were and still are excellent schools.

This threat hung like the sword of Damocles above us, as governess after governess had the misfortune to administer reading, writing, 'rithmetic, the imports and exports of unheard-of places, and attempts to explain to us who won what in 1066.

This could not have been a very good education, because for years I was not told what Latin was. I studied it, declined nouns and so on, but, had I been told, I would rather have declined Latin. As no one had explained that it was a language, I thought it was just another of those tiresome impositions inflicted on children to be done without reason.

My parents' sword of Damocles attitude to the local schools was mistaken. Many excellent citizens have been through those schools; for instance, the accomplished Sue Lawley (of television fame) went to the Dudley Girls' High School, and there certainly aren't any signs of delinquency or ignorance in her.

During the holidays, almost daily I found myself locked up in my room with a pencil, some paper and a potty. It was here and under those conditions that I started to invent games, write little plays and short stories, and generally live in my own head. This curiously lonely upbringing may well have been the essential influence that made me create so many shows – performed, in those days, with imaginary casts with whom to converse and even argue. Later came the privilege of creating shows and writing real plays for real people. So something, good or bad, came out of this solitary life.

Alone, I made a thorough study of the polished, fossil-filled stone mantelpiece, finding one part that looked like a face with a beard; it simply begged to be given eyes and a mouth. With a nail I gave it the face and called it Father Christmas. This did not meet with adult approval.

My parents' reason for this enforced solitude was that, since no one in Dudley was good enough for us to know, we must on no account mix with shopkeepers or their children, and there wasn't anyone else with children of our age. My sister spent similar hours in her room, reading. She was never anxious to make friends and liked books better. She could have been right; however, this was a wisdom too deep for me.

I did have a friend of my own age, Hugh, who lived about five miles away in Kingswinford. But we could meet only after long telephone discussions between my mother and his aunt, his mother having died. His aunt was also a snob, and a worse one than us. I well remember Hugh once asking her for some note paper.

His aunt said, 'No one uses the expression "note paper". If you want to write a letter, you must ask for writing paper.'

'But I only want to write a note.'

And so it went on. These snobberies were made important in the 1920s and, being children, we believed them.

One afternoon we were given the money to go to the cinema with a box of chocolates because, as Hugh's aunt said, we MUST only be seen eating from a box of chocolates.

We were not allowed to sit in the stalls, the cheap seats. We MUST sit in the circle, because people in the cheap stalls smelled, they had diseases and fleas. (The last-mentioned creatures probably did live in the stalls.) This thinking was reversed in the theatre, when only the stalls were good enough, and they had to be seats in the third row. It was ostentatious to sit in the front row, as only successful tradesmen would do anything so vulgar as that.

Hugh's life ended tragically in 1940 when he was twenty. He put a gun in his mouth and deliberately blew the top of his head off because he believed what two girls told him, that he had made them pregnant. He must have slept with them during army leave, or they would not have been able to convince him. Had he not been brought up with such pretentious social ideas and with no 'proper' sense of values, he would have weathered the storm – even if those girls had been telling the truth. In fact they were not, but he never found out that neither of them was pregnant and that both, each unknown to the other, were after his money by trying to force him into marriage. With his unrealistic upbringing he could see this only as a social disaster and disgrace. Others at the time regarded his shame as twofold: first, he thought he had made two girls pregnant and, second, he had been with socially unacceptable girls.

My close friend and confidant at the time was the large dachshund, Sago, whose kennel name was Sancho Panza and whose interests, like those of his namesake were chiefly food and drink. He was not the little yapping lap-dog that so many dachshunds are today; he was a huge German hound with a body the size of an alsatian; only his legs were short.

I loved him like a brother. He was my whole audience for the games I invented. I would read him my plays, complain to him when I thought I had been mistreated, ask him whether he really believed that there was a God, especially the kind, Father Christmassy, bearded God we were told to believe in. He would gaze lovingly at me and wag his tail when asked why a God, who loved us all, still allowed disasters. Like all the wisest, however, the dog kept his own counsel; and he continued to wag his tail gently to show that, even if he didn't approve, at least he didn't disapprove.

One of my father's four brothers was vicar of Kingswinford; when he had time, he would call and rescue my sister and me from our jails. He was one of the very few who called without being invited. Uncle Arden was a kind, considerate and generous man who seemed enormous, for he was about six feet three inches tall. He had a long, solemn, lined face and a parsonical voice with that strange up-turn at the end of a sentence which today is used only by comedy vicars on TV. When asked why parsons had special voices, he said it was so they could be heard at the back of the church.

He would drive us to some church – which took the edge off the rescue – and sometimes he would let me take Sago into the church. But the ride in his car was fun and occasionally we would get a few sweets which we were allowed to eat out of a bag. A favourite sucker was Barrett's sherbet, in a red-printed yellow paper container with a tube of liquorice to suck it through. Sago hated sherbet; he tried it once only, and it made him sneeze; but he liked the liquorice.

Arden's wife, my Aunt Dorothy, was another lovely person. If he was preaching somewhere local on a Sunday, they would always come to lunch. Mother went to hear him very seldom but his mother, Mrs Over-the-road, always went, and we were taken too. My grandmother had her own pew at the church where he preached most often, and her chauffeur would drive us there. He too would attend the service, but in a pew at the back. We could always hear him slipping out as the service neared its end so that he would be ready in position by the car to hold the door open for us when we left the church. Sago was not allowed to accompany us to church on Sunday; no one ever explained why.

Father never joined us in church. One of his regular occupations during the service was to hide all playing cards because it was sinful to see them on Sundays. He was an excellent bridge player, even on Sundays, but only when he was sure his vicar brother would not call. The other item hidden from Arden was my glove puppet of a vicar, complete with dog-collar, just in case it might be considered a blasphemy.

One terrifying adventure with Sago occurred when I found one of Uncle Arden's dog-collars in the top drawer of my father's dressing-table; I put it on Sago over his real collar, from which I hung a small crucifix. Then someone came in through the front door – and, to my horror, it was Uncle Arden. Sago ran to greet him; I called Sago back, but he went on. Being a well-trained dog, he did not jump up. Prayers to Sago and God were answered.

Another of my father's brothers was a sadistic brute. When he was sure no one else was about, he would come up the long stairs to my room and, taking me by the ankles, would hold me, head down, over the balustrade with the stone floor of the hall many feet below. I was too frightened to cry out: he had told me that if I did, he might easily let go, and he would tell everyone that I had fallen over. I knew what was coming next: he would pretend to drop me. He didn't really let go – or this story would never have been written – but when he faked that drop of thirty or so inches, I was always paralysed with fear, and it would still have been impossible to make a sound even had I not been threatened with being dropped if I cried out. On telling Mother about this, she dismissed it with one word: 'Rubbish!' To this day, I cannot stand heights nor even bear to watch anyone else near a long drop. That wonderful Harold Lloyd film in which he staggers along the parapet of a New York skyscraper makes my ankles hurt in exactly the place where my uncle used to grip me.

Mrs 'Over-the-road', my Grandmother Messiter, was another irritant. She had keys to all three entrances to the house, and even to the stables, which were never locked. She would come in without any of us knowing about it. In those days she could sometimes be found in my father's consulting-room, going through his ledgers. She never showed any embarrassment at being caught. Her interest in these books dated back to when Grandfather Messiter died, in 1922. After his death, the medical practice was sold to Father, who had to take it over. Grandmother Messiter did not want the whole sum for the sale given directly to her; instead, she took a percentage of each quarter's income. I have forgotten the percentage, but it was laid down in Grandfather's will. This arrangement was what made her look closely at the books and question my mother from time to time about various expenses. Mother was frequently asked, 'Why did you need so much petrol during that month?' or, 'Why did you have to buy another set of scales for weighing patients?' or, 'What's wrong with the old sphygmomanometer [for measuring blood pressure]?' Every halfpenny was questioned.

Mother and Father were very happily married and were never known to quarrel. A very happy marriage frequently had its roots in a common enemy, in much the same way that war unites a country. Grandmother Messiter was possibly the reason Mother and Father were so happy together.

But Grandmother was strange. After her death, her will revealed a mind that some might call commonsensical, but others might think absurd. She had kept account of everything spent on her five sons. She left equal amounts to each son. Each son had to follow this up by paying back into the kitty all money spent on his clothes, books and education. This money was then redivided among the five sons. As Father and Arden had had the lion's share of education, they had to put in most. Father also had to put in the value of the medical practice and the house, which had been rented from Grandmother, after which he could consider it his own.

In 1929, when I was nine, I was sent away to my preparatory school,

Winton House, in Winchester. I envied Sago, who stayed at home while I was sent away.

This was a horrifying experience that should never have been wished even on a dog.

2
Six bottoms every Sunday

W E ALL MAKE MISTAKES in our lives; one of Father's mistakes probably started with a fixation he had about children in hospitals.

He had already upset the medical profession by saying that nurses, being mostly girls with qualifications, should not have to scrub the ward floors and that hospitals should employ ward maids for this purpose. This practice has since been adopted throughout the whole of the United Kingdom. He was right about that.

He also wrote in an article for a medical journal that he had noticed more diseases of the lungs and related organs among those who lived in smoky towns (Dudley was one) and that these diseases were even more pronounced in those who also smoked. For making such a statement he was ridiculed at the time; he was accused by some of trying to take away from the working man one of his small pleasures.

Now he was prepared to upset even more people by saying that, once a child was admitted to hospital, he or she should have no visitors from outside, because the visit almost always ended in tears and sometimes in a rise in temperature. It's comforting to know that *this* practice has not been followed and that it lasted rather less than a year in the large Guest Hospital in Dudley. It never spread to Birmingham or Wolverhampton, in spite of Father's great efforts.

But he continued this train of thought into my schooldays, which meant that, after delivering me in September 1929 to my prep school, Winton House, Winchester, neither he nor Mother would ever again make the journey from the Midlands to visit me at the school.

These matters were not mentioned as we drove down to Winchester. I must have had a bit of a social conscience even at the age of nine, because when we stopped at a roadside hotel for lunch on the way there, it seemed to me wrong that the chauffeur had to remain in the car and eat his cheese sandwiches and drink cold tea out of an old bottle, until we came out again. He could at least have been given a Thermos flask.

The car, modern for its time, was an Essex; on the front of the bonnet was a round glass disc, inside which was a thin thermometer with some red fluid in it. If this fluid rose above a certain level we had to stop until the engine cooled down again. To my regret, it stayed below this mark for the whole journey to Winchester. Nothing was allowed to stop the inexorable passage into the unknown, not even the scarcity of garages and petrol stations; there were four two-and-a-half-gallon tins of petrol, two per side, held in place with leather straps on the running-board of the car, so prayers that we would run out of petrol went unanswered.

The journey seemed interminable, and there was no way out of it. There was only one occasion for unscheduled halts: when it rained, the chauffeur, Ball, had to cut a slice of raw potato and rub it on the windscreen. This dispersed the water and, helped from the inside by a hand-operated windscreen wiper, it improved visibility.

Arrival at Winton House was filled with shocks and surprises. It was a fine afternoon when the car, which refused to break down or run out of petrol, crunched the gravel down the drive to the small circular lawn with its three or four umbrella-shaped standard roses outside the school front door that was never used by the boys. Parents walked gingerly about, unsure what to do, while apprehensive young sons stood at a wary distance to avoid the embarrassment of kisses and hugs from over-demonstrative mothers and fathers.

The chauffeur helped the school porter with my luggage which mysteriously disappeared, to be unpacked in a dormitory by a maid called Ada. For some inexplicable reason all the dormitory maids were called Ada. There were four of them, three as it happened really called Ada and the fourth, poor woman, therefore had to answer to that name from custom. Their duties seemed to be bed-making, sewing on buttons and mending our clothes. We called them skivvies, poor creatures. New and very young boys had their hair washed by them.

It was the end of an era, as my parents and I solemnly shook hands. One boy called Townsend-Rose, who was only six years old, burst into tears when his parents left; nobody comforted him. I saved my tears for the privacy of the darkness in the dormitory.

I didn't see the car going away up the drive as the headmaster's wife, Mrs Johns, commanded: 'All new boys, stand here!' We did as we were told. She went on: 'Those of you who at home are called by their Christian names will at school be known by their surnames only. There will be no Christian names used here. Which of you is Wilson?'

A small boy put up his hand. 'I am, Miss.'

'You will address me as Mrs Johns. I am not "Miss". Understand?'

'Yes.'

'Yes, what?'

'Yes, Mrs Johns.'

'That's better. Wilson, your two elder brothers are also at this school, as you know. You may have already found out that they are called Wilson

Major and Wilson Minor. You will therefore be known as Wilson Minimus.'

'Yes, Mrs Johns.'

'Now follow me into the lobby.'

We walked nervously behind her, wondering where we were being taken. The boy walking next to me asked what a lobby was. I'd never heard of one either. There was no lobby at home. It turned out to be nothing more than a concrete-floored room where, we were told, we must always change our shoes after coming in from the grounds. We were each allocated a locker and told that in the winter we must keep our rugger boots in it. The word 'locker' was also new to me.

In the middle of this, a boy put his hand up.

'Yes?'

'Mrs Johns, I want to go to the toilet.'

'We don't have any.' She stood and looked at him in silence for four or five seconds, before going on: 'There are none in this school.' She smiled patronisingly as the poor boy looked helpless and puzzled – probably wishing he was at home, as all of us did. Mrs Johns went on: 'But we do have lavatories. The door to eight of them is just behind you.' He started to move towards the door. 'Wait!' He waited, probably about to pee himself. 'Gentlemen,' she said, 'and you are all sons of gentlemen or you would not be here; gentlemen use the word "toilet" only when referring to a lady's dressing-table.'

After supper, the whole school assembled in the common room. The expression 'common room' was also new to me; the same boy who didn't know what a lobby was asked me about the common room; I couldn't help him. Everything was unfamiliar and smelled of floor polish or Jeyes Fluid.

The headmaster, Mr E. F. Johns (who was nicknamed Jumbo, possibly because he was stout, always wore a grey pin-stripe suit and had a rather long nose and huge ears), formally welcomed all the boys to the winter term, and then he told us of boys past who had moved on to various public schools. All of which meant nothing to me, since they were boys I had never met and schools I had never heard of. He smoked Turkish cigarettes endlessly, which was a useful fact to remember later, as the smell of Turkish tobacco meant he was close by.

The common room was a place of horror to some boys on Sunday mornings, at which time every boy's place in his class was read out to the whole school before he went in to chapel. All those who were bottom of the class had to assemble after chapel outside the headmaster's study and be invited in, one by one, to be 'swished'. After being swished we were expected to say, 'Thank you.' I was swished once.

It was a formality but none the less painful for that. The formal part of it was exposing a bare bottom and bending over a chair back – which has since made me wonder about the sexual inclinations of Jumbo. This was his Sunday-morning ritual. There were six forms and, as there had to be someone at the bottom of each form, that added up to six bottoms a week.

The painful part of it was both mental and physical. It started as one stood outside the headmaster's study, being able to hear others being swished. Jumbo would always beat a cushion with three strokes first, then beat the victim with four strokes – unless that victim had committed some sufficiently heinous crime to earn him six strokes. Beatings were never on any day other than that holy day, and always took place in the morning after chapel and before lunch. This meant, as in the case of one boy who I saw break a window on a Sunday afternoon, that his whole week was blighted while he waited to be swished the following Sunday.

There was an unwritten catalogue for swishings. Bottom of form: four strokes. Breaking windows: four strokes. Peeing the bed: six strokes. Fortunately I had grown out of this by now. Impertinence: four strokes. Display of temper to a master: six strokes. And so on.

On hearing that I had been swished, my father wrote to me to tell me that I had to do better or I would end up either in the Army or in the Church. This seemed to make no sense to me, since we had been brought up to revere great generals and bishops, and it also seemed an unkind side-swipe at my reverend Uncle Arden.

What went on in the outside world was a mystery to most of us, even though some daily newspapers were available in the common room. In that month of September, the Nazis were grabbing power unnoticed by almost all except Winston Churchill.

Towards the end of the winter term the name Messiter appeared in the headlines of the national newspapers. Someone read out loud from a paper: 'MESSITER'S CODED LOVE LETTERS'. Being nine years old, I had no idea what 'love letters' were. Codes were different. They could be formed by writing the alphabet backwards; that was all we knew about them.

Another headline ran: 'MAN SHOT IN LOCKED ROOM', and someone read out that a body had been found in a padlocked room. There was no trace of a gun. The padlock was on the outside and the bullet could not be found. An even greater mystery was stamped on the affair when a careful search by the police revealed that the bullet had passed through my Uncle Vivian Messiter's head but had not touched anything else. There was no graze or hole in the wall to show where the bullet had gone. This made it appear that the body must have been taken there after death – until the great pathologist, Sir Bernard Spilsbury, pointed out that this was impossible: death had been instantaneous and the body had not been moved.

There was always a rush at school in the morning to grab the *Daily*

Mirror, Telegraph or any paper, because they all carried the episodic real-life 'whodunnit'. The mystery unfolded day by day, with the morbid thought that eventually the killer would have to meet the public hangman of the day, Albert Pierrepoint, on the gallows.

Most of the boys said that I must have done it because all uncles were rich; having no children of his own, he would have left all his money to me. The facts, that this man was not really an uncle (only a cousin, several times removed) and that I had never met him, did not impress anyone.

The rush for the papers stopped when Jumbo banned them. Every parent received a letter asking that newspapers should not be sent to sons. Some of the boys clubbed together to bribe Charles, the head gardener, to fetch a paper in. Charles was an honourable man and would have none of it.

There was an anxious moment one night when a *Daily News & Westminster Gazette* was smuggled up to my dormitory by a boy, who stood on the end of his bed just before lights off, reading aloud from it to us all, hesitating and stumbling over the long words. He pronounced 'coroner' as the soft drink 'Corona', and we were laughing at him for it, making him blush with shame, when someone shouted, '*Cave!* Jumbo!'

The giggling stopped as if snipped by scissors. It was too late. He could be seen through the open door, ambling his bulk along the corridor with its red shiny composition floor, trailing his blue-grey cloud of Turkish tobacco-smoke, his gold-rimmed glasses sparkling menacingly in the yellow electric light as he drew nearer.

Jumbo's authority was absolute, and we were in awe of him. The boy standing on the end of his bed with the newspaper in his hand was as if petrified – which he probably was, knowing he could not hide the paper or deny he had been reading it to us because he had been acclaiming at the top of his piercing soprano voice.

Jumbo had certainly seen and heard the boy – and, worse, it was Jumbo's copy of the *Daily News & Westminster Gazette*, filched from that *sanctum sanctorum*, the headmaster's study, where hung the infamous half-dozen well-used canes, 'plucked,' Jumbo would say, 'by my own hand from a field near Cannes, and shaped with a handle at one end by immersion in boiling water, a craft only fully understood by Duckforth, the carpentry master.'

As the boy was led away in fearful silence by the poker-faced ambling Jumbo, it could be seen that the poor little rich boy was wearing fine silk pyjamas. Rumour had it that it was more painful to be beaten through silk than on a bare bum.

In spring and summer, great interest was taken in insects and butter-flies. The headmaster was a great collector; he had drawer after drawer of specimens pinned under glass. Some of the prettier boys were unashamedly his favourites, and he would take them with him on night-time moth hunts, when they would mix beer with treacle and smear it on trees to catch what seemed to be endless quantities of hawk moths. This was called bug-hunting, and on these occasions Jumbo was called the Big Bugger. As no small boys knew what this meant and as I didn't find out until long after leaving, it is a mystery how he came to be so labelled.

One master would call boys up to his desk to correct their work; he would put his hand up the backs of their short trousers to fondle their behinds while he marked their exercise books. We hated this, but we had to put up with it, since we didn't know it was wrong. Somebody eventually told Mrs Johns, who asked us all in turn if this were true. When it was confirmed, that master vanished overnight. The talk and gossip lasted well into the next term.

Towards the end of the first term I went down with measles and had to go to the school sanatorium. This was a single long ward and was a converted old First World War army hut. Attached to this was another small building, comprising the lavatories, the medicine room, the kitchen and the matron's room; the latter had a hatch in the wall, which she could fling open without warning, to reprimand any boy who was fooling around instead of trying, as was befitting a pukka sahib, to get better. This brick building was attached to an end-wall of the wooden hut.

The poor woman had no idea that we could all hear it when she used her potty at night. A wicked idea popped into my head, which I mistakenly confided in the others. One boy was put on guard to let me know when she was out of the sanatorium. (This was almost always in the morning, since one of her duties was to sit in the lobby outside the door, behind which was the room of eight lavatories, and ask the boys as they came out, 'Did you or didn't you?' 'Did' earned a tick against the name on the sheet of paper and 'Didn't' earned a cross. 'Did' was more popular than 'Didn't', because 'Didn't' earned a spoonful of syrup of figs. Sometimes boys would be reprimanded by her horsy voice calling, 'Come on out, Smith Minor' – or whoever was in there too long – 'I think you're only reading and I will confiscate your comic.')

The occasion I was waiting for arose one morning when she was doing her Did-you-or-didn't-you routine, and her bedroom was therefore safely empty. I went in, looked under her bed, took her potty out, washed it, carefully dried it on her towel and then emptied a tin of Andrews' Liver Salts into it. Andrews' not only fizzes when put in contact with water, it was also as white as the bottom of her potty so that the salts didn't show. The potty was carefully replaced, and that day seemed interminable, as we all waited for the night to come.

We held our breath as she went to bed, hoping to hear the tell-tale sound of the potty being dragged out.

For half an hour there was not a sound. One of the boys whispered, 'She must have been before she came in.' Somebody else said, 'Perhaps it doesn't fizz with pee.' Some of us dozed off.

Then I was conscious of a boy waking me up. 'She's got out of bed. Listen!' I was wide awake and listening. We all were.

The potty slid noisily over the linoleum floor. There was a few seconds' silence, followed by a scream from matron's room . . . and then silence again, broken only by a few suppressed giggles from the ward. We could hear her going back and forth to the bathroom. We heard the handle of a metal bucket clang down. We heard the floor being wiped. There were a few more giggles, and then sleep.

I never found out who sneaked on me, but a week after I had recovered from the measles my trousers were down in Jumbo's study and I received six of the best.

When the horror of the first term came to an end, we all went home for Christmas, 1929. On that Christmas Day I was given something that was to affect my future.

As was the custom, Mother, Father, my sister Joan and I were asked to the Earl of Dudley's Christmas tea at Himley Hall. I noticed a piano playing: the notes were being pressed by an unseen hand; it was magic. It was the first pianola I had ever seen, and the paper roll feeding it was filled with Christmas carols. While gazing in amazement at this extraordinary sorcery, Father Christmas (the Earl in disguise) made a spectacular entrance to a fanfare of trumpets. The pianola stopped. He started to take the presents out of his red sack and call out the names of the children written on them. Each child went up to him in turn, feeling that lovely mixture of fear, excitement and delight which only a child can experience. Parents' embarrassed voices in the background could be heard prompting, 'Say thank you.'

At last my turn came. I was given a heavy parcel and I could hardly wait to rip the paper off. It was an omnibus volume of H. G. Wells' science fiction stories. I still have it; I can see it as I write. The cover is black with red printing on and it is a little shabby now, over sixty years later. I had devoured *The War of the Worlds*, *The Invisible Man*, *The Time Machine* and so on before the following Easter. The presence of that book during the Easter term at school was a great comfort: it allowed an escape into other worlds.

Years later, it was these stories which inspired me to write fantasy, in the form of twelve plays for the BBC, under the generic title 'The Incredible Misters'. One of them, *Mr Drake's Duck*, was filmed, with Douglas Fairbanks Jnr in the lead; it's about a duck laying an atomic egg and upsetting the balance of world power. I produced the BBC plays myself, and this led them to trust me when I told them I had dreamed up some game-shows.

That same Easter term, 1930, the police arrested William Podmore for the murder of Vivian Messiter. The trial took place during the next term, less than a mile from my prep school. After a fascinating trial, this man, who had been a representative and clerk for Messiter, a director of an oil company, was found guilty. A close study of the case shows that this verdict may possibly be a miscarriage of justice.

At the end of the trial, after the verdict of guilty had been brought in, a small boy almost ten years old went along to Jumbo's study and knocked on his door.

'Come in!' commanded the drawling voice of the headmaster.

The boy gingerly opened the door and said, 'Sir . . . '

'Well, Messiter? What is it? Speak up!'

'S-sir, you know William P-Podmore . . . ?'

'No, boy, but I do know who you mean,' said Jumbo, the gold frames of his glasses glinting in the light of his reading lamp.

'Well, sir, he's going to be h-hung in the m-morning.'

'Hanged!' He stared at me as he brought out his gold cigarette case and lit yet another flattened, gold-tipped Turkish cigarette. 'Hanged,' he repeated. 'Pictures and game are hung. People are hanged,' corrected the headmaster through a haze of blue Turkish tobacco smoke.

'It's g-going to b-be at eight o'clock and I wondered if I m-might g-go . . . '

'Certainly not! You wretched boy. In any case, we had the verdict only yesterday, so he won't be hanged for three weeks. By that time you will be at home on your Easter holiday.' Some ash fell from the end of his cigarette and rolled down his grey waistcoat like a miniature avalanche.

I don't know what had made me ask him such a question, because in fact I had gone to ask about a coming rugger match against some other prep school, and the wrong question had come out.

Mrs Johns later reprimanded me too, for making such a request.

It was during that summer term that Mrs Johns had the eccentric idea that anybody observing lightning in a looking-glass would be blinded for life. When thunderstorms occurred, she and the various maids called Ada would rush round the place covering up what she called looking-glasses. 'Mirrors,' she said, 'are things that motorists use to look behind them and dentists use to examine your teeth.' Lewis Carroll might not have had such good sales if he'd called one of his books 'Alice Through the Mirror'.

3
Speaking for a minute

AFTER WINTON HOUSE at the end of 1933 there was Sherborne, where whacking was still in vogue and one of the perks of the prefects. It took place in the cloisters before witnesses. I was never whacked by a prefect in the cloisters, having learnt to be careful not to be caught doing anything wrong. I was whacked once in a classroom, and it was a whacking that was later to make me a reasonable income.

For my first few terms my sister, Joan, was at Sherborne Girls' School, but we were not allowed to meet. Boys had to be kept strictly separated from girls. This meant that I could not go up to her school to see her, in case my lustful thirteen-year-old eye should fall upon a young maiden; and for similar reasons Joan could not come down to my school to see me.

Even when the various end-of-term plays called for girls in the cast, it was thought better to put powder and lipstick on effeminate-looking boys than to get a few wholesome, pretty girls down from our sister school. Precautions against homosexuality were taken, not by the obvious system of introducing girls, but by the more devious method of removing the lavatory doors.

Sherborne in those days was a great school if you were any good at rugger or cricket. I wasn't. Nevertheless I could run fast and outshoot anyone and was totally absorbed by chemistry, science, mathematics and the school's Astronomical Society, which had a powerful telescope and a good library. There was also a good Musical Society run by a clergyman, Mr Eperson, who earned my gratitude for teaching me that, although sleep is the most sensible way of listening to opera, Wagner is an exception.

I was down for School House, which was full, so I was first put in an overflow house run by Max Westlake, the man who never left the school. He made his debut as a pupil when he was thirteen and, it was said of him, he was such a duffer that he could not go on to a university, but he was such a damned fine sportsman that he was kept on at school until after he was twenty-one so that Sherborne would win more rugger and cricket matches and more swimming cups.

When he reached the unprecedented schoolboy age of twenty-two, no one knew what would become of him as he was unable to pass the simplest exam, and the headmaster was a little embarrassed as one or two other schools had complained of having to compete against a 'boy' of that age. So Max had to be given charge of the overflow house and made Head Games Master; there were no other Games Masters, but the title looked good on paper.

Max's wife, known to us as Minimax, was sensitive to the apprehensions of new boys, as was the matron of the overflow house. Her nickname was Bemax. Between them they softened the blows of arriving at a new school among strangers. The little house was really run by Minimax and Bemax, who produced papers for Max to sign so that he could take the blame for anything that went wrong.

There was some bullying at the little house. Large boys would flick small boys, coming naked from the shower, with the ends of wet towels. This produced red blisters and stinging pain; it was bad enough through thin clothes, but much worse on naked flesh. The area aimed at was usually the private parts, where the pain was excruciating and incapacitating for a time afterwards. I was flicked as others were, possibly because I was still rather small when thirteen years old. A boy struck on his private parts would double up with pain, which spectacle would produce a cheer from the onlookers.

On one occasion a master known as Mr Parry-Jones, or P-J for short, was telling the form about Edward V, or it could have been Queen Anne. A swiftly changing cloud formation outside the window was far more interesting, brushed as it was with the pink of evening.

Suddenly there seemed to be a great explosion under my face. P-J was standing there with his gown wrapped as tightly round him as a sinister black chrysalis wears its chitinous coat. One arm holding a cane was exposed. His lined and moustached face was at its most fearsome. He seemed to have the faculty of changing colour like a thundercloud, and was now looking very dark and dangerous. My attention was drawn to that arm which held the cane forcefully brought down on the desk-lid with a sound like a gun.

'Messiter!'

'S-s-sir?' He was most frightening to me mainly because his real subject was Latin; not only was I rotten at it, I had unwisely insisted on saying that there seemed to be no reason to learn a dead language. Even more unwisely, I had repeated to P-J a conversation I had with my father and mother, during which I had been running Latin down; Mother replied by telling me that Father would never have become Master of Arts, let alone a Fellow of the Royal College of Surgeons and so on, without knowing Latin. Father had commented that Latin learnt at school had not been the slightest use to him in medicine or anything else.

When I repeated this to P-J, with all the tact of a drunken butcher lecturing a vegetarian, he had made it clear that it was something he did not wish to know. As he earned his living mainly from Latin this made a good deal of sense. The conversation had taken place early in that same term, so it was still fresh in his mind.

Now, looking like some mephistophelian horror, he brought out his gold hunter watch. 'Messiter!' he repeated, with such violence that the echo came back from the cloisters beyond, 'Stand up!' My knees shook with obedience. 'You will,' went on P-J, 'in sixty seconds repeat what I have been saying . . . '

No words came out, because I had no clue as to what he had been talking about, and the anticipation of my stuttering magnified the silence.

He continued, 'And you may not hesitate . . . '

'I – er – I – er – I . . . '

'Or repeat yourself.'

It was impossible. Even if the words had been there, they would never have escaped because of physical petrifaction and temporary lock-jaw.

The whacking that followed was painful, humiliating and took place in front of the whole class.

Years later, I remembered that frightening scene, and from it came the panel-game which was first broadcast under the name of 'One Minute, Please'. The panel of six had to speak for one minute on a given subject without hesitation, deviation or repetition. It was the first show format ever sold by Britain to the USA, and it went on television there from coast to coast. The BBC did well out of it and paid me £75 *ex gratia* for everything. The BBC said I had no right to a proper royalty as I had invented it while on their staff, which made it theirs.

When I asked Michael Standing, Head of Variety for proper financial recognition, and possibly a few pennies for my expenses or to entertain some of the proposed cast, I was reprimanded. He said the BBC was not some costermonger's stall from which programmes could be sold like so many cabbages.

One of the cast I wanted in the US version was the inimitable Hermione Gingold. She had played it in Britain and was excellent, off-beat and way out. After telephoning her, I called at her New York apartment and rang the bell.

'Is that you, Ian?' came her voice from the other side of the door.

'Yes.'

'Take your shoes off, dear boy, and leave them outside the door.' Long pause. 'Are they off?'

'Yes.'

She opened the door. The carpet was white. The walls were white. She wore white. In her sitting-room everything, from the flowers to the curtains to the furniture to the piano to the cockatoo and its cage, was white. Even the goldfish weren't gold. They were white.

She didn't ask, she said: 'Now we'll have tea.' She rang a bell and her maid came in with white meringues and white china on a white tray, but a bright red teapot.

Later I changed the format of that game slightly and called it 'Just A Minute', and now the BBC pays for it. It is a game mainly for radio and sometimes features on TV in other countries. It is heard in fifty-seven countries.

It was shortly after the P-J whacking that religion started to become very boring because of the way it was thrust down our throats. There was early morning chapel every day of the week, and Sunday started with Holy Communion, followed by Matins, followed by Evensong.

At one of these services in the school chapel, I was quietly experimenting with the two-fingered barrow boy's whistle, whereby two fingers placed correctly in the mouth and blown through gently would produce a piercing shriek. I had never been able to do it and envied those who could. Puff after puff produced no more sound than a cleric blowing the dust off a prayer book.

Suddenly and embarrassingly, God granted my wish. There was a piercing whistle that echoed round the chapel. It was both a triumph and a shock. Everyone turned around to see who had been responsible. With great presence of mind I too turned around to see who on earth could have been so blasphemously vulgar as to whistle in chapel. No one was deceived. God be praised, this was not followed by a whacking, in the cloisters or anywhere else.

While talking to a friend named either Soloman or Nathan later on, the subject of religion came up. He told me that he was Jewish and what it meant. Naturally, as Sherborne is a Church of England school, I assumed that he did not have to attend the endless services.

His explanation of the Jewish religion occasioned me considerable thought. I slept on it and next day made an appointment to see the Head, Alexander Ross Wallace, who later took holy orders. He was a large man with a pleasing face and a great sense of fun and was respected more than feared.

The conversation in his study went something like this.

'S-s-sir.'

'What is it?'

'A p-p-private m-matter, sir.'

'Sit down, boy,' he said in a kind and gentle voice, as he looked in his diary to confirm what my name was, 'and tell me what's worrying you.'

'Well, sir, it's d-d-difficult to ex-explain.'

'There's no hurry.' He leaned back in his chair and waited for me to speak. At least he wasn't copying the stutter as my mother, sister and some of the boys habitually did.

'I d-d-don't want to g-go to chapel any more.'

To understand the impact this remark had, it is necessary to understand that most people went to church on Sunday in the 1930s, some because of high ideals and faith, but most because it was socially proper to be seen there.

The Head, nicknamed the Chief, was still smiling gently. 'Why? Why don't you want to go to chapel?'

My voice came out as a squeak because it was in the middle of breaking, and anyway the stutter got the upper hand. 'Er, er, er, y-y-you s-s-see . . . '

'Take your time, boy.' He glanced at his diary again.

Suddenly it all came out in a rush. 'I-I'm taking C-Confirmation classes this t-term, as you know, sir, and I don't think I want to g-go on with them.'

'You're saying that you don't think you're ready yet?'

'I-I'm n-not, s-sir. No, sir.'

'Then I'll speak to Mr Bell about it, and I'm sure he'll suggest that you wait a term and go back to his classes later.'

'N-no, sir.'

'You need time to think, and I'm very glad you've come to tell me this. We all find parts of Christianity difficult: it's not an easy religion, it's not intended to be. I suggest that you make notes of those parts that give you the most problems and talk to Mr Bell about them. Or, if you'd rather, come back and talk to me. Your confirmation can easily be postponed.'

'I don't want to be c-c-confirmed at all – ever.'

'You must go on with your religious instruction and make up your mind later. Meanwhile I'll have a word with Mr Bell.'

'T-t-thank you, s-sir. B-but it won't help. You see s-s-sir, I w-w-want to be J-J-Jewish.'

The Head said nothing for a few seconds. He looked up at the ceiling as if he were appealing to God for help, as he probably was, then he leaned forward in his chair and asked, 'Are either of your parents Jewish?'

'N-no, s-sir.'

'Are any of your grandparents Jewish?'

'N-n-no, s-sir.'

He looked perplexed, and there was a long silence. I was tongue-tied and, because of my stutter, could not have added to the conversation.

The Chief drummed his fingers on his desk for a few seconds before saying, 'I'm afraid I can't give you a decision on this at the moment. I'll have to write to your parents about it; if they agree to it, we can arrange for you to have instruction from a rabbi.' By now the Head must have been very puzzled. 'It's very hard work being a Jew,' he said, 'a good Jew; but if your parents agree, I'll send for you and we'll see what can be done. While I wait to hear from them you can get on with reading the Torah. Start this evening.'

'I haven't got a Th-Thora.'

'Torah,' he corrected gently but firmly, and he spelt it for me as he stood up, which was the signal that the interview was over. Walking over to the door, he added, 'There is some of the Torah in the first five chapters of the Old Testament. Start with those. You can begin this evening by finding out what the first five chapters are called. Even without a rabbi, I can get Mr Bell to examine you on the Torah in a month's time. You'll have to work on those books with diligence.'

This wasn't at all what I had intended. Just as I was leaving his study he asked, 'Have you any Jewish friends in the school?'

'Yes sir, s-several.' I thought he was going to suggest that they help me. He didn't.

What came next was a shock. 'This is a Church of England school, as you know. Boys who come here are expected to attend the services. That goes for Jewish boys too. Have you not seen them in chapel?' My face must have given me away. As I went down the corridor I heard him saying, 'Start with Genesis this evening, and be prepared to answer questions on it later.'

He'd rumbled me.

On 18 July 1936, General Franco, who had been sent by the Spanish to an obscure command in the Canary Islands, declared over the radio from there his manifesto for a military rebellion. The same day there was an uprising on the Spanish mainland, and those who had the money and saw what was coming left for safer places.

My Grandmother Messiter was one who agreed to take in two Spanish refugees. They were a boy and his twin sister, both my age, and their names were Jesus and Maria. These are quite common names in Spain, but they caused quite a drama in Woolworth's in Dudley when I came home for the summer holidays, and before we set off to Little Haven.

Jesus was at the other side of the shop when I saw something interesting. At the top of my voice I called out, 'Jesus! Jesus! Come and look at this!' He didn't hear me, so I called to his sister, 'Maria! Get Jesus over here!'

A statuesque woman of imposing presence stood in front of me so that I could not get round her. 'You blasphemous little beast!' she said.

'No, no, he's my friend. Jesus is my friend!' I pointed to him. 'That's Jesus.'

She turned to look at the little Spaniard. 'How dare you take the name of the Lord in vain.' She slapped my face, and it hurt.

'But his name is Jesus.'

'Now you add lies to blasphemy!' She hit me again, thus demonstrating that it is not always right to be right.

History, one of my favourite school subjects, showed that more people were destroyed than were created in the name of God. More and more, the logic of believing that the words 'God' and 'Nature' could be interchanged made sense. Seeing Mr Bell one day I told him that if the letter X were substituted for either God or Nature, one could make some sense of life, because X is kind or cruel, X cares for the whole but not the individual, X moves in mysterious ways but is never miraculous to the extent of breaking its own rules. This was all too much for the solemn-faced man, who said, 'Read Matthew.' Which done, led nowhere.

During a biology lesson we were told that the ichneumonoid wasp uses its rear-end prod, the ovipositor, to lay eggs by piercing the skin and penetrating the gut of a caterpillar. When the eggs hatch, the little wasp grubs eat away, slowly killing the host. Mr Bell, who had never heard of this before being shown it in a book, confirmed that it was God's work, as were all things known to us.

So God did not just create birds, butterflies, sunrises, the magnificent vault of the heavens and all things bright and beautiful; he was also responsible for some very foul ideas. After asking him about that wasp, Mr Bell said, 'Read Genesis.'

'I've read Genesis.'

'Read it again.' Which done, led nowhere.

The Officers' Training Corps was not interesting except to those enthused with enough patriotism to relish the idea of shooting someone. British Army uniforms in those far-off days were designed for marching and fighting in winter only. Our uniforms were no fun in summer. It was here that we were initiated into the mysteries of putting on puttees (khaki-coloured cloth strips that were wound round the ankles to keep the ends of the trousers looking neat). Mine nearly always undid themselves, tripping up the boys marching behind. There was the usual unnecessary bawling of orders, although not one of us was deaf; the usual frowning by the sergeant-major added nothing to civilisation – but a great deal to his animal lust to show he could frighten people. All this was disagreeable, but, with centuries of world conquests behind us, it must have been the right way to go about it. It was accepted as part of our heritage.

One memorable day that summer a field marshal came to inspect us. It was hot, so hot that the sun seemed to hum from a fixed point in the blue sky.

One of the masters was our commanding officer and, in his mistaken desire to add sparkle to the occasion, he had previously had all our bayonets polished by the local blacksmith. The dull, sand-blasted, pitted surface, which had been designed not to reflect light and thus give away a soldier's position, had been superbly removed to expose a glinting brilliance worthy of a jeweller's shop. At the command, 'Fix bayonets!' the reflected sun twinkled from the steel in a scintillating display which dazzled the astonished field marshal as, with military precision, a multitude of glittering bayonets clicked into place.

It has always been considered improper for a senior officer to reprimand a junior in front of the ranks. But the poor man was so appalled, he could not prevent himself commenting at the top of his voice, 'Good God! Gilbert and Sullivan!' He pulled himself up sharply, took our commanding officer by the arm, turned his back on us, and what passed between them must have been known only to them and to the Chief.

There was no bayonet practice the following week, since all the bayonets were back with the lucky blacksmith being carefully dulled to their original state.

Each week we had a lesson called Current Affairs, taken by the Chief; he did his best to reconcile two facts to us: this was the year when Adolf Hitler was visited by Lord Halifax, who was trying to find an appeasement solution to the Sudeten problem; and at the same time our government announced a rearmament programme. For some reason this didn't seem to have anything to do with our schoolboy military parades. He also told us about Mussolini's proclamation of the Rome–Berlin Axis. None of this related to 'By the right, right wheel. Quick – er – march!' He explained why Baldwin had resigned and Neville Chamberlain become Prime Minister. Air-raid Precautions had started, yet he gave no hint of the coming war, and that this war would be timed for the exact moment when most of us boys would be old enough to be killed for something we were not old enough to understand.

We were much more interested in Edward VIII being demoted to Duke of Windsor so that he could marry Mrs Simpson, a union that held even more fascination when it became known that she had once worked in a brothel.

Disney produced *Snow White*, the first full-length cartoon. The BBC produced the world's first radio quiz programme. They were also the first to start a public television service; some said that this was a government spy system which allowed officials to look down the TV aerials into private houses.

Lord Reith, Director General of the BBC, made Radio Luxembourg popular on Sundays by insisting that all BBC music broadcasts on that day should be of 'serious' music. His definition of 'serious' music was never given, but it was generally assumed that it must be with a slow tempo and by someone who was dead.

4

Of coracles and conjuring

A GAIN THE SUMMER HOLIDAYS were spent by my family in the village of
Little Haven in Pembrokeshire. This was where I fell in love for the
first time. She was a fair-haired girl called Peggy from Milford Haven, and
she did not meet with the approval of my mother or father. The affair – if
sitting on a barnacled rock gazing across the beach at her can be called an
affair – did not last long. I had no money except my weekly pocket money
of two shillings and sixpence (13p) – hardly enough to impress a girl who
was earning money and tips as a hairdresser. Even showing her one of my
best conjuring tricks, cutting a rope into four pieces and restoring it again
to a single length, had no effect on her. But it was through her, though not
because of her, that I had my first and only real row with my father, and for
a most unusual, possibly unique reason.

My rival for her affections was a member of the Hitler Youth Movement, a boy my own age (seventeen) called Ingo Schpagne. He had more
money than I. We had met in the same holiday village the year before, and
he seemed to have no family with him. What impressed Peggy most was
the expensive camera permanently hanging from a leather strap round his
neck. So I showed Peggy the four Aces, dealing them out in a row, face up:
Spades, Hearts, Clubs, Diamonds. She then turned them face down and,
after a couple of Abracadabras, she turned them all face up again, to
discover that now they were the four Kings and the Aces had moved to the
top of the pack.

She was not impressed. She thought Ingo and his camera far more
attractive. (We were to meet Ingo again the following year, and again in
August 1939, the month before the war started. He was doomed to enter
my life yet again during the war, in circumstances which were unfortunate
for him.) Being blond, tall and athletic, he swept Peggy off her feet; at the
same time however, the three of us became friends and he was accepted by
our little Welsh and English group who had seen one another for a month
every year since babyhood.

We were a curious set: there was Ingo and Peggy, Gerald Bird from
Bath and his sisters, whose mother's country cottage was predictably
called The Nest, Jim and his sister, Pam, whose father was Mayor of
Halifax and who had secured a government contract for paint when white

lines on roads became compulsory, a couple of others and me. My sister, Joan, was never with us. We climbed cliffs or sailed our boats, mine a twelve-foot dinghy. Jim and Pam used their father's motor boat, with its noisy engine and dirty smoke. We took delight in racing at full tide from the Point to the Lion Rock, the other side of Broad Haven, exactly a mile away. Apart from shooting and running it was the only thing I was any good at. Gerald made his own boat from a washed-up trawler sail and, using driftwood to shape the sail, he made it into a sort of coracle.

In the long summer evenings we would sometimes anchor our boats a quarter of a mile offshore with lighted candles in jam-jars and sing whatever the pop songs of the day were, such as 'Pennies From Heaven', 'I've Got You Under My Skin' and 'I'm an Old Cow Hand'.

It was Gerald Bird's boat that led to my being seriously accused of murder, or at least of unlawful killing. I had got up at about half-past five in the morning because Gerald had spent the previous day arranging a bed-sheet on a pole as a makeshift sail for the coracle, and we wanted to try it out. Before making this improvement, Gerald had always had to accept a tow behind another boat.

On the previous evening we had bought some Mars Bars, apples and a couple of bottles of ginger pop. The latter came in bottles never seen today: they had glass marbles as stoppers, and are collectors' items now. We had a couple of mackerel lines with hooks and spinners. I'd brought a large tin of baked beans, stolen from our kitchen when our housekeeper, Eaves, was not looking. Eaves, always addressed by her surname, was tall, gaunt and forbidding; she had a humourless face supporting an aquiline nose which was two sizes too big for her face. She never motored to Wales from Dudley with us; she was sent ahead by train to Haverfordwest and thence by bus to Little Haven to prepare everything for us. She would have made an excellent poker player, since her face never registered pleasure, displeasure, comfort, discomfort, interest, uninterest, intelligence or stupidity. She seemed to be hiding behind her nose.

Wickedly, I tried her out one rainy day. 'Beautiful weather, Eaves?'

'Yes, Master Ian.'

'Scientists say there will be an earthquake on Tuesday week.'

'They're sure to be right, Master Ian.'

Gerald had purloined a small Primus stove and a frying-pan from his mother's kitchen, and he also grabbed a torch in case we should come across a previously undiscovered cave. We found an old motorcar inner-tube, which we blew up and tested for leaks, because if the boat sank we would need it. We completed our kit by nailing small flat boards on to a couple of old broomsticks to make oars, which we put into the trawler sailboat before carrying it down the shingle into the sea. It was a tough old sail and he had already checked it for leaks. Good stiff canvas like that could safely be assumed to be waterproof.

We climbed aboard and set off due west towards the Stack Rock, an uninhabited island three miles from Little Haven but never more than a mile from the coast.

There was an off-shore breeze; this was normal for the morning and would usually change, as the land warmed up and drew the wind back from the sea; this, we calculated, would blow us out to sea until midday and bring us back in the evening. If it didn't, there would still be no worry since we had the two 'oars'. As we passed the end of the Point we let out our mackerel lines and hung an old compass up near the mast. The compass showed we were travelling due east – which was impossible, because it meant we were sailing over the land.

'We're sailing due east,' said Gerald.

'The compass has gone wrong.'

'Never gone wrong before.' Gerald was so concerned with the compass and his mackerel line that he pulled the tiller towards him. We changed direction ninety degrees and were now sailing due north.

'Look where you're going.'

'We're still going east, according to the compass. Ah!' he said, much as Archimedes must have said, 'Eureka!' He picked up the compass. 'That's better! The damn thing was too near the iron frying-pan. But now we're going north. It's still wrong. Hell!'

'But we *are* going north.'

'Oh so we are. My mistake.' He solved the complex navigational problem like a true sailor and headed straight for the Stack Rock by using his eyes. Simultaneously I caught a mackerel. 'Damn!' said Gerald. 'Have you had breakfast?'

'Yes.'

'Well, have it again.' he said, passing me the frying-pan. 'Have you any matches?' I had, and I reached for the Primus stove so clumsily that the boat shipped water. 'Can you manage a few baked beans with the mackerel?' I asked.

'Why?'

'We forgot the bailer. An empty baked bean tin will do fine, and I've brought the tin-opener.'

Fortunately Gerald also caught a mackerel, so we both had a second breakfast of baked beans and mackerel. We couldn't finish the beans so we decanted them into two mugs. This allowed us to bail, which was our objective.

Gerald, ever the observant one, said, 'That was a bit silly.'

'What was?'

'Eating baked beans we didn't want in order to have something to bail with.'

'What's silly about it?'

'We could have used the mugs and saved the beans.'

We stopped fishing for two reasons: it was going to be a hot day, which would make the fish stink, and trolling mackerel lines would slow us down.

We settled down to the kind of silence only two people who know each other well can appreciate. We had nothing to talk about and neither of us wanted to lose a second of the joy of being on the water.

A mile and a half beyond Borough Head (a headland about five hundred feet high, composed of nothing but rock and bramble) Gerald gently steered the boat towards the coast and pointed at a cave entrance.

At first all I saw was a horsetail waterfall spraying from the top of the cliff down into the sea. Then as we neared the rocks I saw what he was pointing at: three beautiful cow seals with pups, their dog-like noses pointing at us out of curiosity, were moving slowly towards us.

We didn't speak or make any sudden movement because we didn't want to frighten them away. The sun blinked twice as two gulls crossed it. Most seals are filled with curiosity and these, emboldened when they were joined by more of their own, including a couple of smaller bulls, approached us quietly without barking or splashing. Some were less than six feet away, opening and closing their nostrils as they tried to identify us by scent. The cows were taking care that the pups kept their distance. Every now and again, a bull would dip his head under the surface and silently vanish, and then we could see him swimming deep down in the crystal-clear water under our boat, to reappear on the other side and sample the air there.

Gerald slowly turned the boat and headed towards the Stack Rock. When we were well clear of the seals, we lowered the mackerel trolls and watched the sparkling spinners sink slowly behind us. We hooked enough for lunch, which was eaten on the Stack Rock, another breeding-place for seals. Like their relatives we had just left, they too were curious about us.

On this rocky island we were surrounded by cheeky puffins with their pompous, comic clown-like little faces, surprised eyes and orange beaks hoping for scraps; however, as they didn't have the courage to come near us, the bolder blackback gulls swooped in and took the mackerel heads almost before we'd thrown them.

Because it was a calm day we were able to swim among the seals from the Stack Rock. We kept clear of cows with pups because the cows are inclined to bite when with their young. Neither of us spotted that the water was like the surface of a mill pond. The wind had dropped.

We drank our ginger pop, finished the baked beans, ate the last Mars Bar and chewed our apples, but we didn't notice that not only was the sun near the western horizon but the inshore wind had never sprung up as expected.

It was Gerald who first said we ought to start for home. 'We'll have to row,' he said. 'The wind's dropped.'

'It won't be too bad, the tide's in our favour.'

We rowed.

The sun went down in a crimson cloak of glory in front of us, promising another lovely day. We didn't stop to try and spot the green flash which the sun usually gives out as it sets in the sea on a cloudless evening. There probably was no green flash that evening as there were no waves to help cause it.

My paddle was the first to break, so I did what I could with the broomstick; it wasn't much use, so I leaned over the side and used my hands. An hour later, Gerald's paddle gave out and he used his hands too. Eventually we lost the help of the tide because it stopped coming in and after the usual twenty minutes' slack water it was against us as it turned.

Twilight came and dusk turned to dark, showing the stars as flickering pinholes above us.

Now and again one of us had to stop paddling in order to bail furiously with the baked bean tin and the mugs. The boat wasn't leaking in the usual way, it was just that the water seeped in slowly through the canvas. Neither of us mentioned the rubber inner-tube, which didn't feel quite as firm now as it had when we set off. Gerald stopped rowing and tried to blow it up; but this was not possible as it was a car tyre tube. The valve seal was too tight and required a pump.

All sense of time had gone when we reached Borough Head, which we found by looking for the lights of the Little Haven cottages. They glinted invitingly – and irritatingly – on the water; they looked so near, infuriatingly near and stayed where they were, seemingly getting no closer, however hard we paddled. We could not see the top of this wild, bracken- and bramble-covered head some five hundred feet above us.

I told Gerald that our parents would be worried, since we hadn't told them our plans in advance.

'Just as well,' said Gerald. 'If we had, they'd be even more worried by now. Are you?'

'No. And I have a plan. I'll get out here and climb Borough Head. There's a road at the top and I can hitch a lift to the village.'

Gently, because it was quite dark now and there was no moon, I climbed on to a rock to feel my way forward to the cliff which is by no means vertical. I remembered seeing it in the daytime and thinking it merely a steep slope.

So it was, interrupted now and again by vertical rock that had to be climbed or avoided. But this was no fern-covered hill; it was thick with hard, tough, wood-like brambles that tore my clothes off, ripped my skin and cut my face and arms. I was covered in sweat and blood. I lost count of the number of times I fell. It had been a dry summer, so every footstep produced a cloud of dust, which was choking. As I rubbed my skin I could feel the dust turning to sweaty bloody mud.

The exercise was pointless: Gerald would be home by now, since he had only another mile and a half to go to reach the Haven and, without me, the boat was that much lighter. I had spent immeasurable time climbing and stumbling up the Head. He would be at home, and I hoped he would check to see if I was back.

There was little hope of seeing a car at that time of night, but, by some miracle, a gleam of headlights appeared. It was a van. God knows what the driver must have thought as he sped past this ragged bloody figure, waving at him in the middle of the dark road. He swerved, drove on into the night, and vanished.

I walked the rest of the way home, where I was met by my father; he helped me to wash and painted me with iodine. All the cuts and bruises were superficial and, with the blood washed away, Mother didn't look so alarmed.

I got into bed and blew the candle out. Peaceful and welcome sleep took charge.

Women's raised voices and a loud banging at the door woke me with a jolt. I could hear Gerald's mother demanding my attendance. I presented myself in my pyjamas.

'Where's Gerald?' she demanded.

I protested, 'But he must be home because –'

Mrs Bird talked me down ' – there was only one inner-tube between the two of you. I know what happened. That silly boat sank and you took the inner-tube and let him drown; that's why you're here and he isn't.'

I was wide awake and very alarmed. It was possible that Gerald had met with some accident after I left him. He still had a mile and a half to go; and now I was feeling guilty that I had left him to do it alone with no oars and, therefore, no proper way of steering.

I put my bedroom slippers on and, still in my pyjamas, walked in silence with my father and mother down to the beach, where there were three or four cars on the shingle with their headlights on, pointing out to sea.

People didn't seem too anxious to talk to me. In their minds I was already guilty of deserting my friend and of taking the only life-saving rubber ring. It seemed to me that they had already made up their minds: I had killed Gerald.

Jim and Pam were there on the shingle with their father, the paint king from Halifax. He came up to me quietly and carefully asked me in his friendly, warm, Halifax accent where I had left Gerald. I told him it was at the bottom of Borough Head.

'I'm going to look,' he said.

We all helped him down the beach with his boat, it was a long way, as the tide had gone out. He took Jim, his son, with him; as the sound of his motor faded into the distance, I realised that Father and I, both in pyjamas and bedroom slippers were standing up to our knees in water.

It was getting light when we heard the sound of the motorboat coming back. It was light enough to see the shapes of three people in it. My spirits rose.

It was Gerald, cheerful as ever. 'What's all the fuss?' he asked.

'Where have you been?' asked his mother.

'When I rounded the Head into the little Goultrop harbour, I knocked a hole in the bottom of the boat – you know how sharp the rocks are there. I had a torch and the canvas thread with a needle, so I had to stop there and mend it in order to sail the boat back to Little Haven.'

That day, after lunch, Gerald's father and my father set off in a boat with several shovelfuls of shingle; with them was the coracle. At some point well out to sea, they put the coracle into the water, punched a few holes in it and filled it with the shingle. It sank.

Gerald and I didn't watch.

That evening at high tide, we all went swimming off the end of the Point; but Ingo Schpagne would never come swimming with us. If we were running races on the beach or playing beach tennis or any other sport, Ingo would join in, and he always won: he won at rounders; he won running races; he climbed cliffs we thought impossible; prawning at low tide, he caught more than anyone. But we never saw him swim.

I called for him on one occasion at the cottage where he stayed and saw a swimsuit drying on a wall in the sun. I forget how the matter came up, but I mentioned the swimsuit and Ingo said it was his.

'I thought you couldn't swim.'

'Oh yes,' said Ingo.

'We thought you didn't like the sea.'

'I love the voffs,' He always called waves 'voffs'.

'Then come and swim with us.'

'No. I go to swim on my own at a deserted bay.'

Perhaps the truth was that he couldn't or didn't dare swim out of his depth. It was the obvious question.

His answer was surprising. 'In Britain I, Ingo Schpagne, represent my fatherland, Germany. In this village I represent my Fuehrer, Adolf Hitler. I swim: I do not swim as fast as you and your friends. I dive: I cannot dive from so high. I must do nothing to bring shame or criticism upon my Fuehrer.'

'But, Ingo, it's all fun. There's no competition.'

At dinner that evening I mentioned this to my father, who said, 'I wish you wouldn't see so much of that boy.'

'Why?'

'He's a spy.'

'But, Dad, like me, he's still at school.'

'I'd rather you didn't see him. He has asked you any questions about the OTC?'

'What sort of questions?'

'How often do you parade? What calibre rifles do you use . . . ?'

'You wouldn't have to be a spy to find out those things.'

This conversation led to a row. The best arguments come about when each protagonist is sure he is right; Father's instincts told him he was right; mine told me I was right. Rows with Father always ended with me being sent to my room. I ended up in my room on this occasion, too.

Getting back from Little Haven in the car, we noticed that old Sago was lame. We knew he couldn't last for ever; when we found his back legs paralysed, Father gently put him out of his misery and I dug a pit at the bottom of the garden, where I buried him. I could see his grave from my bedroom window every morning when I was at home. I had known him for about thirteen years. He was my best friend.

Just before I had left school, Father and I had a conversation, which between any other father and son would have led to another flaming row. For some reason, ours didn't. I seldom get angry and never raise my voice. Father, though he would never have admitted it, was a stoic. These factors took the steam out of a situation which in any other family would have led to volcanic eruptions.

The words are lost in time, but the gist was that I would follow Father to Cambridge and so into medicine, as he had done.

I said no.

'You could lead a useful, really helpful life if . . . '

'No.' I had seen too much of it, in spite of being away at school most of the time.

He asked what I intended to do, to which I replied I wanted to be a conjuror.

I remember him echoing the words as if in disbelief. 'A conjuror?' There was a long silence. 'Why?'

I had wondered why some wanted to paint, some to dance, some to drive railway engines, or some to work in a bank; but I couldn't express any of this because of my stutter.

I knew why Father was a surgeon: a year before he had shown me when I asked him what made him do it. His answer was to take me to the hospital one Wednesday and tell me to put on a white coat and accompany him to a ward, where we saw a patient who had a continuous twitch in her left arm and most of her body. She could hardly speak properly and was incapable of holding anything in her hands. She had been Father's patient for five or six years but no longer recognised him.

After we left her, he explained to me that tests had shown that she had a tumour under her skull on the right side, and that he intended to operate next day to remove it, adding that it might well kill her but that there was no life for her in the future the way she was. Thursday was his theatre day. He would take me with him.

Next morning, scrubbed up and wearing a white coat (green overalls didn't come in until later), I stood at the back of the theatre near the door and watched as they brought the anaesthetised, unconscious woman in, followed by Father who had himself given her the anaesthetic, a common practice then.

The anaesthetic in those days was alcohol, chloroform and ether, known by its initials as ACE. It was a vicious mix, dripped on to cotton wool held over the patient's nose and guaranteed to give the recovering victim a headache and several attacks of vomiting; it could kill patients who were not too fit. It always made Father smell of ether on Thursday evening when he came home. As the fumes were strong, the surgeon often asked a nurse to use a fan so that he and his assistants wouldn't get high on ACE themselves.

The patient's head had been shaved and I could see clearly as Father prepared to cut into her skull at the place where he had marked it. As the sound of drilling into bone started, I shut my eyes, but hearing the noise still made me feel very ill. I pushed backwards against the theatre doors and discreetly made my exit.

Three weeks later, he took me back to the hospital where I saw the woman sitting up in bed as she poured us each a cup of tea and chatted animatedly. The twitch had gone and her mind was clear.

On our way home, Father said, 'Now you may have some idea why I went in for medicine.'

Father's shoulders seemed to droop when I told him I wanted to be a conjuror. To him this was incomprehensible; it was a bitter disappointment that I could not follow him. Then he smiled a little. 'In this world,' he said, 'you can gamble on horses, go out with women, play cards for money, get drunk – there are plenty of ways of going bankrupt which would be a lot more fun than being a conjuror. The nearest anyone should get to the stage is the third row of the stalls.'

This wasn't mentioned again for a long time – not until the day after I left school for ever. I felt that leaving Sherborne, with its rules which forced all boys to do the same things at the same time and all dress the same, had lifted a great weight. There would be no more prefects shouting and calling for their fags, no more sleepless nights counting the chimes of the Abbey clock, no more sound of desks slamming. Anything that reminds me of that sound turns my stomach over. This was freedom.

I left school in 1938 when one-third of the population was living below the poverty line, one-third on or just above it, and the remainder lived quite well. That last third were probably the only ones who cared that Hitler had annexed Austria. The hungry can think only of their own stomachs and those of their families. Without the money for a wireless set or a newspaper, they neither knew nor cared what Hitler was doing. Nor did they know that the first ballpoint pen had been invented that year by a Hungarian, Georg Biro, or that Howard Hughes flew round the world in three days and nineteen hours, or that the SS *Queen Elizabeth* had been launched.

It was also the year of the hit song, 'Doing the Lambeth Walk – Oi!' and I found out at first hand that the pupils of Roedean Girls' Public School were allowed to dance and sing this, provided they did not say 'Oi!'. They had to sing, 'Doing the Lambeth Walk – Ah!' It was more lady-like.

Father said on my first day home, 'Now about that conjuring business, do you still want to go on with it?'

'Of course.'

He gave me £5 and the cost of a return ticket from Dudley to London, adding, 'And when that's gone you can come home and we'll discuss a proper career.'

5
Show business

HAVING SPENT MOST OF MY CHILDHOOD either locked in a room or away at school, going to London held no horrors for me. Rooms would be expensive and, after inquiring about them, it was clear that one room for one person was out of the question at fifteen shillings (75p) a week. It was essential to avoid the humiliation of having to go back to Dudley, cap in hand, and give way to Father's command.

In Craven Road, near Paddington Station, lived a woman with a huge house; she had turned her large rooms into dormitories and let the beds in them at five shillings (25p) a week, including a slice of toast with margarine and a mug of tea for breakfast. Other meals had to be eaten off the premises. This seemed a price I could afford and the house was clean. There were ten people in my dormitory, one of whom was a loud snorer and kept us all awake.

I found this address through an advertisement, having spent the first night lying on a bench in some park with a name I have totally forgotten. Before you feel sorry for my hardship, you should know that it was a warm early-September night when I lay on that bench with my suitcase containing my clothes under my head, my case of conjuring tricks under my feet, and a determination to conserve money at all costs. September, incidentally, is the month when all major corners in my life are turned.

Finding a journal called *The Stage*, a theatrical paper, was like striking oil; an actor in the same dormitory had a copy. I was pleased to meet a real actor and asked him what show he was in. He stared at me with watery eyes set in a crinkled face which looked as if he'd forgotten to pull the creases out of it when he got up in the morning. 'At the moment I'm resting,' he said, taking a sip from a quarter-bottle of scotch. 'My agent is considering whether I should take an offer from C. B. Cochran or from Anthony Asquith.' The copy of *The Stage* which he was studying with such concentration was out of date, but he said, 'Laddie, this is what you should read.'

'But you're reading it.'

'Forget it, laddie. I've read it. Twice. There's nothing suitable in it for me.'

'With offers from Mr Cochran and Mr Asquith, you won't want any more work.'

'That's why I don't need it,' he said with an air of hopelessness. 'Here you are.' He passed the well-thumbed and grubby copy to me, adding, 'You couldn't lend me a pound, could you?' I lied and told him I didn't have that much. 'Well, a couple of bob will see me through. My agent has fifteen pounds owing to me, and I'll get it tomorrow. I'll pay you back then.' I foolishly lent him two shillings and he left the dormitory.

I read that copy from cover to cover, coming across the name of an agent, Percy Clarbour of Cambridge Circus. There was no reason to choose that one, and I didn't read the name until midday on my first whole day in London. It was quite a walk from Paddington to Cambridge Circus but preserving cash was the first essential.

My behaviour may seem incomprehensible, but it has to be seen against the background of my parents' attitude towards the theatre and the horrifying prospect of going home to eat humble pie and admitting my stupidity. Had Father been angry and thrown me out, I might have faced the return if things went badly for me; but as he had been so kind and had given me the fare as well as £5, I knew he would be unbearably kind to me on my return.

I was aware of what they were doing. Theirs was a wiser course than telling me I had to stay at home; they were letting me go, knowing it could not possibly work out and that therefore I would find out for myself in the end. Father would be wise enough not to say, 'I told you so.' Looking back on it, he had never said it wouldn't work. Nor could I ever claim that he had forbidden me to go or that he never helped me. I had the return ticket and his £5.

I spent the afternoon walking to Cambridge Circus. Immediately opposite the Palace Theatre I saw a notice board reading 'Percy Clarbour. Theatrical Agent'. There was a badly painted pink hand, its index finger looking like an impotent raw sausage, pointing up the stairs.

It was a long climb, up many flights, each a little more sordid than the one below. Eventually I came to a door with a copy of the notice nailed to it. The glamour of the theatre was behind that door. I knocked.

A woman's voice called, 'Come in.' The door was ajar and needed only a small push. The woman behind the desk looked at me over her spectacles without smiling or taking the almost finished cigarette out of her mouth. She was in her middle forties, thin, worn and tired, and her clothes looked as if they needed a good clean and press; her long, clumsily made-up face looked even longer because she had pulled her henna'd hair back into a bun. It was impossible to guess what colour her hair had been originally. There was grey in the red, and the brassy yellow bits must have been the result of experiments with tints.

The office was untidy. A pile of books of photographs, which turned out to be copies of *Spotlight*, still the casting director's stand-by, was capped by a dirty teacup. The ashtray had overflowed and a couple of cigarettes had been stubbed out on a window-sill which supported two more dirty teacups and needed dusting. This was obviously Mr Clarbour's secretary; she would lead me into his presence when he was free – but there was no sign of another door.

'What do you want?' she asked with no smile of welcome, removing her cigarette stub with nicotine-stained fingers so that she could light a fresh one from it.

'I want to see Mr Percy Clarbour.'

'You can't. I'm his widow. I run the agency. What do you want?'

'I want to go on the music halls. Can you arrange me a tour?'

'What's your act?'

Magician.'

'Where have you played?'

'Nowhere.'

'Clubs?'

'No.'

The telephone rang. She said, 'Sit down,' and picked up the receiver, to engage in a conversation to do with a crowd wanted at Pinewood Film Studios. After putting the receiver back she asked, 'Can you wait while I make a few calls?'

I waited while she made about twenty calls. Perhaps a dozen were answered, and to each one she gave the time of the film studio call and the address to go to.

Between calls she asked me where I was from, and I told her. It didn't take much observation on her part to see how green I was. She asked me if I was a member of the Variety Artists Federation or Equity (the two theatrical unions). This was the first I'd heard of them.

'D'you want to earn a pound tomorrow?' And she wrote out a chit for me, which I had to present at 8 am at Pinewood Studios. 'If they ask for your union card, tell them I gave you that note. They know me there. You'll have to join a union later.' She went on to explain that in return for getting me the job I must go back to see her the next day and pay her ten per cent. In this case (with twenty shillings in the pound), I would have to bring her two shillings (10p); at the same time she would be looking out for any other work that might suit me. As soon as the shooting was over, she said, I must queue up at the exit from the studios and I would be given a pound, for which I must sign.

This seemed an easy way of earning a living. During the next half-hour a couple of people called and asked her if she had any work. They went on the list for Pinewood Studios.

Arriving back at the dormitory, I saw the actor sitting on his bed looking unhappy. He couldn't believe my story. He was most plaintive about my finding an agent so quickly. 'But laddie, you've not been here two days and you've found work! Some people have all the luck. What was the name of that agent?' I told him. 'Ah! She'd be no good to me. I'm a thespian with a preference for Shakespeare, laddie. I belong to the serious theatre. You're a music-hall turn. And I must warn you about doing crowd work for the cinema people. A reputable actor wouldn't go near them. They're all thieves. They'd as soon remove your pocket book as look at you. I've had money stolen every time I've done crowd work. Never leave your wallet in the dressing-room. For the same reason, don't take a decent overcoat.' It was pathetically obvious he didn't own an overcoat.

'Oh, you know about crowd work, do you?'

He'd given himself away. The truth was about to come out. He looked slightly embarrassed for a few seconds. 'Well, laddie, I've done a little now and then, to break up the monotony of resting. It's better to turn out for a small fee than put your feet up for nothing.'

His warnings about the film crowd extras were worth the two shillings he had 'borrowed'.

The next day I presented myself at the studios where I was waved in without any questions. No one had asked for my card, so I didn't even had to show Mrs Clarbour's note to anyone. I gave my name to the man at the gate and he ticked it on a list. There were several of us and we were to be a protesting crowd. The make-up man came around, not because we would need make-up but because it was a union regulation.

No one ever told me the name of the film or who starred in it. All I knew was that the set was a street-scene and when a man opened a door and walked into the street we had to boo at him and wave our fists. His reaction to this was to go back into the house.

An important man who seemed to be the crowd director said: 'We're going to rehearse this. Now, when the stand-in comes out of that door, remember he's meant to be a top politician who's been accused of diverting public money into his own pocket. Got it? Think of it as real! Imagine it's your money he's taken and let him have a taste of your anger. You despise him. He's been caught with his hand in the till.' He paused in this impassioned plea to ask, 'Now, is there anyone here who doesn't understand why you've got to boo him?' His question had all the sarcasm of a sergeant demanding something simple from his men. 'It isn't difficult,' he explained patronisingly. 'Let's try it and see if we can get it right.'

Apparently we got it right first time, because he almost smiled as he looked at us and said, 'That's good! You'll make him feel it's personal.'

That was his joke, and he looked at the stand-in for approval; the latter laughed obediently.

There was a long delay while the stand-in was stood down and someone went to fetch the real actor, a man very conscious of his own importance. This last was apparent when he opened the door without any cue to do so and asked that all lights should be used and 'Would the make-up girl come and look at my face. This is totally different lighting from my dressing-room and I can tell my nose is glinting.' A nervous girl turned up with a powder-puff and other accessories to do something to his face, which made not the slightest difference from where I was looking and I was much closer to him than the camera was.

A voice said, 'Let's go for this one.'

Someone said, 'Camera!'

Another voice, presumably the one working the camera said, 'Speed,' meaning that the film was running fast enough.

'Mark it!' commanded someone, and the clapper-board was snapped shut. The name of the film was written on it, but I couldn't read it.

At last someone called 'Action!' and we went through the whole thing again, booing and waving our fists.

Someone said, 'Cut!'

Someone said, 'Print it!' The director asked the sound man if the sound had been recorded properly. It had.

Someone else said, 'Check the gate,' which meant: make sure no bits of dirt were between the camera lens and the film itself.

'Save the red,' came next, and the strong lights went out, only to be put on again as the director called for another shot of the same thing, 'Just for safety.'

We did it all over again. Later they moved the camera to a different position and we did it again; with the camera moved for the third time, it was shot again. After each move there was always an extra shot, 'Just for safety.' Between each take the actor called for the make-up girl.

This scene took all morning to shoot because the man who appeared to be in command changed the angle of the camera several times. Between each take, the actor snapped his fingers in the direction of the make-up girl but without looking at her. She was very patient. It was the work conditions that were forcing her to put up with the actor's rudeness; for every person with a job in the film business there were dozens half-starving and waiting for the chance to get in.

It seemed we were being directed by two people. One man politely directed the actor who opened the door, and the other director yelled at us, the booing crowd, telling us when and how to boo and how to put more sneer into the booing.

I caught sight of the camera once, but it never caught sight of me.

During the lunch break I went back to the room which led to the washroom and saw a man, lying on a bench and looking at the sports page of the London *Evening News*. 'What's this film called?' I asked.

'Dunno,' he answered without looking up. 'I've not been on the set.'

'Aren't you supposed to be in it?'

'Sure, but I've got a hangover and I'd rather have a kip behind these lockers.' I expressed my surprise, so he explained: 'I only go out on the set when it's a small crowd and I'd be noticed. When it's a big crowd like this, there's no point in wasting my time. They never miss me.'

This seemed incredible. It was unbelievable that an extra could be so blasé that he didn't even want to appear in a film.

'D'you go in for racing?' he asked. 'I've a good tip for the 3.30 at Plumpton.'

I showed an interest which I didn't feel, adding, 'I don't know a bookie.'

'That's OK with me,' he said. 'If you give me half a quid, I'll put it on with my bookie. There's a five-year-old called Grasshopper. It's a cert. I've studied the jockey form, and the ground is as demanding as it was last time he ran, and he won then. He's five to one at the moment.' He roused himself enough to stand. 'Yes, lend me a couple of coppers and I'll phone my bookie right away.'

'I don't have any change,' I lied, but I was beginning to see the tarnished side of show business – which was to become quite plain within the next two minutes when another extra came off the set and saw the man I was talking to.

'Sam!' said the newcomer with a note of surprise and a slight threat in his voice. 'About time I found you.'

'What's the worry?' said Sam nervously.

'You owe me a couple of quid. The last time we were together you said you'd put a few bob of mine on Pam's Delight and it came up. You scarpered.'

'No. I lost your address and couldn't find you after the race.'

'Now listen, you bastard . . .'

I made myself scarce. It was a shock to realise that this was not the glamorous business everyone thought it was.

Eventually we returned to the set after lunch, which was a delicious bacon sandwich sold by a studio canteen lady from a trolley; I've loved crisp bacon sandwiches ever since. It was apparent that the set had been lit for a night scene. The property street gas-lamp shone with gaslight and I inquired of one of the extras, a platinum blonde in a beret, what the firemen were doing in the corner of the studio playing cards.

'Well it's the union, duckie,' she said. 'If we have real flames – and that's real gas – the unions say there must be real firemen on the set. Regulations.' To this day I've never found out whether she was telling me the truth.

This time the crowd director explained a little more of the plot to us. Apparently the politician was to be seen at a street-level window in the house at night, and we were to jeer at him again from the road until he drew the curtains to shut us out. The stand-in waiting in the house was carefully lit while we hung about outside, prepared to jeer.

Eventually everyone was satisfied with the lighting as the cameraman minced about with his light meter. He was another self-important man, making the most of his importance. The actor was brought in to replace the stand-in. There was far less light than there had been for the daylight scene in the morning; nevertheless the actor snapped his fingers and called, 'Make-up!'

The nervous girl reappeared and dabbed his face with powder. He made her hold a hand-mirror in front of him for a long time. He pointed to his left eyebrow. The make-up girl did something to it which I couldn't see, but a few minutes later he was satisfied.

Someone yelled, 'Settle down, everyone! We'll have the one rehearsal then we'll go for a take while it's fresh.'

The rehearsal was up to standard and 'Action!' was called. We jeered like mad until someone yelled, 'Cut!'

The director came out on the floor and pointed to one of us crowd extras as he called to his assistant. 'Get the name of that man! See he never works again. He stared straight into the camera. Get him off the set now. Get him out of the studio. We'll have to have a retake.'

The disgraced extra was led from the studio in silence.

We had a retake, and another, and another. The camera was moved and we did it all over again, including a few extra takes 'for safety'. Between each take the actor snapped his fingers for the make-up girl, who obediently and pointlessly powdered his face.

It wasn't quite the film life as described in the magazines, but it *was* different.

At the end of the day I queued up at the exit gates, collected my twenty shillings, signed for them and went back to the dormitory near Paddington Station. It wasn't the sort of day to write home about: they'd never understand it. It was the first money I had ever earned. There was no one to tell except the actor, and I looked for him.

It seemed he'd gone. The woman who owned the house also came to look for him. She was wearing a dirty dressing-gown and a pair of slippers with the backs trodden down. I later noticed that she always wore the slippers, even to go to the shops round the corner. The right side of her upper lip was nicotine-stained from the cigarette which she never seemed to remove except to light a new one. Had I seen that actor?

'Not since early morning. Why?'

'He owes me for four nights. How long will you be staying?' She was holding out her right hand, palm upwards, so I gave her the Pinewood Studios pound note, to secure my bed for four more nights. I didn't mention to her that I'd been silly enough to lend the actor two shillings; but after the woman had dragged her weary frame out of the dormitory I pulled my conjuring case out from under the bed and examined it.

That the actor or someone else had been through it was obvious, because all the coloured silk handkerchiefs were in a muddle; the two white ones, each a yard square for doing the knotted-and-unknotted-silks trick, were missing. The red one, designed to appear magically tied between them, was still there. The rabbit was gone too. This was a matter for some grief, partly because it had been expensive and partly because I had some affection for it. It wasn't a real rabbit, of course, but one made of mole and other fur. It was very soft and could be squeezed into a space under a black disc in an opera hat.

In those days every conjuror worth his salt was expected to produce a rabbit from a hat. This rabbit had a hole in the back of its head so it could be made to nod in answer to commands such as, 'Nod once for a black card, twice for a red. Red? Yes, now nod once for a diamond and twice for a heart,' and so on . . . a tediously time-consuming way of arriving at the identity of a chosen card.

Next morning it was back to Mrs Percy Clarbour at Cambridge Circus to pay her ten per cent for getting the film job. She gave me two or three more crowd-extra jobs for later days. They were enough to make me think of buying a diary, but September was a bit late in the year for that sort of expense; a piece of card was good enough.

Mrs Clarbour became a temporary mother-figure. I went to her office every day looking for work, and discovered that while her late husband had had an agency of some worth, by 1938, it was very much on the skids. I found this out when she offered me seven shillings and sixpence (37p) to sit in the office all day to take the bookings and collect the ten per cents, while she went down to some studio as a crowd extra, for which she would get her pound. It was obvious that after deducting my seven and six, she would make only twelve and sixpence (63p) for herself. On top of that was her fare. (She always took her own sandwich.)

I had to make a note of every telephone call; if it turned out to be a lucky day, with a call for a crowd, I was to take the number needed to form a crowd, then choose as many men from a list as women, ring them and book them. I had enough sense to know that if men only were wanted I used one list, all women came from another, women with babies from a third, children from a fourth list, and so on. She said it was never necessary to ring the same number more than once, if it was answered by a film extra's friend or relative, get that extra to call back to confirm; it didn't need much brain. Getting the extras to call back was only one economy.

Mrs Clarbour also gave me a list of names linked with pencil lines: linked people were friends who would call one another to say they must call us if they wanted the job. This also saved her telephone bill. Some extras called every day on the off-chance; they would get preference, since they too saved the cost of a call.

I was to hold the fort for her several times, and we got on well enough.

One Friday I was in the office while she was there too (there was nothing like being on the spot if a studio rang) when she answered the phone and seemed to be talking to an old friend; they talked for a long time. I had been retyping her list of crowd extras with their phone numbers on to cards for a box which, I suggested, was easier to handle than lists on sheets of paper, and had had to stop because she couldn't hear over the clatter of the typewriter.

'Yes,' she said, 'I think I can help you. I'll call you back in twenty minutes. Please don't call anyone else until you hear from me.' Then she put the phone down. I knew it was important since she never called anyone back except producers and people who could bring her work. 'Ian!' she said, opening her eyes very wide, 'don't get excited, but I may have something special for you. The Queen's, Poplar, is stuck for one act for next week. They want a double act, a novelty act of some sort.' Not seeing how this could affect me, I listened politely. It turned out that the Queen's was a music hall theatre in the East End, and the management had just had a let-down for the coming week starting on Monday. 'I'm going to take a chance on you,' she said.

'But I'm not a double act.'

'I know that; but you can become one.'

'How?'

'If you're prepared to work all over the weekend with a pretty girl I know, then I'll get you the job. I know I'm taking a chance. What does it matter? I shall go on with crowd work if this doesn't work out. What about it?'

I didn't need asking twice. There was to be a pretty girl thrown in and I was at an age when all pretty girls were appealing.

Mrs Clarbour picked up the phone again and dialled a number. 'Hello, Gwen? Sylvia Clarbour here. Is Daisy in? Good.' A short pause. 'Daisy, now listen carefully, what are you doing this weekend? Good. Cancel your boy-friend. Are you working anywhere next week? Good. I've got a boy in my office who says he's a magician. No – he's done a couple of card tricks in the office for me, and I've no idea how he did them – that's all I know. I can probably get you both a week at the Queen's if you can work together.

You'll have to practise all over the weekend, starting early tomorrow morning.'

I could hear the pulse beating in my ears. She was putting an act together and it looked as if she might sell it too.

'Hang on.' She looked up from the phone. 'Can you and Daisy rehearse at your place?'

'No, sorry, it's a dormitory.'

This information was conveyed to Daisy. There was another pause, followed by more conversation on the telephone, then she finally hung up.

'Daisy's mother, who's an old pro herself, says you can go to their place and rehearse there tomorrow and again on Sunday.' She sounded as excited as I felt. 'I've been asked to supper there on the Sunday so I can see how it all fits together.' Her mood suddenly changed. 'For god's sake, Ian, don't let me down. I've never booked an act unseen, and although the Queen's isn't exactly the London Palladium, it's a start. All down one side is a bar, which can get a bit noisy. It's a tough date, but it might lead to something for you – ' she smiled as she added '- for Daisy and, for that matter, for me. I'd rather book acts than mess about with this sordid crowd work. Don't let me down. Have you thought about what you want to be billed as?'

I told her. She told me to write it down.

She picked up the phone again and spoke to the man at the Queen's. 'I've got the double act for you, a magician and his assistant. The magic is fine and the girl will get the men whistling. They'll do ten minutes on the Monday first house and spread to fifteen for the rest of the week if you like them. Will you be putting a sticker over the name of the act that cancelled? You will. Good. Here's the name to get to the printer tomorrow: "Cassan the Mystic and Daisy". Ten pounds the week between the two of them.'

I could hardly believe my ears. That was a lot of money. I wondered how it would be divided. She put the phone down.

'Well,' she said, 'you'll be opening there on Monday night first house – whether you last until the Saturday is up to you. You'll be getting six pounds for the week and Daisy will get four, less my commission, of course.'

'Of course.' Privately I thought that seven to three would be a better division, but I didn't know then that Daisy would save the act.

6
Getting the bird

DAISY AND I REHEARSED in a house somewhere off the Edgware Road, a few miles north of Marble Arch. She was a pretty, vivacious, blonde girl with a broad grin, good legs, bright blue eyes, a trim figure, and a wicked sense of fun that combined well with a cockney wit. She didn't realise at first that I was an amateur. She had had plenty of experience in the chorus, both singing and dancing, so she knew all the theatre jargon. This was impressive. It was news to discover that, in the theatre, 'flies' were neither insects nor trouser buttons.

Her mother was worldly-wise and didn't leave us alone for a minute. Being a pro herself, she became an unofficial producer, and very useful too. There was one line I delivered badly after deliberately producing the wrong playing-card. The line was: 'You can't expect me to get it right first time. You should see my contract: it was carved on ice and filed in the boiler-room.'

Not exactly a belly laugh, but Daisy's mother told me my timing was wrong and that, playing it that way, it would never get a laugh. 'You must pause longer between each sentence, so it sounds as if you don't know what's coming. You do know, of course, but it mustn't sound like it. Bring out the three words 'carved on ice', pause longer, it's just possible they may laugh there without realising what they're laughing at; and get that tag-line, 'filed in the boiler room', much slower. After that, try looking into the wings as if you've said something wrong.'

I did exactly as she said, but she still didn't look convinced that this was going to be the greatest thing since George Robey. She frowned for a while; I worried, because I didn't know what I was doing wrong. Suddenly she came out with it. 'You sound posh,' she said, 'Can you lay it on a bit as well, so that the audience thinks that sounding posh is funny?'

I had no idea what she was talking about. She explained with great care and asked me if I'd ever heard of the Western Brothers. I had. She said that part of their fun was imitating what the audience thought of as the public school accent. 'You have one,' she said, 'and what you must do is exaggerate it and get a laugh with it. Project more. Put it over.'

I understood; I tried, but she still looked worried.

Daisy was wonderfully inventive; for example, there was another trick that involved a card being chosen by someone in the front row and shuffled back into the pack after which I would throw the pack across the stage so the cards would shower over her. She was to reach up with her right hand, miss the pack but catch the one needed card. She said it was predictable and it would be more fun if she were to say she'd missed it, but then, after a few seconds of sexy wiggling and saying she could feel its 'fluence' all over her, produced the missing card from her cleavage. It was good, but she added a mystery line: 'It'll be a lot better after the band call.'

What on earth was a band call?

Band call, she explained, took place on the Monday morning at 10.30 when the orchestra assembled in the pit to try to discover what music each act needed and had brought with them. Such music had to be very adaptable, because no two theatres of this type had the same kinds of instruments in the pit. These scruffy bits of paper were called band parts, and we didn't have any.

We arrived at the theatre at about a quarter past ten, and I was happy to see a man pasting our billing, 'Cassan the Mystic and Daisy', over the name of the act that had fallen by the wayside. We were right at the bottom, in quite small type, and couldn't be read from the other side of the road; but we were there.

Going into the theatre, we sat in the front stalls with the other acts while the orchestra started to assemble. 'Orchestra' – well there was a decent collection of drums with a very keen and noisy drummer, a double bass, a trumpeter doubling on the slide trombone, and an upright piano which didn't need tuning badly because it had already been tuned badly.

There was a conductor who doubled as the piano player. He was stout and seemed to sweat continuously as he laboured for breath. His cravat was wearing thin at the corners, showing it to be cotton stretched over cardboard or some other stiffener. There was no means of telling where his chin finished and his neck began. I looked at him in some alarm and hoped he would last the week. Whispering my apprehension to Daisy she said, 'Let's hope we do, too.'

Mrs Smith kindly took charge of our act. We'd had a discussion on the bus about the lack of band parts, and she agreed to brief the 'orchestra' to use 'Colonel Bogey' to play us in and play us out. Band parts would not be needed since everyone would know it. 'Colonel Bogey' usually cheered any audience because of the vulgar words that had been put to it within a year of its publication in 1916. Any other musical emphasis needed could be supplied by the drummer or the man on the slide trombone. Big tricks with dramatic finishes would be built up by a roll of drums, finishing with a good wallop on the biggest drum. I didn't have any big tricks with dramatic finishes.

In 'the business', an illusion is sometimes distinguished from a conjuring trick: the former uses plenty of elaborate and large apparatus, while a conjuring trick is usually no bigger than a magical effect with cards, ropes, billiard balls, silks, glasses of water and so on. I had no illusions.

And any illusions I may have had about the theatre were fast vanishing. Those on the same bill as 'Cassan the Mystic and Daisy' were now gathered in the stalls. I can remember only three other acts. One was called the Bently Sisters; they sang and danced. They weren't sisters at all, they were mother and daughter – and looked it. A second act was a comic who had evidently pinched his material from Max Miller, billed himself as 'The Poor Man's Max Miller' and wore a suit made of curtain material with huge flowers all over it. He was the star, had a dressing-room to himself and smelled of brandy and garlic. The third act comprised a couple about our age, a brother and sister – or so they said – who would have been good if they'd managed to perfect their most difficult stunt: she leaned decorously against a large red post-office-type letter box while he, from quite close, threw three-ply wooden letters across the stage, trying to get them into the letter-box slot. The slot showed signs of having been greatly and recently enlarged.

They were scared stiff. Daisy discovered that they had never done their letter-posting act in public before. At the band call, with the drum-roll and the thump at the end of it, the boy managed to get only one letter out of the total of eight into the slot. It was humiliating to hear him saying that it would be all right when there was an audience. We just hoped he would get one in and then stop while he was still winning. He also juggled rather badly with just three balls.

The whole show was billed as 'Twice Brightly – 6 pm and 8 pm. Wednesday and Saturday matinees at 3 pm'. The Queen's with the bar down its side was a leftover from Victorian times when the music hall had developed from tavern entertainments, with some inns meeting demands for humble entertainment and others enlarging their premises to take a stage. It was this development from the 1850s onwards that persuaded men, women and children to leave their usual wage-earning work and join in the business of entertainment, and risk having bottles, eggs, cabbages and rotten fruit thrown at them.

Daisy was a pro all right. At the 'rising card trick' she asked the trombone player to make the appropriate ascending sound as each of the three cards rose from the glass, with a drum beat as I finally plucked the risen card clear of the pack. With the trick in which I threw the pack so it would shower all over her and she would appear to catch the chosen card in her cleavage, she told the conductor to tickle the high notes of the piano as if he were tickling her, and so on.

The Bently sisters opened the show at precisely six o'clock, which coincided with the bar opening. The bar posed quite a noise problem, as

well as causing many of the patrons to be facing the wrong way. The girls
were followed by the letter-posting act, during which not one letter went
into the slot even though the poor boy took a pace closer to the letter box
after each failure. I don't remember the rest of the first half, except that it
was closed by the 'Poor Man's Max Miller', who was brash enough to tell
the line of boozers to 'face the front or buy me a pint.'

The Bently sisters also opened the second half; they were followed by
us. No, there was no overnight stardom, and I was so scared I've no
recollection how it went. Mrs Clarbour was there for the eight o'clock
show, when the letter-box trick was still a failure and, as the evening was
older, more drink had been consumed by those leaning against the bar,
thus encouraging drunken cat-calls.

Going back on the bus, I was astonished to hear Mrs Clarbour saying
that she had spoken to the management and that they would not be
wanting the letter-box stunt on the Tuesday. The Bently Sisters were
asked to put an extra number into the first half and an extra number in for
the second half. Would 'Cassan the Mystic and Daisy' make their act last
another five minutes? Would we? We certainly would – and I knew exactly
what those five minutes would consist of. Daisy wanted to know in detail,
so I agreed to meet her at the theatre at two o'clock the next day, to run
through the new part of the act.

I spent the next morning looking for a pet shop that sold pigeons.
Finding one, I chose a nice-looking, lively bird and asked the owner to clip
its wings so that, if it was made to jump off a shelf a couple of feet above
my magic wand, it would have to land on it. He did this. Then he put the
pigeon on a shelf and clapped his hands, and I held my wand about a foot
below. The pigeon landed on it. We did it three times and that bird never
missed.

I met Daisy as arranged, and she winced a bit as she saw the pigeon. I
should have noticed that wince right then; I was to regret getting involved
in this part of the act for many months afterwards. She called the bird
Leonardo from Aristotle because, as she explained, he was the man who
flew too near to the sun and burned his wings.

The trick was simple enough. I explained to her that I would ask 'any
lady in the audience to please hold up a ring she was prepared to lend me
for a short while.' Daisy would be looking through a hole in the curtain
with a a pair of opera-glasses so that she could see exactly what sort of ring
it appeared to be. Back stage she had a set of Woolworth's rings which I
knew inside out. If the 'lady in the audience' produced one that looked
nothing like anything we had, I would pretend I hadn't seen it.

When the right type of ring was found, Daisy would take the duplicate
in her right hand, make her entrance, take my magic wand from me, go
down into the stalls holding the wand in her left hand and ask the lady to

slip the ring on to the end of the wand, where it would appear to remain. As she turned to remount the steps to the stage, Daisy changed hands, allowing her right hand to slip the duplicate Woolworth ring on to the wand while the real ring vanished into her left hand. She did this half a dozen times so well that, even standing in front of her, I could not see her make the vital switch of rings.

She was to come up on to the stage and drop the duplicate ring into a screw of paper. Then she left the stage with the real ring while I stuffed the paper into the muzzle of a small stage pistol. We spent half an hour practising that and nothing else.

While I was taking my time doing this, Daisy would be off-stage tying the ring to one of the pigeon's legs with a red ribbon and putting the bird into a box, which she then slid on to a string, stretched across the stage. She was to use a pulley to hoist the little bird-box to centre stage; the pulley also concealed a thread which, when pulled, would let the door at the front of the box drop down and swing on its hinge, thus releasing the pigeon.

Phobias weren't fashionable in those days; the word was not even in my vocabulary. Daisy had a phobia; she hadn't fully realised it herself at that time. I had noticed her wince when I put the wooden bird-cage on a crate, back stage; but this was a big phobia: she was frightened of birds and terrified of birds fluttering.

It was fortunate that this was a Tuesday, with no matinée. We spent the whole afternoon getting Daisy and Leonardo acquainted, and it wasn't easy. I had to take him out of the cage, hold him firmly so he could not flutter, while she – after half an hour of looking at him and shuffling closer – finally touched his head with her little finger. Two hours later, she accepted that she could hold him.

While the Bently sisters cavorted about to the strains of 'I've Got My Love To Keep Me Warm' and other pops of the day, Daisy finally managed to tie a ring to Leonardo's leg with no help from me. This was really the eleventh hour. I could have kissed her. I said so. She kissed me instead. Then it became mutual. This was in the days when boys and girls kissed. They didn't eat each other in the way they appear to do on television today.

We had had no time to rehearse her next task, operating the pulley; as the audience was already out front being entertained by the Bently Sisters, she had no chance to practise pulling the box to the centre of the stage, at which point I was to make much of taking careful aim at the box and pulling the trigger with my left hand.

As the pistol went *pop!* Daisy had to pull the door release so that Leonardo could flutter out, with the ring tied to his leg, and settle on the magic wand held in my right hand. The next part was simple. Leonardo, with the ring still attached by the red ribbon to his leg, was to be carried by me on the wand down to the owner of the ring for positive identification, after which the red ribbon would be untied and the ring returned to its owner. Leonardo couldn't possibly escape as his wings had been clipped.

While the Bently Sisters were opening the second half of the first house I kept looking at Daisy – not with desire, but with terror that she might collapse at having to hold Leonardo all by herself.

But she managed. The trick was such a success that for the second house we decided to finish on it. It was such fun we spread the 'business' in order to give it the build-up we thought it warranted. It was a success for the rest of the week until Saturday night, second house. This was our last performance at the Queen's.

Daisy had been to see the drummer between first and second house. She told me that she had suggested to him that I should count 'One! Two! Three!' before I pulled the trigger and she pulled the release, and he could do a drum-roll with a good big drum wallop and crash of cymbals at the end as the pigeon appeared. This was a splendid idea. Her phobia had left her and it seemed now that nothing could possibly go wrong.

Between us we got through the cut-and-restored-rope routine, the multiplying billiard balls, a couple of card tricks, burned-and-restored (borrowed) pound note, Chinese rice bowls and so on. We were now about to start the ring and pigeon trick.

'Will any lady or gentleman kindly hold up any ring they are prepared to lend us for our next experiment, known as Material Television.' (There were only about two thousand television sets in the whole of the country at the time. They were the miracle of the age, and 'television' was the buzz-word of the 1930s, just as 'electricity' was the buzz-word in late Victorian times and 'green' is the buzz-word today.) The patter went on to describe how television could transport a picture from one place to another; but this new form of television would transport a solid ring from one place to another . . . Glorious rubbish that scarcely even related to the effect of our trick; but that was show business.

A girl near the left-side gangway held up a gold ring which held a small diamond. We had a duplicate which Daisy quickly picked up as she made her entrance. Passing me she took my wand, looking confident as she went down the four steps over the 'orchestra' pit to the fourth row back, where the girl was holding up her ring. Daisy held out my wand and the ring was slipped over its end. She came back up on to the stage, making the switch as she did so, and dropped the duplicate ring from the end of the wand into the square of paper I was holding.

As she left the stage to tie the ring to Leonardo's leg there were no worries there; she had done it nine times before with increasing confidence. I prattled on about cathode rays and other nonsense so she would have plenty of time to tie the ring on, load the box, hitch it to the waiting hook and work the pulley to hoist it up to centre stage.

The box arrived, about a foot above my head and a yard to my right, in exactly the right position. Daisy was getting ready to pull the cotton that would release the door and expose Leonardo so he could jump down on to my magic wand.

Aiming the pistol at the box and dramatically demanding total silence for a few seconds (which I didn't get because of the boozy bar), I said, 'One!' The drum-roll started softly. 'Two!' The drum roll was building perfectly. 'Three!' I fired. There was a crash of cymbals, combined with the boom of the big drum and the sound of the pistol. Daisy pulled the cotton. The door opened as I leaned towards the box, holding the magic wand exactly where Leonardo was to fall.

Clipped wings or not, the noise was too much for that bird; his adrenalin took over, enabling him to shoot off like a white streak. I just caught a glimpse of the red ribbon and the ring as he vanished into the dim recesses of the back row of the theatre. I stood there, paralysed, hoping to see Leonardo perching on something in front of me.

We never saw Leonardo again . . . or the red ribbon . . . or the ring. Someone must have grabbed him, had pigeon-pie for supper and sold the ring on Monday.

I made some lame excuse or other and said that the bird would appear 'as if by magic' before the end of the show.

The girl's father appeared instead, and not by magic, before the end of the show. We had a subdued conversation back stage, during which the offended man tucked his chin into his chest and, with permanently raised eyebrows furrowing his brow, seemed to be silently saying, 'All right. Go on. Hit me.' He moaned about the cash value of the ring, plus the sentimental value, plus the nuisance of having to go out and buy a new one. 'That ring is worth ten quid. It's a real diamond.' That was too much in those days, as I checked later by looking in jewellers' windows. I knew that he knew he'd got me and, taking the area into account, I assumed he was going to swindle me. Most of the poor, like most of the rich, have this constant desire always foremost.

There was nothing I could do except be thankful that I had been doing quite a bit of crowd work and was wise enough not to leave my money at my digs but had it with me, such as it was. I could pay the man his money, which was in my back pocket – but his raised eyebrows and defensive stance told me that he was lying. I told him that if I claimed on my insurance, it might take weeks to settle, but we could call it quits if I gave him £7 there and then. (I had no insurance; it was just a bluff.) It worked. He grabbed the seven pound notes with such speed, I knew he'd have settled happily for five or even less, as the ring had looked suspiciously like the fake from Woolworth's.

In the summer of 1939, because I had volunteered for the Territorial Army, I went to summer camp with the Royal Horse Artillery, where I noticed with some apprehension a brass plate on the field gun reading '1912'; a few inquiries revealed that we had no shells to fit it, as they weren't made any more. What is more, we had no artillery other than that one old field-gun. This period was followed by a happy month in Little Haven with people I knew, loved, respected and enjoyed. When that holiday ended, I was unknowingly to say goodbye to most of them for ever.

We had motored back from Little Haven to Dudley on Tuesday, 29 August 1939, a little earlier than intended because Father, having read *Mein Kampf*, said war was coming. I, not having read it, said it wasn't.

On 1 September, a Friday, I walked into the town of Dudley to buy a wireless set for Mother, as she said the news was important. Father couldn't stand the wireless, saying that as all the news was read by actors who could not be trusted, it would be better to wait for *The Times* and read the truth. Father read *The Times* and took the *Daily Mirror* for the servants.

I arrived back home just before lunch to find a green envelope on the hall table addressed to me, 'On His Majesty's Service'. As I was already a Territorial, it was not my calling-up paper but my mobilisation paper.

Father and Mother both read the mobilisation paper and said that no one at the barracks could possibly know that I was even in town, therefore it would be perfectly all right to stop to lunch, to tea and to dinner, and report at the barracks at five minutes to midnight.

With that in mind, one of the maids was dispatched to buy a chicken. Father went down the cellar to choose a bottle of wine for dinner and opened it there and then to 'let it breathe'. Before lunch he gave me a large whisky and a cigar, neither of which was appreciated.

From time to time Mother commented that our cook would probably join up and our dear Evelyn, the parlour maid, would get a job in a munitions factory. (Why she made this distinction I never discovered.) Furthermore, the daily would just not show up in the morning. (I failed to see the logic in that.) The gardener, Tonks, would be sure to leave, as would Ball, the chauffeur. Mother suddenly said she would join the WVS and drive an ambulance, which she did a few weeks later.

On Sunday we declared war on Germany. It wasn't put like that: the Prime Minister said on the wireless that if the Germans didn't clear out of Poland, they could consider themselves to be at war with us. As we all know now, they didn't clear out of Poland.

We were at war with Germany.

7

Puddle on the stage

ARRIVING AT THE DRILL HALL just up the road at five minutes to midnight, I was issued with additional kit and directed up to the local roller-skating rink, which was a huge hall with a jet-black shiny floor.

Large numbers of young men from Dudley and surrounding areas were milling about; there seemed to be no accommodation of any kind for them. At the rink there were two lavatories: one marked 'Gentlemen', a one-seater with three standing urinals; and the other marked 'Ladies', a one-seater only. There was no hand wash-basin in either. It was a curious comment from the architect, saying tacitly that men pee four times more often than women. There seems to be no reliable research on this subject and it is possible that the architect thought that men drank more beer than girls, who were pleased to be seen in a pub in those days, drinking gin and lime held in the left hand with the little finger raised.

A lance-bombardier looked at the 'Ladies' notice and said, 'That's a special one and it will be reserved for the Nancy boys.'

Looking at the men milling about, it was difficult to imagine how they would all cope. Lights were scarce and any switched on were greeted with 'Put that bloody light out!' because black-out precautions had started. The few lights that were switched on had blue bulbs in them, giving little illumination. It was clear before the night even started, especially as some of the men arrived very drunk, that there would be a filthy mess in the morning. There was.

To add to the smell of vomit and urine, the confusion at sunrise was reminiscent of a Hogarth low-life picture. Most men who had arrived in the pink now had black hands and faces. The black was from the floor. Everyone and everything was either dirty grey or quite black because no one seemed to know, until glorious September daylight flooded in, that roller-skating rinks were black-leaded to keep the surface smooth.

In most minds we were there for neither King nor Country. It was neither patriotism nor love of our monarch that held us there. No one at that roller-skating rink had ever met him, and it was impossible for them to love someone whose image they had seen only on postage stamps and coins. Few, if any, were there for patriotic reasons; for some, it was just a job with regular food, free clothes and pay. Unemployment was high. The motive others had for being involved with the military was a fear of ridicule if they dodged it. Most simply had to be part of it, whatever it was.

We were right to want to stand in the way of the monstrous Nazi regime. The sad part is that most of us had no idea what the Nazi regime stood for; few even knew it was monstrous. Equally sad is that most of the Germans who called themselves Nazis were just as ignorant of what the Nazi Party represented.

We sat in our barracks, glorying in the knowledge that we were the 268th Battery of the 119th Regiment of the Royal Horse Artillery, with one gun (that would not fire as we had no shells for it) and one horse so that we could qualify as Horse Artillery. Nobody ever sat on that horse; looking at its sagging back, it really didn't measure up to it. Each morning someone was detailed to take it for a walk, but no one was allowed to ride the poor creature. The day came when the horse was no longer about. It will not be mentioned how tough the stew was for a week afterwards.

My first professional venture in uniform was mercifully short, and in retrospect it was probably just as well that I developed double pneumonia, which revealed a heart murmur; this in turn, when the pneumonia was gone, resulted in the regimental doctor telling me I was no longer fit for duty.

To my delight, I was told at the time I would never be fit and my illness would be a handicap to the army. In my frame of mind that was just great; but I was a little put out to be told I might well not make forty years. The heart murmur led to my being advised to lie rather than stand, to stand rather than walk, to walk rather than run, and to carry nothing heavier than a walking stick. That this was all rubbish was not revealed until medical science after the war showed that there are thousands of people with heart murmurs who don't drop dead; to the chagrin of those who made such medical prophecies, they have been found to live to ripe old ages. The only effect of my personal murmur had been to load my life-insurance payments.

So there I was, back in mufti, no longer worrying about puttees. Dudley looked the same. Mrs Over-the-road had a special long face for me as she waited for signs of my dropping dead. She always put on this face if anyone was ill; and with it went a special voice, which was probably cultivated when my grandfather was in practice and he would naturally lose a patient or two from time to time. I caught Mother also looking at me with that special face once or twice, but I had to disappoint them both.

An armaments factory called Rubery, Owen and Company of Bilston took me on as a clerk, my main employment being to try to estimate the amount of scrap metal they were producing and to ensure that it was loaded and checked out by rail to some destination whose name I never discovered. I wondered once or twice why they did not deal with it themselves, since they could have melted it down and re-used it. The job had no compensations except that of a vague feeling that it was a war job, and someone had to do it.

My twenty-first birthday was on 2 April 1941, and there was to be quite an assembly of various uncles, aunts and cousins, whittled down by the calls of war to just a handful. War or no war, Mother managed to find a couple of capons and, as Father had always kept a well-stocked cellar, wine was no problem. Father decreed that even though it was wartime we would dress for dinner; as I could never tie my black bow tie properly, I went into Mother's room for her to do it for me. (In those days, wearing a made-up tie put one quite beyond the pale.) I was standing there, holding the tie in one hand, when she looked up at me, wearing her most serious face. She seldom wore any other face, but, as it was my twenty-first birthday, I worried a little when she said, 'Sit down, Ian, I have to talk to you.'

I sat, wondering if some girl's mother had telephoned to announce that her daughter was pregnant and it was my fault or, worse, the army had discovered that I had acquired some of their equipment. Perhaps it was my night for sitting on the roof of the town hall, watching for incendiary bombs.

'I have,' Mother said, 'something serious to tell you, now that you are twenty-one.' She sat down, which I knew meant she was about to say something that she considered to be of significance. 'Every family has a skeleton in its cupboard.' There was a long pause during which she looked around, either to ensure that no one else was listening, or else she was wondering how to break such dire news to me.

I looked as po-faced as possible, to stay in harmony with her mood. 'What is it, Mother?'

'One of the Messiters, your great-great-great-grandfather, was vicar of Wincanton.' She stopped again.

'Never mind, Mother. I'm sure we'll live it down.'

She didn't smile; Mother never had a proper sense of fun. 'That man, in spite of the cloth . . . ' She was clearly delaying telling the dreadful tale as long as possible because it was so shameful.

'What cloth?' It was a new expression to me. I thought she was talking about a table cloth.

She explained patiently the significance of the cloth before going on. 'While he was vicar of Wincanton, he fathered twenty-six illegitimate children . . . ' She didn't like to look at me as she said it. I didn't like to ask if bicycles had been invented then.

I was looking at her as I remembered a few words from Genesis, my favourite book: 'Be fruitful, and multiply, and replenish the earth', but all I could say of consequence was, 'Gosh!' I was totally unprepared for her sense of timing, her low-key delivery of the line that will live with me for ever.

'But,' she added, as if to make the whole disgraceful chapter in my ancestry respectable, 'he was never unfrocked.'

It was impossible not to laugh. Mother looked appalled. I apologised and mumbled something about her lack of a sense of humour. To accuse her of having no sense of humour was equivalent to saying she took sneaky kicks at the dog or stole the budgie's millet.

'I don't want you to think,' she said, 'that I don't see what you are laughing at. I know perfectly well. But I think you're being very vulgar.'

Mother was driving an ambulance, my sister was a Voluntary Aid Detachment nurse. The maids were thin on the ground. There was one new one called Daffodil whom we called Daffy because she was simple – so simple, indeed, that on the night of 14 November 1940 when we were all down the cellar during a noisy air-raid, she suddenly jumped up and screamed. Father asked what was wrong.

'I've left my bedroom window open,' she said, 'and a bomb can get in that way.' Mother told her to leave it as it would make no difference.

Father never hurried or panicked, and we both knew that, while one or two bombs were dropped in error on Dudley, the target was probably Birmingham or the factories round it. The noise was mostly made by the anti-aircraft guns, one of which was strategically placed on a lawn about fifty feet from the house. Every time it went off, Mother said, 'Oh Lor'! I hope they don't break our windows.'

Now and again Mother wanted to fetch something from some other room; if she had to cross the stone hall, she would take someone with her, not to accompany her across the hall but to stand at the top of the cellar steps and listen for enemy aircraft. The huge glass dome above her was now a very real danger: a loud explosion could have caused the whole structure to collapse, with shards of glass showering down and bouncing up from the stone floor. So, at the shout of 'Now!' she would scuttle across the hall to get whatever she thought was worth risking life and limb for. She would then repeat the process to get back to the cellar.

As Mother was in the Women's Voluntary Service, she would come up yet again from the cellar to telephone the local branch, asking if she were needed. She was. The HQ was just up the road, so she walked there and I went with her.

The only alarming part of that was hearing the shrapnel from the exploded anti-aircraft shells whirring down, to ricochet off the buildings and ping in the road.

Back home, Father was waiting for me in the car. 'Come on! Jump in!' he said. 'It's Coventry. They're getting it badly.' With that we were off on the thirty-mile journey and, after the first five miles or so, Father told me to look in the back of the car under the seat where I would find two flasks of whisky. 'Put one in your pocket and the other in mine.'

Most history books mention only that single huge raid on Coventry but in fact there were several, as it was a centre for the manufacture of aero-engines and machine-tools. The main error of those raids was ignorance, in that the Germans bombed the town itself, while the factories were located round the edge.

Coventry on that night of flames was a shambles of fire, fallen masonry, dazed, dead, dying, saddened, bewildered and injured people. The various services – police, fire, ambulance, Women's Voluntary Service and others – were overwhelmed in this night of terror. Over seventy thousand houses were destroyed; four hundred people were killed and two thousand were badly injured under the rain of German steel and explosives estimated at six hundred tons of high explosive and an uncalculated quantity of incendiaries. The town was virtually wiped out and a new verb was created for towns badly bombed: 'Coventrated'.

My job allowed me Saturday afternoons and all day Sunday off. This was no time to be thinking of entertainment; but the conjuring tricks were still with me and I had made a good friend at the factory; Derek, my co-scrap-metal checker and magical conspirator.

Cinemas in those days would show a main film, a newsreel and a short, such as a Charlie Chaplin, a Laurel and Hardy or whatever. They also had an organist who would rise apparently from the bowels of the earth as he played his mighty organ. Because of the war, untold thousands of people were away from their home towns with nowhere to go except the cinema. New films of the year included *Holiday Inn*, *Mrs Miniver* with Greer Garson, *Rembrandt* and *How Green Was My Valley*. The Marx Brothers' last film, *The Big Store*, was going round again, following its opening the previous year. Cinemas became very big business and they vied with one another to attract the largest audiences. Some of them employed a stage variety act or two between the films in order to enhance their attractions.

Derek and I discussed the possibility of becoming a variety double act and touring the multitude of cinemas in the Midlands during the evenings and at weekends. To that end we worked out an absurd routine.

As he was very tall, we got him a wig with a bun on top, like that of a pantomime dame and through this bun were thrust two big knitting needles. This made him look like a giant. He also blacked out some of his front teeth and grinned broadly. He wore a black satin blouse with georgette sleeves, a red pleated short satin skirt, short green socks with suspenders and hobnailed boots, built up to increase his size even more. I was the dude in white tie and tails with a red-lined black cloak.

We weren't very good but, because of the shortage of live entertainment, we made as much with our act as we made in the factory. Two episodes of this act are worth recording.

The first concerned the sack trick. Derek was handcuffed with a trick pair of cuffs and put in a sack, with two members of the audience on stage to tie the sack firmly and seal the knot with red sealing-wax. After this, I would stand in front of the sack, facing the audience; I held a large cloth behind me with my arms outstretched so they could not see how he got out.

There was a large clock to show how long it had taken to handcuff and get him into the sack. The audience noted the time and were told it would take him less than half that time to get out.

The tying of the neck of the sack was similar to the tying of a pyjama trouser cord. It could be pulled tight from the front, and this squeezed the neck of the sack shut. Unknown to the audience, there was a small slit in the tube through which the cord was threaded; Derek had plenty of slack hidden in that tube and tied with a slip-knot. While the knots were still being tied he would get the slip-knot undone and hold on tightly to the loop. At a signal from me in the patter, he would let the slack go, expand the mouth of the sack, escape, retie the knot, pulling the sack shut again and poking the spare cord back into the sack. 'Hurry, hurry' music gave an illusion of speed.

With a chord in C major he would pull the cloth from my hands to throw it over me. He would pass the sack to the members of the audience who had put him in it to show that it had not been cut and that it was still tied and sealed.

One night, two really tough soldiers jumped, invited, on to the stage. They handcuffed Derek and put him in the sack. Then, with great strength, they pulled violently at the ends of the cord. The cord stopped at the point where it should have been tied, but then suddenly they pulled it some more, and all the slack needed for the escape came out. Derek had not been holding it firmly enough and the slack was lost. He was tied tightly in.

I saw what had happened and wondered what would or could possibly happen next. The clock was now an appalling embarrassment. They had taken only two and a quarter minutes to put him in. Five minutes had passed since then. The organ played the 'Hurry, hurry' music over and over again. The illusion of speed was now a delusion of slowness.

I could hear the audience shuffling and making unfriendly noises. People don't boo or cat-call today; they did then. We were getting the bird. In the background I could hear Derek calling for help. 'Have you a razor blade?'

'No,' I half whispered.

'A penknife?'

'No.'

We were followed by a girl singer. We took the whole of the stage and her act was to be in front of the tabs (curtains). I signalled for the tabs to be pulled, then I dragged Derek, still in the sack, into the wings.

'Oh for Chrissake!' I heard him saying as the girl started her act. 'Open this bloody thing! I'm suffocating!'

I had a better idea which Derek never really forgave me for. I managed to find a large card with RESERVED printed on the front. The back was blank and white. On this I wrote: 'NEW ASSISTANT WANTED'. Much to Derek's relief, he was then let out. I talked him into getting back in and put him on a settee in the foyer when the audience was coming out. The notice was pinned to the sack. We never discovered whether the audience thought the whole thing had been planned for their amusement, but that cinema never asked us back.

The other episode also involved the sack trick, and it landed us in court. Prior to the trick itself I would ask for a volunteer to come on stage and be tied up. There never was a volunteer, which led naturally to asking the audience if they had any ideas as to who should be tied up and put in the sack. Derek, at this point, had to look alarmed and, the more alarmed he looked, the more the audience liked it when I pointed at him and asked them 'Her?' 'Yes!!' they would yell back. This could be played up to get them all shouting, which is always good entertainment.

At this point he would feign tears. To complete the illusion, he had a wet sponge concealed inside a handkerchief, tucked up his knickers; the handkerchief was to be pulled out to wipe his eyes and then squeezed to show the tears running down and falling on to the stage.

One Sunday we had reached the point where the audience cries out 'Yes!!' when the water from the sponge started to trickle down his leg and on to the stage. He felt it running and looked down. Then he looked up at me and, foolishly, I looked down at the growing puddle on the stage. We then both looked blankly and innocently at the audience, who by then were crying with laughter. This sort of thing was unknown in the theatre at that time, unlike today. We completed the trick, leaving a highly delighted audience holding its sides with laughter.

I hadn't reckoned with the local Watch Committee. Appearing before the bench on the Monday morning, we were fined £1 each for public obscenity.

One Saturday night, after we had done our turn in a cinema, we were up in the manager's office being given our money when the telephone rang. The manager answered it: it was a panic call from Another Midland Theatre in a small industrial town near Dudley. He was being asked if he had seen any act recently that could take the second half of the bill in his theatre for a week. He suggested us and put me on the phone.

We couldn't do matinées because of the scrap-metal business; however, because of war work, they no longer had a matinée except on Saturdays. This was perfect, because we had Saturday afternoons off; we could do it.

There's an old theatrical expression: 'The ghost walks', which is slang for 'salaries are about to be paid'. It is an allusion to Shakespeare's *Hamlet* Act I, scene i, where Horatio asks the ghost if it 'walks' because

> Thou hast uphoarded in thy life
> Extorted treasure in the womb of earth.

At that theatre, by custom the ghost walked on Fridays between first and second house. In other words, we expected the owner, a fat little bald man with a mean manner and an even meaner pencil-thin moustache, to come round to our dressing-room with the £14. He didn't turn up.

A few inquiries from the other acts at the end of the evening showed that, not only had he not paid all of them, those he had paid had been given less than their agreed money.

Derek and I were worried at first, but he had a plan. As we had the matinée and the two evening shows still to come on the Saturday, we would waylay this man. We did – or rather, Derek did. We sat with the dressing-room door open after the matinée and waited for him to walk past. As he did so, Derek, who was always braver than I and much bigger, seized him by his coat and said bluntly, 'What about our money?'

The owner hadn't expected this. 'We've had a bad week,' he pleaded.

Derek dragged the little man into our dressing-room, slammed the door and said, 'Balls! We've been counting the house. There's been hardly a seat vacant.'

'That was paper,' said the owner. (To 'paper the house' is a theatrical expression meaning to fill the theatre with 'deadheads', non-paying people who have been given free seats. They are often friends of the cast, theatrical landladies, the press and so on.)

'Balls!' Derek repeated. 'People like you don't have that many friends.' He grabbed the owner by the front of his jacket and, doing something usually seen only in films, shoved him up against the wall and held him there, pressed against the wall, with his feet a good twelve inches from the ground. The owner could do nothing. 'Well, do we get our money or don't we?'

The little man looked thoroughly frightened. After some moments of hesitation while I wondered if Derek would hit him, and he probably wondered that too, he said, 'All right.'

Derek lowered him to the floor but kept a tight hold on him.

'Let go!' said the owner. 'There's people out there in the corridor.'

There certainly were. As Derek opened the door it was plain they had been listening with some delight.

'Ah!' said Derek with pleasure. 'We're off to try to get our money. Anyone want to come with us?'

We went to the box-office, where the owner was temporarily released. 'It was ten pounds, wasn't it?'

The chiseller would not give up.

'No,' I said, 'it was fourteen pounds.'

'I haven't got that much in the till. I banked it this morning.'

'Let's look!' Derek was really angry now. 'Come on. Get that bloody till open. Get it open! Go on! Open the thing!' He grabbed the owner's left arm and started to push it up his back. Two people suddenly appeared at the box-office window to buy seats.

I asked them to hold on a bit while we were being paid our wages. People never react as one would expect. They waited, and as they waited they watched, but without much concern; it was almost as if they expected this sort of free entertainment at the theatre. Their faces were quite expressionless.

I worried now that Derek might break the owner's arm. The chiseller opened the till with his right hand. He counted out the money. There were three other artists with us. Derek asked them each in turn what they were owed. The owner paid two of them what they claimed. After that, the till really was empty. To cut a long story short, Derek extracted the money due from the owner at the beginning of the second house, since the money was now in the till from the sale of tickets, and this was handed over to the grateful artists.

Mother had her wireless, and the programmes seemed fascinating. The lure of London and show business, now in the form of a carrot dangled by the BBC, was a temptation impossible to resist. I gave a month's notice to the factory.

This time I didn't have to borrow from Father. I found a fairly decent room in Chelsea through an uncle of mine who was already living in the area.

Before I had unpacked, I wrote to the BBC. Great care was taken over that letter, which is still in the BBC files. It went:

November 2nd, 1942.

BBC
Broadcasting House
London W1

Dear Sirs,
I would very much like to work for you. But as I have had a good
education I do not know anything.
    Can you help me?

Yours truly

I don't know what I expected. I certainly didn't in all seriousness expect to
get a job with such a mighty organisation, which was known and respected
all over the world.

    It was also an organisation about which I knew almost nothing, as
Mother had listened only to classical music and Father disliked what he
called 'that infernal noise machine'.

    To my astonishment, the reply came back in three days. It gave me a
telephone number and an office to ring, to make an appointment. I had
twopence, so I telephoned at once. In those days the number was Welbeck
4468. It is engraved on my heart.

8
Shoving discs

APPOINTMENT MADE, for no particular reason I put a pack of cards in my pocket.

I experienced a great sense of occasion going though the heavy bronze-and-glass doors of Broadcasting House and up to the reception desk; at least I was treading the hallowed ground.

To be punctual, I arrived three-quarters of an hour early, presented my letter to the security-conscious reception desk, and was asked to wait. Various important-looking people coming and going exuded a god-like air. Each man was surely some famous broadcaster, such as Stuart Hibberd, and all important-looking women must be Audrey Russell. After forty minutes had gone by, a girl at reception gave me a square of paper with my name on it and the number of the room in which the frightening interview was to take place.

The lift shot up to the third floor, to spill the occupants out on to the carpeted, hushed corridors with numbered doors on each side. Finding the correct number, I stood outside and took a deep breath before knocking. My timid knock was not answered. A second and louder knock produced sounds of laughter and, 'Come in!'

Three happy-looking people were sitting behind a table, all smiling. One was a very quiet and pleasant woman. 'Mr Messiter?' she asked.

The old stutter was back in a big way. But as all stutterers find, it was no good just nodding and sitting down, so I forced myself to say 'Y-y-y-es.' This must have impressed upon them immediately that I had not come for a job as an announcer.

'Please sit down.'

The tallest, a man sitting in the middle, was holding my letter. He had a red face, short-cut greying hair, a sports coat with leather elbow-patches and a friendly attitude which seemed to say, 'There's nothing to be afraid of.' They all looked even happier when he asked me, 'Do you really think that having a good education automatically ensures that you know nothing?'

'No, not really.' All this was punctuated by the stutter. Stutterers who raise their voices stop stuttering, which was why, when I addressed an audience from the music-hall stage I almost lost this most humiliating incapacity; but it would not have been seemly to shout at an interview, especially in Broadcasting House.

He laughed as he asked the next question. 'Where were you at school?'

'My prep was Winton House, the prep for Winchester.'

'Oh, you have an academic background.'

'No. I went to Sherborne.'

'Failed Winchester?'

'No. I never sat for it.'

'You didn't learn anything at Sherborne?'

'Yes. I learned a lot about rugger, cricket, the army, history, gymnastics – oh yes, there was Latin and so on. But nothing which I can use to get a job.'

'No, I've never seen a Latin script around here. I went to Wellington. My Greek is splendid still, but the BBC haven't used it – yet.' The other two laughed.

I was scared stiff, not knowing whether he was being very kind or sending me up. Panic and a desire to escape as quickly as possible welled up.

'As you must be able to guess, we have hundreds of applications for jobs here . . .' He paused and waved my letter, as if trying to make up his mind whether to keep it, throw it away or throw it at me. He spoke instead. ' . . . but this letter . . .' They all smiled again. By way of an amusing diversion, they had just wanted to see what sort of a lunatic would write for a job in that fashion.

He asked to see my military discharge papers and identity card, which he examined closely before handing them back. He asked a few relevant questions to which the answers, when I could get them out properly, seemed acceptable. 'Would you mind waiting in the next office for a few minutes?'

Miss Loom, a lady with prematurely greying, neat hair and a well-cut coat and skirt, was sitting close to the adjoining door, and she opened it for me. I went into an empty office which overlooked the Langham Hotel, the hotel to which Edward VII was reputed to have taken Lily Langtry and several other bedworthy ladies.

I heard Miss Loom laugh, but the conversation in general sounded like a low hum, broken now and then by a cough; the words were too indistinct to be heard. The men laughed a couple of times, so it was only natural to assume they were laughing at me. The desire for escape became more urgent.

It seemed hours before Miss Loom opened the adjoining door. 'Please come back.' It was not possible to read her thoughts in her face; she was inscrutable.

The man with the leather elbow-patches spoke first. 'How would you like a month's trial as a recorded programmes assistant?'

Having no idea what a recorded programmes assistant was, what the hours were, where the workplace was or how much pay there would be, I grinned from ear to ear and accepted it at once.

'When can you start?'

It seemed wrong to say 'at once', so Monday was named.

'What work are you doing now? Today? This morning?' asked Miss Loom with a smile that seemed to tell me she knew I was out of work and didn't want to admit it.

'Nothing.' Owning up wasn't easy, and only happened because of my lack of speed in thinking up a convincing lie.

'Right then!' said the man with elbow-patches and a happy smile. 'Let's start now. Here's a form for you to take into the next room and fill in. While you're doing that I'll find someone to show you around and teach you what you have to do. When you get to the bit that asks what job you're applying for, just fill it in with the letters RPA. They stand for Recorded Programmes Assistant. You will be paid weekly at a rate of two pounds ten shillings.'

Ten minutes later I had joined the BBC.

The aura of Broadcasting House was more suited to a church than to the hub of all British broadcasting. To this day, try as it has, it has never quite shed that atmosphere.

Lord Reith had been the first General Manager of the British Broadcasting Company in 1922 and Director General of the British Broadcasting Corporation, which replaced the Company on 1 January 1927. His influence on broadcasting lingered on long after he had gone, like the smell of Jumbo's Turkish cigarettes. When audience figures were collected to find out who listened to what and whether or not they liked what they heard, the Fun and Games Department (then known as the Variety Department and now as Light Entertainment) was drawing the biggest audience; but there was a feeling that that side of broadcasting was not quite respectable when seen through the eyes of Lord Reith. (This was curious, when it is remembered by those who knew him well that his own private life could have done with a little clean-up. Under the pious exterior was a womaniser with a ruthless and occasionally vicious streak.) His strength and saving grace was that he was a magnificent and powerful administrator.

At the interview it had been made clear that many people, who started as Recorded Programmes Assistants, used the introduction as a stepping-stone to other departments and better jobs within the corporation. 'You, Mr Messiter, would not do that, would you?'

'No,' I agreed, and my expression said I would not dream of such a thing. How could anyone think it possible? I was so excited to have got even that far that such an idea had not occurred to me – until it was put into my head by that chap with leather elbows who sat, pink-faced and smiling, in the middle.

Someone was detailed to show me round the parts of Broadcasting House that might concern me in the future. I saw studio doors with lights over them: some were off and some were illuminated with brilliant red lights. Again the solemnity of the surroundings gave one a strange feeling of being on the verge of a spiritual experience. My guide's voice took on a tone of reverence as we stopped within a foot of one of these doors while he pointed to the bright red light over it. 'Never,' he said in exaggeratedly hushed tones, 'go into a studio when you see that light actually on. It means that they are actually broadcasting or recording in there.' He raised his right arm towards the studio door and let his right hand flop, to demonstrate his meaning.

Finding myself standing within a few yards of someone broadcasting, I was too overawed to reply; I took a step backwards, as one might on discovering the unexpected presence of the Pope.

My guide was a thin man wearing a double-breasted jacket with lapels so flat that they seemed to have been pressed on him. He had a pencil moustache, below which protruded an unlit pipe, which he sucked at noisily. He found an empty studio, which was divided into two: one part of it was the control room; the larger part, separated by a door, a wall and a double-glazed, sound-proof window, was the microphone section in which hung or stood the magic microphones themselves.

'Nothing said in this actual room part can actually be heard the other side of that window.' He waved his arm around to show the extent of the room.

I nodded as intelligently as I could and said, 'Oh.'

'But on this control panel is this switch. When you press that down, it will, or should, actually cut off the microphone in there so you can speak to the broadcaster without the listeners actually hearing you. Note that I said 'should cut off the microphone'. It doesn't always work and that's led to a few disasters in the past. You simply can't imagine what a mess that can make of things. The engineer has to keep a log book and enter up any mistakes. For that reason it's absolutely forbidden to swear in here or,' he flapped a hand at the studio, 'or in there. Even if you think the microphone is dead, you still mustn't swear.'

More intellectual nodding, with the sort of face that was meant to express horror at the thought of swearing within a thousand yards of Broadcasting House, not even in Regent's Park, well up the road.

'I think,' said my guide, looking importantly at his watch, an unnecessary procedure as there were two accurate clocks in the studio, 'that I've just got time to show you something of what an RPA actually does – you are going to be an RPA, aren't you?'

'Yes.'

'Good. They're all ever so nice. Ever such nice people. I was one myself once until I was promoted.' He took a large disc from an envelope. The disc was silver on one side and the other side was black with grooves in it. 'This is called a Watts disc, named after the inventor.' For a moment he looked thoughtful. 'His names is Watts.' He paused while that bit of enlightenment had time to sink in. 'This is an actual recording of a Major Hastings war report. It'll be your job to play this sort of record on a cue from the announcer in the studio.' He pointed to some yellow wax-pencil marks on the surface. 'Those marks show where the needle must be placed if the whole disc is not to be played.'

This was before the days of iron-oxide emulsion tape, and it appeared that the discs and scripts were supplied together. The RPA's job was to mark the discs with the special pencil. Sometimes there would be more than one mark, to show where paragraphs of speech had to be edited out; to do this, the needle had to be lifted at the first mark and replaced at the second mark without the listener noticing the blank as the patch was jumped. This took some skill. First, the 'pot meter' (potentiometer) had to be turned down with the left hand so that anything affecting the needle would not be heard. Next, the pick-up arm holding the stylus had to be lifted with the right hand, dropped within a split second into the next yellow-marked groove, and the pot meter turned up again. It was almost impossible for left-handed people to do it. It required a steady hand, perfect eyesight, considerable dexterity, a keen ear, a good memory and no brains.

The next two days were spent finding where the Disc Library was where the Watts discs were held as distinct from the Gramophone library (which held commercial gramophone records), which was different again from the Sound Effects Library of street noises, trains, guns and so on.

Everything had to be signed for so that, in theory, everyone knew where everything was at any moment. In practice, there was a fair amount of chaos and few people knew where anything was.

The first programme in which I had to drop a needle on to a disc was on my third day in Broadcasting House, and the music was that used to introduce 'Farming Today'. That part I managed beautifully, because playing a gramophone record then was as easy as it is now, after which I lapsed into few seconds of silent self-congratulation.

The announcer from behind the double-glazed window waited for the music to finish; as it did, the programme engineer turned up his microphone and gave him the green light to speak, whereupon he spoke his lines to introduce the farmer, who was not there.

This farmer's speech was on a Watts disc, and I had the announcer's words of introduction on a cue sheet in front of me. He arrived at the cue words themselves, which are engraved on my mind even today: 'And here he is.'

There was a long pause because I was still congratulating myself for getting the music disc on. Becoming aware of the silence and of people looking at me, I became paralysed with fright; I had forgotten what to do and then, suddenly remembering, I couldn't move to lower the needle into the right groove.

The programme engineer looked up at me. 'Now!' he said.

The producer nudged me. 'That's your cue!'

The programme secretary nudged me and said, 'Go on, drop it!'

It was the sort of remark made to Sago when he had a stick in his mouth. I dropped it.

I expected to get the sack after what was in reality only a three-second pause but which seemed an hour to me, but it wasn't even entered in the engineer's log book.

At the beginning of December, I was sent to another set of BBC studios about a five-minute walk away, at 200 Oxford Street. The offices were upstairs, the canteen and entrance was on the ground floor, and the studios were in the basement.

It was from here that the programme 'Radio Newsreel' originated; it is still running. This programme was to make up about nine-tenths of my work. If you sleep badly and fiddle about with your radio at night, you may have heard it and know that it consists of an 'anchor man', who introduces various speakers on a variety of subjects. In those days the show was liberally peppered with war reports, all on Watts discs. It was my job to collect the discs from the library, check them against the scripts in order to know where the jump-cuts had to be marked with yellow pencil, then play them twice: once for rehearsal and once for transmission.

Mysterious people from upstairs would dictate the policy which determined the 'must' recordings and the 'must' reports, which were read live from the studio. The 'must' items were firmly set, they were all serious war stuff, and there was to be no deviation from them. The programme was half an hour long and the 'must' items took up about twenty minutes of that time. The producer was allowed the ten or so spare minutes to introduce lighter subjects of his own choice and so help attract an audience, which might otherwise grow bored with continuous war reports.

The programmes was heard in English in Canada, the USA, Australia, New Zealand, India and in all parts of the world where English was understood. This meant several transmissions were made within the same twenty-four hours, with slight variations in each programme to fit the country aimed at. To accomplish this, we had a shift routine; three twelve-hour days on, followed by three twelve-hour nights on, followed by three days and nights off. That is equivalent to seventy-two hours' work in six days; but it was the three nights following immediately on top of the three days that were punishing. A couple of RPAs broke down because they couldn't take the alternating sleeping habits.

In the RPAs' room we had a huge sofa, and at any time of the day or night one, two, three or four of us would be asleep on it. In the rare event of being off duty for four hours or longer, there was a dormitory in which beds could be booked. I managed to save several weeks' rent by booking a bed there in various names. As I have always disliked sleeping in my clothes and several other members of the staff also disliked this, many a night-time 'Radio Newsreel' went out with some of the operators wearing pyjamas or nightdresses.

For one transmission which went out at 3.30 am, the announcer was in his pyjamas, the programme engineer was in his best (and probably only) suit, I was wearing my pyjama bottoms only, because it was a hot night, and the producer was wearing his swimming trunks rather than waste clothing coupons on pyjamas, as it was summer.

It was on this occasion that the administrators, who were known as buffaloes, chose to send a senior member of the BBC staff to the studio with an important visiting Canadian air marshal. It is curious how clothes affect people. Instead of the air marshal addressing his questions to the producer, who was in swimming trunks, he spoke only to the programme engineer, who was engaged in the difficult business of balancing the sound.

It was impossible to be at war without some appalling personal sadness happening almost every week. There was a young, most likeable man, about twenty-three and a war corespondent whom I got to know. His name was Kent Stevenson and his idea of fun was always over the top and rather childish, like slipping a tomato on to a chair in the canteen just as someone was about to sit on it. His philosophy was simple: death always happened to someone else.

We sometimes walked down Regent Street during air-raids while others scuttled for shelter. We were stupid and young – and convinced we were immortal.

I knew that Kent sometimes went on aerial bombing raids over Germany, taking with him the cumbersome Watts disc recording machine with its carefully balanced cutting arm. As planned raids were always top secret, sometimes announced at the last minute, private arrangements often had to be cancelled without explanation.

Kent had many problems over dating girls because he had many girlfriends. Frequently girls who knew that we were friends would ask me if I knew where he was. I almost never knew – and if I did happen to find out, it would have been dangerous to let on, because we were warned that spies were everywhere.

I didn't know until later that he had one special girl.

On the afternoon of 17 May 1943 we were in the Oxford Street canteen when he suddenly looked up at the clock. 'Jeeze! That the time?' He jumped up and searched his pockets for something that turned out to be a little china pig, smaller than a field-mouse. 'D'you know Sadie?' he asked.

I didn't know Sadie. But I knew that Kent was always surrounded by pretty girls.

'You'll recognise her when you see her. Give her this if I don't get the chance.' I called after him, to ask if Sadie was on the staff. He didn't hear me. He'd gone.

Nor did I have the wit to realise the significance of those last words of his to me: ' . . . if I don't get the chance.'

That was the day of the massive RAF bomber raid on the Ruhr, the huge German factory area. All that was ever found out about him was that he was a commentator in a bomber that was shot down. Whether his plane went down in flames to crash on German soil, or whether the plane was hit and dropped into the sea, I shall never know.

I put a notice on the BBC staff notice-board, asking Sadie to please contact me, as I had something for her from Kent Stevenson. No one replied.

One night, during a break between 'Radio Newsreels' two months later, some of us were in the canteen and I heard the name Sadie called out. It wasn't a common name, so I went over to the table and asked which was she.

'I am,' said a girl of about nineteen.

'Did you know Kent Stevenson?'

'Who?'

She wasn't the girl, but I told her the story and asked her to keep the pig just the same; I would keep in touch with her for a while, just in case the real Sadie turned up. She understood and kept it.

The real Sadie never did turn up; but it seemed to make sense that a girl with the same name should have it – if anything during a war makes any sense at all.

In addition to Watts discs, there were some slow-speed discs of enormous diameter which could not be edited. Instead of spinning at seventy-eight revolutions a minute, these giant discs, which looked about three feet across, turned at less than half that speed, allowing one disc to take a half-hour programme. They had to have special, very heavy, lead-lined turntables to cope with their size. All the gadgetry was on the top of a grey monolith in the middle of the continuity studio, from which all programmes on one service were linked.

It was my fate to have to take one of these giant discs, which held a talk by the Archbishop of Canterbury, and put it on to the turntable. I knew that as soon as Isobel Ann Shead, the continuity announcer, had completed the announcement, it was necessary to give the heavy turntable a shove; this was to get it up to the correct speed straight away, as the needle had been set at half a groove before the speech began.

Isobel introduced the Archbishop with a note of gravity in her voice to match his exalted position and, as she finished, I gave the huge disc a shove as usual.

Unfortunately, I shoved too hard; this jolted the monolith, which in turn made the needle jump out of its groove and slide across all the grooves, making a '*Pppppppppppppppppp!*' noise, uncommonly like a raspberry. The needle came to rest on the last groove, which had one word left on it. That word came out loud and clear: 'God.'

Fully expecting to be carpeted for that, it came as a pleasant surprise to me when nothing happened. Isobel didn't log it, nor did the duty engineer, who had fallen asleep.

There was a regular programme from Oxford Street called 'Junior Bridge Builders', chaired by Alistair Cooke, one of the most delightful of all broadcasters; he introduced teenagers from both sides of the Atlantic, with the idea of building a bridge of ideals. Some of the programme was from youngsters recorded on Watts discs, which was why I was involved to play them, and some of it was live.

The producer was a girl called Miranda Dulley, and one day she asked me if I could find a female teenager who would be suitable for the programme, so I telephoned Mrs Clarbour, who still had her old office in Cambridge Circus, and explained the problem to her. She was happy that I had rung her but surprised that I was alive and in London because she had heard that I had been lost at Dunkirk.

I felt almost ashamed to tell that that I never got as far as Dunkirk. She didn't sound disappointed and said she would send a couple of teenage girls along to 200 Oxford Street at four o'clock two days later.

I warned Miranda Dulley to expect a couple of girls at that time in her office, and I told the commissionaire that there would be callers whose names I didn't yet know, but who should go up to the producer's office. He pointed out that this was most irregular, as names of callers had to be known in advance, since the BBC came under some wartime secrets regulation, which I had never heard of, but whose guiding principle apparently was that no one was allowed in who had not 'passed scrutiny'.

I showed the commissionaire my pass with my regulation Identity Card and, looking as po-faced as possible, said I would be glad to be the scrutator of the couple of girls expected.

The first girl appeared at the reception desk at a quarter to four and was clearly most scrutable. I asked her to wait with me so I could show them both the way when the other girl arrived and, sure enough, the second girl arrived a couple of minutes later. A *third* girl followed her in, after her came six in a bunch. Suddenly fifteen more arrived all at once.

It was a worry. Various sober buffaloes and other members of the staff were coming and going through reception. At the same time they all seemed to be saying either, 'You lucky bastard,' or, 'What the hell is Messiter up to now?' The older ones were as full of disapproval as the younger males were approving.

Mrs Clarbour must have put out one of her crowd extra calls. I knew that at least one of the girls present would fit the bill, so, with as much dignity as possible, I told the commissionaire that there were now enough and that if any more came from Clarbour's Agency, to tell them the job had gone. With a horrible presentiment that I had abandoned the commissionaire to yet more girls advancing upon the reception desk, I led this glamorous bevy of sweet-scented, tittering, whispering, nervous girls through the maze of corridors upstairs to Miranda Dulley's office and knocked a little apprehensively.

'Come in.' She was seated behind her desk and looked up in horror as the giggling galaxy flooded in. 'Oh,' she said, 'this is far too many, Ian. Where did you find them?'

'By telephoning a theatrical agency.'

'They're not really what I want. I just want a pleasant girl, who has some sort of routine job in London and who can . . . ' She stopped and stood up to make a short speech of apology and thanks to the girls for their presence and to ask them all to go away.

Those lovely girls, who had all been ogling me before, now looked at me as if I were something nasty, fit only to be left on the side of the plate. I took them all back to reception, saying, 'Sorry,' every other word. They were mercifully and quickly absorbed into the anonymity of Oxford Street while I went, shamefaced, back to Miranda.

'No, Ian,' she said, 'go and find a nice ordinary girl between seventeen and twenty who can talk, someone with brains. You must know someone.'

As I was not a Londoner I didn't know any girls who were not on the staff. So that evening I went to a dance hall near Covent Garden, partly because the wonderful Glenn Miller was playing there, and partly because

I thought that there I would find the right type of girl with brains who could talk.

I found the right type of girl, who had plenty of brains and who still talks.

I know because I married her.

9

'What job?'

THERE HAVE BEEN many imitations of Glenn Miller; while some have been good, none has conjured up the atmosphere of the master. His was the definitive popular young music of the day.

I was in that crowded dance hall, with no more than five shillings in my pocket, hoping to meet 'the right type of girl with brains who could talk'.

I had noticed one girl, taller than the average, who was wearing a pale-coffee-coloured lace frock. She was fair, with a broad happy face, and I couldn't keep my eyes off her. During a Paul Jones, every time that the circle moved round and the music stopped, I always found myself opposite someone else; of course, these were the normal odds in a large and crowded dance hall. Fortune eventually almost smiled on me when the circles halted once more; but, even now, close as she was, that girl was still not opposite me but some distance to my right. However, she was nearer than ever before, so I thought that, if I didn't grab her at once, I never would. So I pushed the competition on one side somewhat rudely and we found ourselves dancing together.

It was my turn to be dumb: this was not just the girl for the radio programme – she was the girl for me. No one had ever affected me like this before, and she made me feel small, though she was only half an inch taller than I; it was something about the willowy grace with which she moved. She was talking about something which I have now completely forgotten; I couldn't take it in because of her proximity. She said she was eighteen years old and was there with a group of friends.

I found the courage to tell her what I was there for. There was no means of knowing whether she believed me, but while we were spending the rest of the evening together we must have made a date for two days later, to meet at the reception of 200 Oxford Street.

The day for the recording arrived. I remember telling Miranda Dulley about the girl, Enid Senior, and how she would be fabulous, great, terrific, a knockout; as I went on, Miranda looked up curiously to interrupt my enthusiasm to say, 'We are only looking for a straightforward girl in her teens, who can tell Americans of the same age what it's like living in a country subjected to air-raids, food rationing and clothes rationing, and how she gets to work each day.' She was saying everything she had said before, just as if it was forgotten . . . It was. She added, 'I do hope, Ian, you haven't gone over the top again as you did when you asked that agent to send hordes of chorus girls. They were not the sort of people we wanted at all.'

About half an hour before the time appointed for the recording, I met Enid at the reception desk and took her rather nervously up to Miranda's office. I knocked on the door and introduced them. They seemed to get on fine together and chatted easily. I went down to Studio 3 in the basement and lined up the six gram banks (a row of turntables, each with its pick-up arm and pot meter. This row of six turntables was known as a TD7. No one has ever discovered what those initials and that number stood for. I knew that Enid and Miranda would be coming down in a few minutes; I hoped Enid wouldn't be too disappointed to find out what a humble job I had, changing the needles and putting on the discs; with luck, she wouldn't even notice. It was just as well that I hadn't lied to her about the importance of my job; but I hadn't said what it was either.

Alistair Cooke was sitting in the studio itself with two other participants, talking to them and making notes on his script, when Enid and Miranda came in. After the introductions were over they went through a little rehearsal.

Enid talked her way competently through that first broadcast; it must have been a success, as she was asked back several times, on one occasion for political comment on the Beveridge Plan (the 1942 report on which the Welfare State legislation was based).

Because she worked for Sir Richard Acland, who had founded the Common Wealth Party the previous year and was engaged in writing his book *Forward March*, we were both drawn into political consciousness. Enid, as a high-speed shorthand writer, spent much of her time in the House of Commons, getting the talk, the argument, the political rows and remarks of the political doyens, creepers, dullards, show-offs and sparklers written down. This also made her politically very aware.

Until then I had always supposed that Hansard, the Bible of the House, was a printed record of what had been said in the House. We were both a little surprised to discover that, if a Member of Parliament regretted having made a particular remark which might damage him or his Party, it was possible for him to go to the Hansard office (if he hurried) and have the remark removed or even altered. We were both growing up fast. This was all mysterious stuff and, like most young, politically conscious people, we turned strongly socialist. There is an old saying: if you're not a socialist before you're thirty, you have no heart; if you're still a socialist after thirty, you have no head.

In London many of us used the underground stations as air-raid shelters. Officialdom did not like people sleeping in the deep stations at first, but Londoners thought otherwise and, soon after the start of the heavy air-raids, people were down there in their thousands with their children, their blankets, their sandwiches and flasks of tea. It might be thought that this cheek-by-jowl living would put an end to snobbery once and for all. But one evening, when I was in the flat of a couple of friends, the siren went off. We weren't a hundred yards from Knightsbridge Station, so I suggested that it might be a good idea to go to earth until the all-clear sounded.

'Good Lord, no!' said my hostess, 'Those places are full of riff-raff and I'd rather be bombed than mix with the plebs.' She meant it. Her husband agreed and poured himself a stiff black-market whisky. And so, stoically and quite unnecessarily, we sat and listened to the distant *crump* of high explosives. This was selfish because, if we were not killed outright, we would still be a liability to the overworked doctors, nurses and ambulance people.

The bombs were getting nearer and I sat there, thinking it was stupid to die for snobbery; but I did not have the courage to tell my friends that we should get out quickly, in case they thought I was afraid. And I *was* afraid. The next bomb, just along the road, brought the sound of a landslide, which was the collapsing of buildings. Fear was real – but it must not be shown, so still I sat there nonchalantly, waiting for the next thump; when it came, there was an immediate crash and a shattering of glass, some of which fell into the room and ripped a curtain. 'Oh damn the bloody Germans!' said my hostess. 'That stuff came from Liberty's. I'll have to go round tomorrow to see if they've got any more.'

'What about the coupons for the material?' asked her husband.

'Oh, I know a little man round the corner who can sell me some.'

The black market was indeed widespread.

Enid and I were soon in love; we planned to marry as 1943 became 1944. At the time I had moved from Chelsea, into a house owned by a Mrs Winston whose Christian name we never knew, so we called her Winnie.

The war tide had turned; in February the Allies landed at Anzio. When April came, the daffodils, wide-eyed and open-mouthed in the sunshine, nodded at each other in astonishment at the spring, a spring when the allies dropped over 81,000 tons of bombs on Germany and German-occupied Europe.

The Germans sent newsreels to neutral countries as propaganda, and we took copies from them, as had been intended all along. These showed us that concrete and steel fortifications made Europe an impregnable fortress; guns could emerge from any hole in a cliff face.

We had our bag of tricks too. Broadcaster and commentator Audrey Russell contributed to one particular trick and I went with her; we had to take a car from London down the Dover Road and stop about half way. We were several miles ahead of a mass of tanks going the same way on the same road.

There we waited until the convoy started to pass us. In my capacity as an RPA I had to hold the microphone while Audrey's commentary was telling the listeners how this was only a small part of a mighty Allied army travelling to the coast in an efficient manner. The squealing rumble of tank tracks could be heard in the background, as well as the various engines of the cars and halftracks. At no time did she say, nor did she ask any of the soldiers interviewed, why we were all heading for the Dover area.

We knew the broadcast would be picked up by the enemy and give the impression that, were we to invade northern France, it would be via the Pas de Calais area. The tanks and other pieces of mobile equipment went back north after dark, in order to be seen next day in broad daylight travelling down the Dover Road again. From the point of view of German reconnaissance, we were stockpiling arms around Dover. Reconnaissance planes later confirmed that the Germans were swiftly bringing reinforcements to the Calais area.

Shortly after that trip of deception down the Dover Road the pleasant Miss Loom, who had been at my first BBC interview in 1942, asked me to go to see her. When I was a child and when Father sent a message through one of the servants that I must see him, I always assumed that I was in some sort of trouble, and I was nearly always right; he never sent for me to congratulate me about anything. I remember hoping that he would congratulate me on some exam I had passed. Day followed day, and my success was never mentioned by anyone. Both Mother and Father told me over and over as a child that my life would be one of continuous futility unless I did something about it. What that something was they never said, but they left me feeling inferior at all times. If there was a snub going that would suit me, I got it. The result of this has been for me to assume that, if anyone with control wants to see me, it is because I have done something wrong.

Miss Loom had been formally responsible for my appointment as an RPA. I knew, as I walked up Regent Street from Oxford Circus towards Broadcasting House, that I was about to get the sack, so I comforted myself with the thought that changing needles and records had been fun; it was different and, more important, had been the foundation for some good friendships.

She had the same gentle smile and manner as before. 'Please sit down. Would you like a cup of tea?' Being apprehensive by nature, by now I was wondering whether I had done something so awful that I would not even get the customary week's pay in lieu of notice . . .

It was nothing like that. She told me that our current conversation was not under any circumstances to be repeated. Curiouser and curiouser. From that moment on, I was to consider myself under some sort of oath of secrecy. There was no formality involved, and anyway I thought I was already under some oath, because there had been something about it in the paper I had signed on joining the staff. The mystery deepened. The conversation became more complex and I was well into my second cup of tea (free) and fourth biscuit (free) when she came to the point. 'Would you consider a very special job?'

When you're just twenty-four years old, broke, and your future is in the hands of one person, however gentle her smile and manner, there is only one reply,

'Yes.'

'Good.'

'W-w-what job?'

'I don't know.'

This was even odder. Here she was, offering me a job – but she didn't know what it was.

I said I'd take it. What possessed me to agree I will never know.

'Officially you won't have this job, so we shall continue to pay you.'

There was a clue there somewhere. 'Y-y-you mean I shall be leaving the BBC?'

'Not officially. Officially, you will have been transferred to Manchester. It was going to be Birmingham, but your family lives near there – and we want you to disappear.'

This was gripping, *Boys' Own Paper* stuff. At any rate, I was gripping the sides of the chair. 'Are you s-sending me to M-manchester?'

'No, but that's what you tell your friends.'

'Where am I g-going?'

'I don't know.' She smiled innocently.

I looked at my much-pawned (and always redeemed) wrist-watch. 'I have to go now,' I said, standing up, 'because I'm on a programme at four forty-five.'

'You're not going to do it. We'll have someone else on it now, since you've been taken ill.'

'I feel very well.'

'No, no, you're not *really* ill; but we said that, if you agreed, a message would be sent to get a replacement for you, as you've been taken ill.' (I never found out who the 'we' were who agreed to all this.)

She picked up the telephone and rang the RPAs' room at 200 Oxford Street to tell them that I'd been taken ill, and would they please have a substitute to stand in for me.

I wondered what the hell I had let myself in for. She had said 'if I agreed'; but I was wondering what it was I'd agreed to. I couldn't remember agreeing to anything . . . Perhaps I had . . . but if I had, I couldn't recall what it was. Miss Loom had said she didn't know what the job was, so it was impossible for me to agree to it.

She was looking at a piece of paper; the light from the window behind her was shining through it, showing the heading printed on it, and the one word I could read in the mirror-writing was 'Ministry'. However, there were so many ministries. That word offered no real clue.

'Have you got your army discharge papers?'

'Not w-with me.'

'Are you living in rooms?'

'A room in Woodside Park.'

'Go back there now, collect your discharge papers and your Identity Card, if it's not with you, and report to this address in Duke Street, St James's, where you will ask for Major Heinrich Dehn. We'll see to it that you don't lose your room in London. Write down the name and address of the person you pay your rent to.' I did that and she handed me a sealed envelope. 'That's your reference from us. The major will want to see it.'

It was time for me to ask a question. 'What does it say about me?'

'Nothing except that you are "punctual, honest, reliable and sober, as far as is known".'

I resisted a cynical, 'Thank you very much.' On my wages, no one could be a bleary-eyed drunk. It didn't sound like much of a reference. The name and address of the major were typed on the envelope.

I took the tube to Woodside Park, a suburb about nine miles north-west of central London. I told 'Winnie' Winston that the BBC was transferring me to Manchester, that they would continue to pay the rent and so to keep my room for me. After packing a case, two hours later I found myself being ushered into an office block in Duke Street by a uniformed guard.

Major Heinrich Dehn (who was eventually caught by the Germans and shot for spying) was a most efficient man. He was the sort of person the French would describe as being very correct. He could have been thirty years old or thereabouts, lean and already losing his sandy, thin hair. His freckled skin showed he had been much exposed to the elements. He welcomed me coldly and without a smile and asked me with a slight French accent what I knew of the job.

'Miss Loom has told me nothing.'

'Who is Miss Loom?'

'A Personnel Officer at the BBC.'

'Her room number?' I told him. 'Describe her.' I did. 'You saw her this afternoon?'

'Yes.'

'What was she wearing?'

I described her coat and skirt as best as I could – but, not knowing taffeta from sailcloth, I don't suppose I made a very good job of it.

He picked up the telephone and, getting through to the BBC, asked for her. 'Miss Loom? I have a Mr Messiter here in my office. You saw him this afternoon? Good. What are you wearing?' There was a long pause. 'Thank you.'

Replacing the telephone, he opened the envelope I had given him, inspected my Identity Card, looked at my Artillery discharge papers, read my BBC reference and almost smiled as he put them all in a drawer. 'You'll get them back later. Where have you been living for the last few months?'

I told him.

'A Mrs Winston? Have you the telephone number?'

He wrote it down and dialled it at once. Fortunately she was in. 'Mrs Winston? May I speak to Mr Messiter, please? He's out. I see. Manchester. Did he tell you which train? No? Never mind. Thank you. No there's no need for him to ring back.'

None of it made any sense. He seemed to be checking my identity with care. He had confirmed my story and now appeared satisfied enough to allow himself to relax slightly, leaning back in his chair with the back of his head in the palms of his hands. Then he spoke to me rapidly in French; it was almost incomprehensible. Next, he said a few words, which could have been Dutch or German but which were totally incomprehensible to me and left me looking blankly at him. He picked up the telephone again and spoke in French to someone somewhere and all that I could pick out was my name, *oui*, *non* and *merci bien*. He was frowning, not so much in anger as in puzzlement. He listened intently and made a note on a piece of paper. Returning the telephone to its cradle, he looked at me in silence.

This was embarrassing. There was long pause before he spoke. 'It's no secret to anyone that the invasion of northern Europe is imminent.' He stared at me as he said this and I stared back, not knowing how I was meant to react. It looked like the beginning of a spy story, but it couldn't be, since I spoke no German and my schoolboy French was sufficient for me to understand only Parisian French spoken slowly. I spoke nothing but English – except for a few rude songs in Welsh.

'Are you prepared to go back into uniform for the invasion of Europe?'

The answer to this was a non-committal, 'Oh.'

'There will be two or three others from the BBC with you; your job, which is called Psychological Warfare, will be to help spread the news of the Allies' success and drive home the stories of Axis defeats.'

'Undermine enemy morale and c-c-confidence?'

'Exactly. We want people with practical broadcasting experience.'

'How can that help?'

'Suppose we capture a radio station . . . we would need people to run it. Suppose we do not capture a radio station, we would need people who know how to set one up.'

I didn't feel confident that I could run a radio station, let alone set one up from scratch; and it never occurred to me to tell him that the BBC already covered Europe in all European languages most competently from Bush House.

Instead I asked him, 'When do we invade?'

At last the man laughed; it was at my expense for asking such a naïve question, but he was human. 'I can't tell you that because no one has told me; it is top secret, and it can't be known until the last moment, as it depends on many factors, especially the weather.'

I heard myself saying, 'I'll go.'

'Good. As from now, you will go into training and be addressed as Captain Messiter.'

I had no idea what I was letting myself in for.

10
To Omaha via Kilburn

I WAS FAIRLY SURE NOW, WHEN MAJOR DEHN handed me that slip of paper he had written while on the telephone, that I had been vetted for spying, had been found wanting in language, and was now being passed on to Psychological Warfare.

I didn't see how I could possibly tell the Germans how badly they were doing when all I knew was, '*Ja, gehacktes Fleisch, und nein,*' which means, 'Yes, minced meat and no.' I also knew a phrase in German which means, 'This is my aunt, will you please change the tyre on the back left wheel of her car,' but I couldn't remember it any longer.

The paper he had given me had the name of someone else and his room number on it. As I was not allowed to go there alone, a military guide came into the room to escort me to the lift and thence to the room number written on the paper. I had no illusions that I was important. It was rather that Major Dehn didn't know me and so couldn't trust me to wander alone around in this most sensitive of buildings.

Once again I was vetted, this time by an Englishman who addressed me as 'Captain' and who told me to report to the corner of Duke Street and Jermyn Street at 5 am the next morning, where I would be met by others and collected by an army truck. He said he knew I was supposed to be in Manchester, and for that reason a room would be reserved for me at a nearby address; I was to go straight there, not to wander about London, not to go to a pub or to telephone anyone, as it could be an embarrassment if I were seen in London when some people thought I was in Manchester and others that I was so ill as to be at death's door. Life was getting very complicated. Once or twice I thought I might wake up and find the whole thing had been a dream.

I don't think that now, all these years later, I could be prosecuted under the Official Secrets Act for something done in 1944: between the office and the hotel, I found a telephone box. Just before I reached the kiosk, a nicely cynical almost theatrical, touch occurred when a girl presented me with a white feather for cowardice because I was not in uniform. I smiled at her and said something like, 'You're quite right. I'm much too scared to fight.' She made a sound of disgust and went her way.

I telephoned Enid, using one of my most dramatically disguised voices so she wouldn't know who it was, and told her that her friend Ian Messiter had to go away for a while but that he would be perfectly all right. The disguise was so brilliant she immediately said, 'Oh, Ian, where are you?'

Surrounded by posters outside the box and by stickers in the box, all of which read 'Careless talk costs lives' and 'Even walls have ears', I told her; this was very silly of me, but at that stage I didn't know how clever she was.

Enid, at seventeen, was the youngest woman ever to pass the Final Examination of the Corporation of Certified Secretaries, and also to be awarded their Gold Medal for achieving first place. She had completed this degree course in eighteen months (instead of the normal three years) and it qualified her in Company Law, Accountancy, Commercial and Mercantile Law, Economics and many other subjects. She was too young to realise her commercial value on the business market. As she was too modest to explain it, she was interviewed by prospective employers with substandard qualifications themselves, who did not know what her abilities really were. It wasn't until years later, when I was working as Head of TV with Mather and Crowther, one of the biggest advertising agencies in the world, that I realised that their own highly paid Company Secretary had precisely the same qualifications as Enid. She could have had a great career in commerce. In our working life together we would not have survived without her professional knowledge, since I am incapable of signing a contract on the right line, of reading a bank statement or, faced with a balance sheet, of distinguishing between profit and loss. I can never remember what anyone ever pays me for anything or, if I lose the receipt, what anything costs.

I found the hotel, about three minutes' walk from where I had to meet the army truck next morning. Presented with the register, I stupidly almost asked to use the telephone to inquire from the office I had just left whether I should sign my own name or make one up. I signed my own name and arranged for a call at 4.30 am. After a horrible stale brawn sandwich, expensive at threepence, I went to bed.

There were one or two things that I should have asked before leaving that strange office. A truck would be there on the corner of Duke Street: what truck? How would I recognise it? Did it have a number-plate? Why had I not been given the number? Others would meet me. What others? What were their names? Why had I not been told? More to the point, what had prevented me from asking?

My precautions and knowledge were crassly inadequate. As I dozed off, my stupidity seemed to stand in front of me like an accusing ghost.

I opened my eyes and could just make out that I was in a strange place; nothing seemed familiar in that half-light, and there was a banging sound very close to my head; it was someone hammering at the door. Oh yes, this was the hotel room and a voice was saying, 'This is your four-thirty call.'

Twenty minutes later, I was on the corner of Duke Street and Jermyn Street. There is only one word to describe my movements there: lurking. Several others were prowling and sneaking about just as suspiciously, while we all eyed one another apprehensively. Two people did seem to know each other, and they spoke in tones too low to be overheard as they kept their distance. No one was in uniform.

There was the sound of a motor close by and everyone peered into the darkness of the blackout to see what it was. The sound went on and faded into the night. It could have been the truck, checking that we were there, and it might turn and come back. It seemed that others thought so too as all heads, only just visible in the gloom, turned in the direction of the fading sound.

At about ten past five a covered truck pulled in by the kerb and two people in uniform climbed out. One, the driver, went round to the back and unlaced the cords that held the green camouflage canvas cover shut. The other, an officer, went over to the two who were talking and said something, after which they climbed into the back of the truck. One by one, the early-morning street lurkers disappeared into the truck.

The officer came to me last. 'Are you waiting for anything?' He had a New York accent.

'Yes.'

'What?'

'Possibly that military truck.' I thought this would give the impression of being cautious, although it was a bit late for caution.

'Name and rank?'

'Messiter. Ian. Captain.'

'What was that name you gave before you said Captain?'

'Ian.'

'How's that again?'

I repeated it.

'Spell it.'

I spelled it. He said there was no such name and he'd got me written down as Jan. To all Americans from then on I was Jan because the name 'Ian', to my surprise, was then almost unknown in the USA.

He presented me with a brass disc on a thin chain and explained it was my 'dog tag' with my name stamped on it and I was to hang it round my neck. I looked at it, and my first name there was still 'Jan'. The problem of my name, he explained with much patience, could be resolved if I would admit that Ian was just a fancy way of spelling Jan. There was no choice. I admitted it. 'OK. Get in.'

There were eight of us in the back of the windowless truck, four on one side facing four on the other. The driver reappeared and laced up the canvas at the back. The engine started and when we moved off we were thrown about a little, not much: without knowing when the truck was about to take a corner, however, no one was ever prepared.

The American officer in the front passenger seat, who was now invisible, called through the canvas that he hoped we'd all been to the bathroom recently, as we were not going to stop for some hours; if anyone wanted a piss, the small board in the centre of the truck was removable, exposing the road, and that must be used as the bathroom. That was the first time I had heard the euphemism 'bathroom' used for 'lavatory'. I wondered why he bothered as he had no reticence about using the vernacular in the twelfth-century English word 'piss'.

All eight of us introduced ourselves and I discovered that the two who had been whispering together in the road were both BBC employees like myself. One was Archie Campbell, a drama producer; the other, Imlay Watts, who ended up with the OBE (and who was no relation of the Watts of Watts discs), was from Administration. It was Imlay who brought up the question of recording machines. We didn't have one. Out came his notebook and pencil and the fact was written down; he was obviously from administration. We had no programme engineer to work the machine we didn't have; out came the notebook and pencil again. It came as a surprise when he asked if anyone knew where we were going, because he looked like the sort of person who would automatically know that – or at least he would have a note of it in his book. Imlay turned out to be a lot of fun and well worth knowing – even if at that moment he had no idea where we were bound or what we were to do when we arrived at wherever it was.

The American officer in the co-driver's seat called out to us that if we were hungry or thirsty we would find K-rations under the seats. K-rations were lightweight US army emergency rations comprising chocolate, coffee, sugar, powdered milk, Spam, powdered eggs and other compacted, nourishing substances. One man, it was said, could live on one K-ration box for a week – either in theory or in emergency, but certainly not in luxury.

We had been travelling for over an hour and a half when someone – I think it was Archie Campbell, the fastidious to a fault BBC Drama producer – suggested that we all try to estimate the speed of the truck. We tried lifting the loose floorboard and looking down at the road as it whizzed past, but it was too small an area to allow us to guess the speed, so we settled for thirty miles an hour. So, someone said, if we had been travelling at thirty miles an hour for an hour and a half, we should have travelled at least forty-five miles. Where would that get us? No one knew. Someone suggested Colchester, but no one agreed. Someone else said that, as the jumping-off place for the invasion would be the south coast, we must be approaching Tunbridge Wells. I was hopeless at geography, so

I listened and tried to nod intelligently at the mention of various coastal towns' names.

After three hours' guessing, we gave up because it was fruitless. Somebody pissed through the hole in the floor and, in trying to put the loose floorboard back, let it drop through on to the road.

'The cost of that will be deducted from your pay,' said a man called Sullivan, brother of the actor, Francis L. Sullivan. He was a happy man with a quick wit and a ready laugh.

'What pay?' said the offender. 'The British army aren't paying me, nor are the Americans.'

That meant that we were all unofficial soldiers if we were not being paid by either the British or the American army. I knew that no government would, and still won't, acknowledge spies, therefore there can be no regular method for paying them; so I worried. I'd be hopeless as a spy. If we weren't to be trained as spies, then why were we all being paid in such a roundabout way? Perhaps it was all a fiction that we were to set up a radio station.

The truck skidded to a halt: we had arrived at wherever. We heard the American officer jump out and run round to the back; he unlaced a small part of the tarpaulin and stuck his head in. 'What was that?' He added that he had heard something drop into the road.

The culprit owned up to dropping the board. I said that it was wonderful to arrive because I was dying for a piss but could never do it under these wobbly conditions and in front of other people. (This, I learned later, was to do with having been beaten for bed-wetting as a child.)

The American said we hadn't arrived at wherever; we'd stopped in order to get the bit of board and put it back. I volunteered to go and find it, not because I'm the volunteering kind, but because I hoped for some hint as to where we were and I felt cramped, sitting still for so long. And there might just be a chance to relieve myself.

He said we must stay where we were and not look out through the back; he would get the board himself, just to be sure it had not been dropped with some message attached to it.

So it was like that: we were not to be trusted.

While he was gone, Sullivan kindly suggested that I should try to pee through the hole since the truck was no longer lurching about and that, if I would attempt it, they would all whistle to help me. It was no good. The more attention this silly disability of mine attracted, the worse it became.

Somebody tried to see out of the back by pulling the canvas open. A respectful American voice from outside the truck immediately said, 'I'm sorry, sir. I have my orders, sir, to see you don't do that, sir.' It was the driver; he'd been put on guard. That was that.

The officer found the piece of board with apparently no suspicious messages either written on it or thrown out with it, and it was handed back to us through the canvas.

We were off again. Sullivan said there was something funny about the countryside here because we kept slowing down and even occasionally stopping. This type of driving went on far too long for it to be the natural slowing and stopping which would be inevitable if we were passing through country towns from time to time. This was a large city. We could also hear buses constantly now.

We came to a gentle stop. Someone said we would now probably all be blindfolded – but we weren't. The driver came round and unlaced the canvas and we gazed out at what looked like a suburb of some town. Most of us probably thought we were by the sea.

Nobody shouted, 'Fall in!' or, 'By the right, right wheel, quick march!' We ambled a little sloppily along the road and turned into a smaller street that was lined on either side with detached houses. I was well to the rear and alone. The two Americans were leading the way; if they didn't trust all of us, one of them should have been behind us to watch. Had there been, I would not have been able to open the door to a telephone kiosk on the corner.

It was clear that we could not make phone-calls, although no one had specifically said we may not. Nor had anyone said we could not go into telephone boxes. In the first part of the war, when some of us thought the German invasion was imminent, many people had gone to a great deal of trouble, pointing signposts the wrong way and putting up the wrong names of towns here and there in order to confuse the enemy, should they get that far. It was a wonder they never altered the telephone boxes. In those days, the town's name, such as Bournemouth, would be written in the middle of the telephone dial in every telephone kiosk in Bournemouth. London telephones were generally similarly inscribed with the names of the area, such as Mayfair, Knightsbridge and Hampstead. I had opened the door to that red-painted kiosk and was now looking at the centre of the dial, which read 'Kilburn'.

We had travelled for hours, using up valuable petrol and at pointless discomfort, to have swapped Duke Street in St James's for Kilburn, only five or six miles to the north-west. Under the umbrella of Supreme Headquarters Allied Expeditionary Force (SHAEF for short) it had not dawned on the Americans or the British that Londoners might be able to recognise their own home-town. A little unintentional humour at a time of tension was important for sanity: this was enough to make a parrot laugh. Wartime stupidities of the Allies were exceeded only by the wartime stupidities of the Axis, otherwise we might well have lost the war.

I closed the kiosk door gently. No one turned around to discover my secret, and I followed the others past some pretentious saluting; here we discovered that not all Americans realised that a British soldier not in uniform or not wearing his military headgear cannot return a salute. There was some mumbling in the background about, 'If it's backwards, its British' and 'Stupid limeys.' Few of us, however, were real soldiers; the Americans, just like us, were simple civilians dressed to kill. Saluting over, we were shown into what had been a pleasant, large, detached house before the normal soldierly obscenities were scribbled on its walls.

American soldiers were issued with booklets to tell them how to behave properly in Britain; these were a valuable contribution to the friendship between us. They were told, for instance, that England, Wales and Scotland are one island and that the Scots and Welsh can get upset if they are labelled English. They were told that in the UK, if someone says, 'That's a lorry,' the American must not correct him by saying, 'what the hell is a lorry? Can't you say "truck", like anyone else?' It was loaded with terms like 'pavement' for 'sidewalk', 'garden' for 'backyard', 'railway' for 'railroad' and so on.

We English were not so far-sighted. We accepted the Americans as they flooded in, but we had no booklet on how to become and stay friends with them; this led to many misunderstandings. I was told of one, in which an English girl told her American boy-friend that, if he got up early enough, he could call round at her house and knock her up. The girl's father nearly killed that GI Joe, who thought she had invited him to jump into bed with her.

The Frenchman, Major Dehn, came up one afternoon and gave us a lecture on the ease with which one could extract information from strangers. One of his examples was as follows. Groups of French girls from the same resistance organisation but unknown to one another were instructed to go into cafés at a naval port, Brest for example, and each would pick up a German sailor or two. Each would make a date for the next evening and would then report back to HQ each time a date was or was not made. It was never difficult to find out which ship each sailor was from. Eventually one or more girls would report that her sailor could not make a date for the following evening. By correlating those girls whose sailors could not meet them again, it was an easy matter to predict the sailing of a German ship. What made the procedure even more subtle was this: the girls were never questioned about their targets together. Those asking the questions hardly knew one another, so only the top person whose job was to signal England was privy to the information, and even that knowledge was extremely restricted. Properly used, this kind of scheme could target the assembling of U-boats and other information of equal value.

A spy, so we learned, was not a shabby individual in a dirty raincoat who hid in a dark corner with his hat pulled down over his eyes, but a man, or girl who worked in a group out in the open and made friends with the lambs before the slaughter. We too had to be careful.

The major also demonstrated that it was fatal to be mysterious. Someone who obviously has something to hide is more likely to be found out than someone who can tell a whopper, provided that whopper is somewhere near the truth and is always credible.

During that lecture in Kilburn he suddenly pointed at me and said, 'Where are you, Jan Messiter, now?'

'Manchester.'

'Who are you working for?'

'BBC.'

'Good. Are you in rooms there?'

'No. Can't afford it. I'm in one room . . . ' and so on, giving my landlady's name and the name of the street. He delivered a slight reprimand because I had given information he had not asked for; but he seemed generally pleased – so I felt even more guilty, sneakily telephoning Enid that evening from the box down the road. I even did what I had particularly been told not to do: I looked up and down the road to make sure no one saw me go into the kiosk; that might have attracted attention.

Suddenly and without warning, we were all transferred to Clevedon, a seaside town on the Bristol Channel near Bristol. We were all under canvas in filthy weather, all eight of us in one bell-tent, with our heads round the edge and our feet in the middle, near the centre-pole. The fastidious BBC producer, Archie Campbell, didn't care for this, and nor did anyone else.

I made a very curious and loyal friend of an American sergeant, Chuck Collins; at first I thought he was sending me up, but he was not; he was old enough to be my father and always addressed me as Capt'n Limey. He was in charge of the field-kitchen; if I had been out on some duty and came back at any time, late or early, he would call out, 'Capt'n! Gimme fifteen minutes and your tea's all set.' The sergeant must have heard somewhere that all Englishmen drink tea on any occasion. Where he found this tea is a mystery, because it was rationed in the shops and was not sold at the American PX. Nevertheless, the minute he saw me, he would grab a saucepan, empty half a packet of tea into it, add a tin of Carnation milk, sugar and a pint and a half of water, which he measured with great care. This concoction was boiled for ten minutes, beaten with an egg-whisk and strained through a fine sieve into another saucepan, where it was allowed to simmer on the stove.

I was so touched by his concern for my welfare and his obviously friendly action that I found myself almost every day gulping down this extraordinary liquid and having to smile at the same time remembering to say, 'Thank you'. He would stand in the background, watching with pride and occasionally calling out, 'Now don't forget to finish up.'

During our time at Clevedon we were lectured on various forms of psychological warfare, two of the strangest of which were being tried out in Italy at that time. One was the cinema projection on the clouds of images, some religious, others propaganda messages. The other odd way of disseminating news was by means of a silent glider at night. This took considerable skill. A glider would be towed up to a sufficient height so that it could be neither seen nor heard. A disc player and a pair of amplifiers were placed in the craft, one under each wing. As the plane glided over what the pilot hoped was the target town, the speakers were switched on to 'broadcast' the recorded message.

It was decided not to use any of these methods on Germany or France because the inhabitants were considered not sufficiently illiterate to be frightened by disembodied voices from above. What the major concentrated on was far more practical. Psychological warfare is simpler to wage when you're winning than when you're losing: tell the enemy to give up and save his own life, so that he can go home after the war to help rebuild his country – that about sums it up; also, you must never tell him a lie unless there is no chance of being found out.

Early on the morning of 6 June 1944, we learned that the invasion of Normandy had started. The Allies were landing, protected by terrifying fire from the navy and from the air force, just as Hitler had said we would.

Hitler was literally caught napping – but not with his trousers down, because at this stage of the war he never undressed for bed, remaining always in uniform. He had gone to bed on the night of 5 June, having had weather reports for the northern French coast and the Channel which showed that all probable areas would be too rough for landing. (It very nearly was so.) He left instructions that under no circumstances was he to be wakened. So, with the invasion in full swing, no one dared disturb the Fuehrer.

Not only that; because of the weather, Field Marshal Rommel also thought it would be impossible for sea borne troop movements, so he had departed to visit his wife in Stuttgart. As soon as he heard about the invasion, he tried to get back as fast as he could; however, Hitler had ordered that no senior officer should fly because of our overwhelming airpower, so Rommel had to return to his command by car. Again his progress was hindered, this time by blocked roads, and he did not arrive at Army Group B until the evening of 6 June, when the Allies had been ashore almost a full day.

We had also dipped into our bag of tricks. The French resistance had received large quantities of coded messages, indicating that invasion was imminent. German High Command had maps showing little movement of Allied troops in the West Country; but they could see by reconnaissance large quantities of tanks, guns, tents, etc., in the Dover and southeast area of England. These war-machines were not what they seemed: they were railway engines made of wood, inflatable rubber-and-canvas tanks and guns, and all the materials of war, from shells to bombers, made by theatrical prop mechanics. They were a well-kept secret and were totally realistic, even at fairly close range. Naturally they were barricaded and the people living close by were barred from approaching with such notices as WAR OFFICE – KEEP OUT . . . NO ENTRY . . . ALL PASSES MUST BE SHOWN.

On the south coast we not only had masses of dummy boats, which from the air looked exactly like troop carriers, we kept up continuous and spurious radio conversations, systems of easily broken codes and signals to give the hungry enemy ear all the information he could hope for prior to an invasion in the Pas de Calais area.

On 8 June (D-Day + 2), without warning, so I could not telephone Enid, our Psychological Warfare unit was driven to Southampton. On 9 June we went aboard a Liberty Ship, which was to transport us in daylight across the short stretch of water to Omaha Beach, on the east coast of Normandy; from talking to others I discovered that Omaha was taking a severe hammering from every conceivable German warlike device.

It would be a downright lie to say I was not afraid. I was terrified; as with most of us, the fear of showing fear was more fearful than the fear itself. A few of us sat in solitary shivering silence of terror, counting their beads or just staring motionlessly in front of them. But for the majority, because of the very present terror, voices showed a little more strain; they were pitched slightly higher; jokes were more frequent and flowed constantly: feeble jokes, filthy jokes and old jokes, all drew howls of tense laughter from these frightened men, each hiding his feelings under an outward show of merriment. An issue of condoms was made to each man, which drew a flow of ribaldry.

This was followed by a grave psychological mistake. The ship's padre announced he would conduct a service for those who wanted it. The joking died immediately as we assembled for the service, which naturally opened up to thoughts of death. Holy Communion would follow for those who wanted it. This was the voice of one about to give the last rites. It had a disastrous effect on the attitudes of the men: they clammed up. They would have been better off seeing a Betty Grable film. When the service was over, the high-pitched jokes were no more.

Progress across the Channel was alarmingly slow. I tried to blot out any thoughts of Doenitz's U-boats, the dangerous and efficiently run side of the German defence which, unlike the Luftwaffe, was capable of delivering sledgehammer blows to the Allied shipping. They were the silent, sinister sharks sliding through the deep waters, well below the ruffled surface. The area had been swept clear of mines – or so we had been told. Nevertheless a careful watch for them never let up.

So we were going in on D-Day +3, and as we drew nearer to the Normandy beaches gunsmoke was visible and gunfire was audible.

About half a mile off the beach, our engines were silenced, and for a few minutes we drifted in the turbulent sea, a sitting duck for enemy aircraft, for enemy gun emplacements which were still in evidence, and for any U-boat cruising silently below us. Down went the anchor. The time the chain took to rattle down was so short that the water must have been very shallow. I prayed that it was too shallow for a U-boat.

I was looking apprehensively at the activity, the life and the death on Omaha beach, when an American colonel, probably just as frightened as I was, came up beside me, put his right arm round my shoulder, and with his left hand pointed at the shore.

'Son' he said kindly, nodding his head solemnly as if he were about to make a profound statement, 'this,' he paused and his left hand opened as it swept it round the panoramic view in a grand gesture packed with dramatic significance, 'is it!'

For some reason I thought this was hilariously funny; it was exactly like a line from a second-rate American film. It was a superbly corny line, dramatically spoken. It helped break the mood created by the religious service earlier on. I didn't laugh. The man must have had a couple, and I wished I had had a couple, too.

But the moment had come. Scrambling-nets of thick rope were lowered over the side, for us to climb down to the landing-craft that surrounded us like ducklings round the mother duck. These were US-designed DUKWs, and indeed were referred to as 'ducks'. When it was my turn to climb over the side of the ship, it became apparent that the further down the net, the rougher the sea looked. It was another Allied bloomer that we had practised this in harbour conditions but never in the open sea.

The man in front of me had been telling me, while we queued up, that when the war was over he was going to open a bakery with his wife and teenage son near Washington; he missed his timing and fell between the landing-craft and the mother ship, to be crushed to death. I sometimes wonder if his widow and son ever opened that bakery.

My jump was better timed and it could not have been more than a three-foot drop while the DUKW rasped, clanged and thumped against the ship. After much incomprehensible shouting and swearing, the DUKW was full and, casting off, started to move us the few hundred yards to the beach.

Suddenly and for no apparent reason the engines stopped, and we found ourselves in comparative silence, broken only by shouts from the Liberty Ship and explosions from the gunfire, shells and mines on the beach. Nearby, other Liberty Ships were unloading men and cargo. But we had stopped. The noise close by was mostly the constant slop, slop of the water and a slap from the tip of a wave that occasionally made it over the side. It was cold and because of the wind, it was getting colder. It was also late and was growing darker.

There seemed to be no reason for stopping and riding the swell; one or two were unfortunate enough to feel seasick at this movement, and they threw up. The American army captain sitting next to me suggested that we sit in the back of one of the jeeps, which had been allocated to us anyway. I didn't know that, and I wondered how he knew. However, this was no time to question his knowledge.

From the jeep he pointed to the reason for our stopping in the growing darkness: to our right and about fifty feet away floated a vicious-looking horned mine, waiting to be detonated by a bump from an unwary craft. If there was one mine about, there would be others which would not be visible in the gloom. The irony of that mine was that it could have been laid by us, some time in the past, against German naval excursions; nobody could identify it for sure. We all watched it. Some said it was drifting towards us, others said it was anchored. One man volunteered to dispose of it by shooting it. The man sitting next to me gave an abrupt order to that soldier to put his gun away as a mine that size, exploding only fifty feet from us, would probably kill us all.

There was no question of dozing; it would have been like sleeping with a rattlesnake in the bed. We just watched and prayed that the German shells from the coast would continue to miss us and that mine.

At first light, cold, wet and rapidly losing morale, which I probably never had much of in the first place, we were cheered slightly by the sound and feel of the DUKW's engine starting. As the morning sun rose higher, we could see we had been joined by many other ships disgorging their men and machines into various landing-craft.

The noise coming from the beach was of spasmodic firing and the occasional deep-throated crump of a shell. I was happy to note that shells were largely wasted on sandy beaches because the sand stops much of the flying shrapnel.

After the chill and uncertainties of the night it was a luxury to land. For some reason I thought that we would have to go, cold as we were, into the inclement water and wade ashore. As the DUKW scraped the beach, its huge front was dropped forward and we drove ashore in style, looking for a pair of white parallel tapes that marked the mine-swept part of the sands. We had to drive between them, well beyond the high-water mark. There were notices every few yards warning men to stay between the tapes, as there were mines still buried in the sand. There was no certainty that every mine *between* the tapes had been cleared.

Four young Americans, high on scotch which they were drinking straight from two bottles, were in a jeep in front of us, a-whoopin' and a-hollerin' as they drove a meandering path. Some commanding voice was yelling at them to take it easy and keep to the swept channel. It was too late. A wide curve to the left in their jeep – and there was a great explosion as the jeep leaped up, turned over in the air and fell, to crush those boys underneath and burst into flames. The petrol tank had been full and there was more petrol in cans at each side and at the rear.

War is waste and foul enough. 'Its glory,' said General Sherman in 1879, 'is all moonshine. War is Hell.' This was France in 1944, already abused by the Germans, about to be further abused by the Allies in the name of freedom; and in a strange way that accident seemed to sum up the futility of war. Being so repetitive, war is natural. God is Nature, or vice versa.

This could have been a moment to weep. You can't cry in wartime. There aren't enough tears.

11

'War is hell'

IT'S UNLIKELY THAT YOU'LL FIND a beach on a French map called Omaha. The locals will tell you where it was, and it is marked with a huge and beautiful war memorial. Such structures should be ugly, as a constant reminder of the ugliness of war.

In 1959, Enid and I went back to that beach. We had with us our thirteen-year-old daughter, Susan, and ten-year-old son, Malcolm. My purpose was to carry out a promise I had made to myself on landing there. It was to find the exact spot on which I had landed, and there to drink a bottle of champagne, should I live to return. We all left the car to go down on to the sand by a tiny stream I had noticed in 1944. We opened the champagne and took out the glasses. There I tried but failed to drum up a feeling of 'This was the very spot'. There was a slight drizzle and it was cold.

The only thing that was warm was the champagne.

It was just bad luck that we were given this beach on 10 June 1944, because it had been more trouble than any of the others. Heavy surf had made landing conditions formidable, and the lie of the land prevented a clear view inland from the beach. It was also packed with too much equipment, too many jeeps, bewildered soldiers looking for their units and a muddle of crates which had been landed below high-watermark so that the advancing tide was ruining whatever was inside them.

The muddle which bedevils all wars was back with us. In the confusion of disembarkation I had no means of knowing who the other three in the jeep were. The driver was a sergeant I had never seen before, the man next to him was a major somebody-or-other, next to me was a captain who, like me, wasn't quite sure what his precise and immediate job was.

We moved inland slowly and with caution. As I was in Psychological Warfare I was not armed. Of my immediate colleagues, only the sergeant carried a weapon; the major suggested that, as the sergeant was driving, it would be more sensible and practical if he, a passenger, should hold the only gun we had between us. The sergeant was excessively polite in his refusal to hand over his weapon. The major tried taking a vote from us as to who should hold the weapon, and the sergeant sensibly refused to give way.

I never gave my opinion on who should be in charge of the gun because I didn't really have an opinion, so I mumbled. The major thought I had agreed with him; the sergeant took it that I thought the weapon should stay where it was. It was rather a sneaky way of keeping both as friends. The fourth chap mumbled too.

After less than a mile, we steered through a gate and into an orchard; where there were others like us, so we dismounted and wandered among them, looking for familiar faces. Finding our own Commanding Officer, I asked for orders; he said that our orders were to wait for orders. He was perfectly, humourlessly serious. K-rations were being distributed and were very welcome.

The Germans were finding that they could not contain our bridgehead at Omaha, although they had us bogged down at Caen; however, we had our problems too: we were landing far more men and material at Omaha than we could disperse competently. The orchard was filling up. As more and more men arrived, latrines were constantly being dug with poles for seats. Inevitably, but fortunately rarely, a man would lose his balance and fall backwards into the pit, to lose all his friends for at least the next twenty-four hours.

We remained in that orchard for two days while nothing happened except for the sound of shells, bazookas and small-arms fire, and the squeaking rumble of recently landed equipment being moved forward. There was no talk of 'the front', as there didn't seem to be one. There were places where the enemy was and places where the enemy wasn't. Occasionally and with a nasty shock we would discover places where the enemy was when we had been told he wasn't.

We also saw some horrifying sights, such as flame-throwers turning soldiers into short-lived balls of fire. I sometimes wake at night even now, thinking I can hear the screams of dying running men before they fell, writhing, to the ground to perish far too slowly in unimaginable pain.

Even at this late date, von Runstedt was not going all out to drive us back into the sea because of our bag of tricks department, to which Audrey Russell and I had made our minor contribution on the Dover Road. Tremendous German reserves were still held in the Pas de Calais. It's easy to look back now and say how silly the Germans were in not seeing that our huge armada, being so large, must have been the only invasion force.

By the end of the second day, 12 June, the day after the capture of Carentan, our PWD (Psychological Warfare Department) unit had assembled and assessed what transmitting equipment we had and what our wavelength should be, and we were scratching about for something to transmit that would annoy, demoralise or mislead the enemy. We still lacked the powerful transmitters which had been promised us; at this stage, however, it didn't really matter, since nobody had any brighter ideas than those that were emanating continuously and efficiently from the BBC at Bush House.

I met a Frenchman who was desperate for money – he didn't tell me why, and even if he had, I might not have understood him because his French was larded with a strong Normandy *patois* – nevertheless he made his needs plain by showing me a ring, which he assured me was a pale sapphire. I had a few francs and, remembering that I had never given Enid a ring, I showed him this money. He made that curious dismissive nasal sound that only a Frenchman can make, because the value of the franc was all over the place due to the fluctuations of war. I showed him a few pounds, the ring was mine, and I found out later that I had done well; but it was an aquamarine, not a pale sapphire.

That evening I joined some American friends for a good poker game (still my favourite card game) and won what I had paid for the ring, even though I broke the golden rule of poker: never drink and play. I drank more than was good for me and was very lucky.

Two of the boys had laid their hands on something called French whisky. I didn't like the smell of it to start with, and the field padre shared my opinion: he didn't like it either. He, good God-fearing soul and excellent poker player, had a large bottle of Calvados. In spite of drinking the stuff and occasionally having to shut one eye so that the Two of Spades didn't look like the Four, I kept being dealt good hands, and so won and won.

I'd had the sense to put up my bivouac before the game, using an earth mound surmounted by a hedge as protection against any stray shell, bullet or bazooka, so that when we had all had enough of cards and booze, all I had to do was crawl in and nod off. That night I dreamed I was back at school, and the desks were slamming with their unforgettable bangs. Eventually the banging of the desks became intolerable and I woke up, to realise it wasn't desks banging but Germans advancing all round us and firing at the same time. I had disliked school so much that it was the most enormous relief to discover that it was only the war.

Being cowardly by nature and not being armed, I thought it inadvisable to emerge from my bivouac, so I peeked timidly out instead. German tanks were plunging down my side of the mound, under which I had been sleeping. The horror uppermost was that one might go right over my bivouac and squash me. One did come over so close that my kitbag was crushed, and I found out later that the ring I had bought for Enid had also been crushed but the stone was safe.

Because of this German advance I found myself on the wrong side of the lines, which would be embarrassing to have to explain to a German. A few German infantry milled about round my tent, but none was curious enough or brave enough to have a look in it.

So there I stayed for the rest of the day, praying to remain unseen or judged to be of no consequence. I tried to work out what sort of attitude I would adopt if discovered; would it be one of brave arrogance or of meek surrender? Would I be taken to some Nazi headquarters and questioned? This too would be awkward, since I had been briefed never to make a mystery of anything as that only makes interrogators more curious. But what harmless facts could I tell to satisfy the inquisitors?

As I wasn't quite sure what my brief really was, even the truth would seem vague and futile and would be assumed to be a lie. I pictured myself at the wrong end of a gun, being ordered to tell all or be shot. The rules said that all a captured man had to tell his captors was his name, rank and number. I had a name. I had a rank. I had no number. I worried.

By that evening, the Allies had captured half the advancing Germans, had killed a few, and the rest had scurried back the way they came, probably as relieved as I was.

I took a long cautious look around to be sure the battle was all over; as darkness fell, I crept out on my hands and knees and progressed in that fashion for a long way, remembering my old army drill: 'Whatever else you do – keep your head down, and keep your bottom down.' Head and bottom were still as close to the ground as possible as I snaked along in the semi-darkness, when I bumped into something soft. It was an American soldier, who was peering with binoculars over one of those hedge-topped banks.

He looked down at me. 'What's up, bud? Lost something?'

Acutely embarrassed, I stood up and said I'd lost my unit.

He explained that they wouldn't be down there on the ground, and I agreed, quickly producing my paper that had been signed by General Eisenhower. God bless that signature; he became more respectful and directed me to my unit, where I joined the others, bursting to tell them my story. But I didn't, because no one had missed me and it seemed out of place to inflict it on them.

There had been a few casualties on our side. None of our unit was hurt by enemy action, but in the midst of this horrifying war one of our unit had died needlessly, and another was blinded. These casualties were needless – as are all war casualties – but some are more needless than others. They were the two who had formed part of our poker school with the padre; the filthy whisky turned out to have been made with methyl or wood alcohol. I don't know if the blinded one ever recovered his sight because he was soon shipped home, somewhere in the USA. They were just as much casualties as if they had gone down under enemy fire, because they had been lifted bodily from their normal pursuits and dropped into a war which they neither wanted nor understood. When a man's surroundings are totally changed, a change must be expected in him too.

We seemed to be stuck for a very long time on this bloody peninsula. The French of Normandy whom we had 'freed' were not the cheering crowds so often seen in old newsreels of liberated Frenchmen. The local people were unquestionably surly and unsmiling. Politics aside, the German invasion of Normandy had damaged no buildings, and had supplied the locals with reasonable rations. Backstreet scum the Nazis may have been, but they were disciplined. The occupying forces had been trained to behave and they saw to it that the German military would be respected. In addition, the educated Germans have always had instinctive good manners.

But after 6 June 1944, along came the coarse British Tommy with a belief culled from the music hall and cinema that all the French girl wants is to be laid and to say, 'O la la!' Add to this the sex-starved GI Joes who had been away from home even longer. This mixture gave the Normans an appalling but true impression of what the new invaders were like.

One afternoon, while I was still trying to find out what I was meant to be doing, with what, with whom, how, why and where, two quite well-dressed women and a man asked me in very good English if I would talk to them for a moment. Naturally I fell in with their suggestion. They asked me to accompany them to a hospital.

I went to one ward only. In it were twenty children, aged between two and about twelve, in ten beds a side. One of the women asked me to go quietly from bed to bed and look into the face of each child. I did as I was asked and noticed to my horror that not one child had all its limbs; some had also been blinded.

Back at the door of the ward, one of the women asked me whether I had seen.

I couldn't speak. I nodded.

She went on, 'You did that.' The other two looked at me to see if I understood.

The man spoke. 'That wasn't done by the Germans, and those children will suffer for the rest of their lives from what you have done. That and worse was all done by your bombing and your shelling. The Germans never hurt us. Now go back to your people and tell them what you've seen and ask them what they're going to do about it.'

It was impossible to speak. I couldn't start a political argument there. Nor had I the wit or the knowledge to bring these people any comfort. On my way back to my unit, I could think only that this was hardly even the beginning of what would have to be done in order to reach Germany, all those hundreds of miles, thousands of houses and hundreds of thousands of children away.

I went straight away to see my commanding officer and told him what I had seen. He was sympathetic but added that Hitler would have done worse, had he ever reached the United Kingdom. 'What was the name of that hospital – the address?' I gave it to him, asking what he could do. 'We'll send them some cookies and candy.'

Cookies and candy! That was about it. But there was nothing else he could do; we were in the business of total war, not Bundles for Britain.

I am not being unpatriotic in saying that the German soldiers were better fighters than the Allied soldiers; they were better trained, better disciplined and infused with a passion most of us seemed to lack. They lost the war because we had better supplies, were better organised and outnumbered them in men and materials. That is a generalisation and it must not be allowed to detract from the exceptional bravery and selflessness of many of our men and women. This has been recorded, but regrettably many more of our sacrifices never came to light.

I still didn't have a job, because our powerful transmitter had been lost during the storm of 22 June while being transferred from ship to shore. As I wandered about, I heard the friendly and familiar voice of Sergeant Chuck Collins: 'Capt'n Limey! Hey! When was the last time you swallowed a mug of tea? Or are you a convert to coffee?'

I was pleased to see he had survived so far, when so many had not, and watched with mixed feelings as he tipped half a packet of tea into a saucepan, blending it with spoonfuls of Carnation evaporated milk and sugar, before adding a pint of water and boiling it furiously while pounding it mercilessly with an egg-whisk.

Should we make contact with the enemy, our theme was to be that we assumed our victory was inevitable and that loyal Germans who loved their fatherland must not die for it but should live for it, because so many of their towns would have to be rebuilt. Meanwhile we wrote pamphlets which were translated into German and distributed to the enemy, letting them know that surrender would mean no more war worries, no more fears, just reasonable food and a dry bed every night. This was our mission. All we lacked was the radio to put the message across. In practice the first things given to each prisoner were an orange, a bar of chocolate and a packet of cigarettes.

Churchill, Roosevelt and Stalin had made an appalling blunder. They had ensured that many more Germans and Allies would be killed before the war was finished. They had done this terrible thing with the absurd declaration that the German surrender must be unconditional; no terms could be negotiated; no quarter could or would be given. The enemy, be he ordinary German or fanatical Nazi, now had no choice but to fight to the end.

I did meet one fanatical Nazi. It was one afternoon when I was watching the prisoners being herded into cages before being given their oranges and so on. There he was, the one who in Little Haven had said, 'I, Ingo Schpagne, represent my Fuehrer!'

All is muddle in war, but now was a moment to take advantage of it, so I went up to the officer in charge and said it might be useful if I could talk to one of his prisoners because I had known him in civilian life, before the war. I produced my papers and my document signed by Dwight D. Eisenhower. A document signed by God Himself could not have been more impressive. Ten minutes later, I had been given a corporal as a guard, I had a tent to myself, and someone had been detailed to collect Ingo. In the tent was a small table and a chair for me. There was nothing else.

Ingo came in and raised his right arm. 'Heil Hitler!'

I restrained myself from laughing, mainly because it wasn't funny. I said, 'We don't do that on this side.'

There was nowhere for Ingo to sit. 'Corporal,' I said, 'please fetch a seat for Captain Schpagne.'

'I have orders not to leave the immediate vicinity of this tent.'

I produced my card, signed by Eisenhower, for the corporal to see; surprised by the signature, he just said, 'Yes SIR!' returning a minute later with a far more imposing chair for Ingo than the camp stool on which I was squatting. Ingo knew he was beaten, and with being beaten went humiliated manners; he immediately offered me his chair and would have accepted my stool. This was the Nazi way of thinking, so I left him with the better chair.

I told Ingo I would rather we were at Little Haven than in this French field. He didn't react. I reminded him of Peggy and Sago, but still he sat there, staring at me without smiling.

'What will they do to me?' he asked.

'You'll go to a prisoner-of-war camp and be shipped to either the USA, the Isle of Man or some such place, and when this misery is over for all of us you'll be sent back to Germany, where you'll be needed to help rebuild it. Your Luftwaffe fellow, Goering, has let you down rather badly and his promise that not one Allied aeroplane would ever fly over German soil has not been kept.

'We've done more to Hamburg, Bremen, Berlin and other places than your lot did to Coventry and the rest.' My lack of tact was deliberate. 'But more important than that is that you should live to help rebuild Germany.'

Ingo was still very tense; I was too young to be able to tell whether this was pride or fear. Whatever it was, I felt I wasn't getting anywhere on any level.

'Am I now to be castrated?' he asked.

'Certainly not!' I laughed. I knew why he had asked this but, pretending I did not know, asked, 'Who told you that we did that to our prisoners?'

'It originated in Dr Goebbels' department, which means it is true.'

'I've heard that when you Germans take prisoners you're civilised and treat us fairly?' He didn't reply. 'We shall treat you the same way.' He still would not relax and he didn't even seem to remember our old friendship. So deeply was he infected with the poison of the Nazi creed that I alone could not possibly wean him off this lifetime drug in a half-hour talk.

Remembering Father's warning that Ingo was a spy, I cold-bloodedly asked him about it. At last he started to open up. 'No, I was not a spy, but I was told to photograph the beaches and to take the pictures back with me. That was why I went on long walks on my own.'

'And with Peggy.'

'She came with me. She had no knowledge of what I was trying to do. But that was not spying.'

'You needed the information for possible landings on Welsh soil?' He didn't answer that one. So Father had been partly right.

Post-war studies of the German plan have confirmed that in 1940 the Fuehrer had considered using Southern Ireland as a jumping-off place for a landing in Wales. Many German 'students' had spent their summer holidays round British coasts in order to take photographs which would show the landing possibilities.

I asked the corporal, standing dutifully by the tent flap, to mount guard over Ingo while I went to see the commanding officer with a proposition. Nothing ever happens as it would in a film; first of all, I couldn't find the CO, then when I did he was in a military conference in a heavily guarded house. I had to hang about. When he came out, he was in a filthy temper and just glared at me and said, 'Well?'

With something sensitive to discuss, this was not a good opening. 'I have a prisoner, sir . . . ' I started.

'Congratulations!' he said sarcastically. 'Shove him in the cage with the others.'

Getting straight to the point might help. 'No, sir. I want to ask him to dine in the mess with us?'

'That means you've got either Rommel or von Runstedt,' he replied in a bored voice as he turned to walk away.

'No, sir.' I managed to walk round in front of him, barring his way. 'This is an old German friend.'

'We don't have German friends. What the hell are you talking about?'

I quickly told him about Ingo and suggested that if we wined and dined him, with everything served from silver and on tables laid with the best table-linen we could raise, we could then let him go back to his own people who, I knew, were short of food. After he had seen how we appeared to live, he could tell a most convincing story, and a large number of those weary, homesick, hungry Germans would be only too willing to believe him. 'What do you think sir?'

'Balls!'

However, I did manage to get more chocolate, oranges and cigarettes. To this loot I added some sausages, a recently killed pair of chickens, a duck, half a dozen pairs of boots and some other necessities, and managed to get permission to send Ingo back to his own people. He was also armed with white papers, for his men to stick on their bayonets if they wanted to surrender. It was never known whether this ruse worked; but after that, and in that area, we had an epidemic of surrendering on the part of the Germans.

I wish I knew if Ingo survived the war.

On 20 July it was raining persistently near St Lô. Boots squelched in the mud; motor tyres could be heard spinning in mud until many hands shoved the vehicles into motion. Someone said that Hitler had been shot dead so we could consider the war to be at an end. I asked for the source of this information, but before I could get a reply I heard that our commanding officer had sent for everyone to pass on some important news.

The crowd of curious soldiers at the meeting-place was large, too large for safety. At last a very important-looking officer was driven up. Standing on a temporary podium, erected from old crates, his speech was brief: 'Gentlemen, an attempt has been made on the life of Adolf Hitler by one or more of his own people. Reports on the German radio say that the bomb, placed under the table on which he was studying maps, killed several of his staff, but he himself walked out of the building unaided. You will be kept informed of any developments.'

To my relief the meeting then broke up, so we were no longer a sitting duck for an enemy plane.

As the Allies managed to fan out to the west and south I found myself (for no remembered reason) once again in the back of a jeep, being driven to St Malo. As we reached the causeway to Mont St Michel, I remembered my father telling me that there was a restaurant there run by a Madame Poulard, who made the finest omelettes in the world. I put it to my companions that we might drive up the causeway and find out if she had survived the war so far and if she was still making omelettes.

We drove up. We had no idea how recently the Jerries may have left. Madame Poulard was still there, beaming with pleasure and telling us that lunch would be ready in forty-five minutes. Oh yes, she said, the Germans had left about an hour before, having had a good breakfast.

I have a great regard for the practical French. The meal was excellent, made from the first fresh eggs any of us had eaten for some time. Madame Poulard apologised for the German white wine, but by now we didn't care.

Suddenly we were alerted by the screams of a girl just outside in the narrow cobbled street. We jumped up and ran to the window just in time to glimpse a naked girl covered with tar and feathers which, we were told later, had come from Madame Poulard's hens that were kept at the back. The girl had been sleeping with a German colonel, and this was her punishment. The crowd jeering at her was composed almost entirely of women. I saw one French man. The girl died later. She was not the only French girl so treated, but fortunately she was the only one I saw. The primitive process of tarring and feathering is more disgusting to witness than to write about; the tar prevents the pores of the skin from working, and death comes slowly unless the tar is speedily removed. Should we have gone to the poor girl's rescue? Were we not just as vicious in ignoring her plight as her accusers had been? Suppose the girl had not slept with him like a prostitute, in order to get favours from him (and plenty of English girls slept with American soldiers for just that)? If she loved him, what then?

Sometime early in September 1944 I found myself in Le Mans – the town now famed for motor racing – with nothing to do. While listening idly to the municipal band in a park there, I had a feeling that I was being watched. The war had now left Le Mans far behind, as the Allies were crossing the German frontier. All was peaceful in this part of France; relatively few people in uniform were about. Out of the corner of my eye I noticed an unfamiliar uniform which, from what I already knew, looked extraordinarily like that of a German *Standartenführer* (colonel). The man was staring at me and then he took a couple of paces towards me. I knew this was no silly Allied soldier dressing up; no one would go to the trouble of dressing up as a Jerry colonel in well-polished shoes and properly creased trousers. He could see the two golden arrows on their black-lacquered brass backgrounds which were fastened to my uniform. As he edged closer, he was probably wondering what they were.

It was odd that no one else seemed to have noticed him, since his uniform was quite distinctive.

He was now about three paces away from me, so I went up to him. '*Guten Morgen*,' I said. That was all I could say in German that was relevant, as none of the other three words I knew would have been appropriate.

And in perfect English the colonel replied, 'Are you American?'

'No, English, attached to the American army.'

'I'm finished,' he said. 'There is nothing more I can do.'

'It's a bloody awful war. I hate it,' I said.

'So do I. I have had enough.'

'Have you had breakfast?'

He looked very surprised. 'No.' I think for a second he may have believed I was going to take him to a café for a croissant and coffee.

'Then you must be hungry.'

'I am.'

I felt almost apologetic as I told him I would have to take him to my commanding officer. 'When you've seen him you'll get something. It won't be bacon and eggs, but you'll be looked after. Are there any more of you?'

'No.'

'Have you been hiding a long time?'

'Since the fighting stopped.'

'Where?'

He gave me the address of a farm, which meant nothing to me, then he added that the farmer had had no idea he'd been in a barn loft, living on stolen eggs and fruit. I respected him for ensuring that the farmer would not get blamed for housing him. It didn't occur to me to ask how he came by such a perfectly pressed uniform and polished boots.

I commented on his perfect English, only to discover that he had been at Cambridge, as Father had been. They were, however, at different colleges, and I didn't ask if they had been there at the same time. To my curiously snobbish outlook, this made him quite acceptable, and therefore he must be treated as a gentleman. I write those words with shame. (I said earlier that this book would be a confession. The truth is often shameful.)

He said he was bitterly humiliated at surrendering and had considered shooting himself. I gave the standard talk about a true German patriot living for the fatherland, not dying for it, because it would need rebuilding. By now, I completely believed in it myself, and still do so today. The Psychological Warfare Department must have saved quite a number of lives.

He was anxious for news so, as we went back to our HQ, I told him all I knew: that the Allies had crossed the German frontier at Trier the previous day. He betrayed no reaction to the news; he looked thoroughly beaten.

Standing to attention before the CO, he was subjected to a search which immediately revealed that he was carrying a heavy automatic and a very large butcher's knife, both of which were placed on the desk by the sergeant who had searched him. The sergeant and the CO both looked at me as if I must be a simpleton not to have disarmed the prisoner. I was about to explain that, as he seemed such a decent chap, I didn't like to ask if he was armed, especially since he had been at Cambridge, as had my father; then I remembered that most Americans at that time had only heard of Oxford, so I thought better of it and kept my mouth shut.

That night was unforgettable, because an American and I found an empty house which we cautiously 'liberated'. We took adjacent rooms and, after demolishing half a bottle of scotch, retired to bed on mattresses for the first time in months.

In the morning I felt groggy, and at first I wondered if I had overdone the scotch. I wrote a note, thanking the owner for the night's rest, and left it on the dressing-table, using 'BBC, London' as my address . . . but unfortunately I never heard from him or her. My colleague also wrote a thank-you letter and left it on his dressing-table. By midday I felt really rotten, so I went to see the Medical Officer. He listened to my heart and promptly sent me up north, to the hospital up Cherbourg.

In Cherbourg I felt splendid again, but another doctor examined me; he also said that my heart murmur made me a liability. By now I concluded that it must have been the scotch, since I was in good condition.

The next thing I knew, I was being shoved on board a Dakota cargo plane that was returning empty, having delivered its goods somewhere in France. In all innocence I asked the pilot for a parachute. 'There's only one,' he said, 'and I'm sitting on it.' He was, too; I saw it. 'Didn't you ask for one at the PX?'

'No, I didn't think of it.'

'Then I tell you what we'll do. If we get shot down, I will put her down as gently as possible on the water. Do you swim?'

'Yes.'

'Good – these planes sink darned quick. You scramble out and swim for it, after first asking me for the compass, which I'll give you so you know which way to swim to England.'

By now I realised I was being sent up and I felt very small. Fortunately the noise of the engine made further communication impossible as we took off from a bumpy field. My feeling of embarrassment stayed with me the whole of the way over the Channel.

The minute I arrived in London, I telephoned Enid at Inveresk House, which is a short distance from Simpsons-in-the-Strand. She was free.

Over lunch (which I swear was gulls' eggs, but Enid says was a goose egg which we shared), I raised the idea of marriage. She told me that, as she was under twenty-one, she had had to get special signed permission from her mother to go overseas with PWD. It was now impossible to get out of it, so my suggestion that we should marry was naturally turned down.

'When do you go to wherever?' I asked.

'September the nineteenth,' she replied between mouthfuls of duck/ goose/seagull/quail egg.

'Today is September the fifteenth.'

'I know.'

'Where are you going?'

'I don't know yet, and if I did I wouldn't be allowed to tell you.'

The rest of lunch was spent bewailing the fact that we would have to remain spinster and bachelor for ages.

There seemed no way out of this impasse.

12
Noises off

ENID was a popular girl in her PWD unit and neither of us had counted on the number of friends she had. It had been suggested to her that if her guardianship was changed from her mother to me, then I could legally stop her going abroad and get her out of PWD; marriage would change her guardianship. Another friend told her that, under certain circumstances, a special marriage licence could be granted by the Archbishop of Canterbury.

When she told me this I was grateful – but not as elated as she, because now it all hung on getting her mother's permission to marry. Enid said she thought she knew a way round that one. I made no comment and, a pessimist by nature, frankly didn't believe her.

I telephoned my mother in Dudley to say I was back, not mentioning the so-called heart problem, to discover that my father was very ill indeed and that I ought to travel up as soon as possible. It wasn't very helpful of me to say that I was also going to get married as soon as possible. Mother said that if I didn't get married I had to see Father at once, and if I did get married I was to bring Enid with me to honeymoon in Dudley.

If you know Dudley, you will believe me when I say that Enid and I were probably the first and last people deliberately to contemplate Dudley for a honeymoon. This must not be misunderstood as a slight on the admirable town, which is every bit as charming as Tipton, Bilston or Hanley.

While unpacking that evening in my old room at Winnie Winston's, I became aware of a new nightmare. Buzz-bombs or doodlebugs, properly called V-1s, had first hit London on 13 June 1944 while I was in France. I was hearing the sinister droning for the first time. I ran out to catch a glimpse of it as it chugged over.

Going back into the house, I saw that Winnie had now come out of the broom cupboard, after hearing the explosion, and was answering the telephone.

It was Enid for me with some good news. 'I've done it!' she said. 'I've got Mummy's permission.'

'How?'

'Can't tell you over the phone. It was rather naughty.' She told me how she had asked a senior officer at PWD for help; he had seen an army

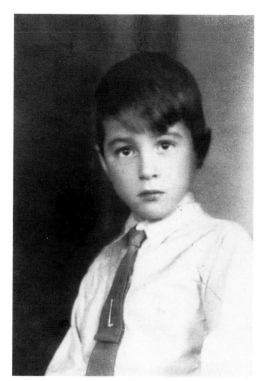

(Above) Me aged seven.
(Below) My father at Littlehaven c. 1935.

Myself and friends on holiday in Pembrokeshire before the war (my sister seated).

Gerald Bird and his trawler-sail boat (see Chapter Four).

The *Twenty Questions* team arrives at Hamburg to entertain the forces just after the war.

Gilbert Harding, human Stromboli and chairman of *Twenty Questions*.

(Above) Peter Waring in 1946.
(Below) Barbara Kelly and Bernard Braden in *Leave your Name and Number*, 1950.

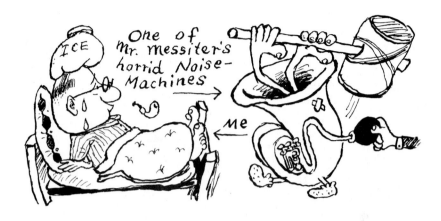

'Mr Hoffnung's Terrible Nightmare': Gerard depicts his fears about
One Minute Please.

Typical misbehaviour by the remarkable Gerard Hoffnung on
One Minute Please, 1952.

Roy Plomley, myself and klaxon (*One Minute Please* 1952).

The audience's view of *One Minute Please*: behind the three 'jurywomen' are (l. to r.) Margot Holden, Violetta and Martina Mayne, Roy Plomley, myself, Frank Muir, Philip Harben, Gerard Hoffnung.

Many a Slip, 1966: David Nixon and Richard Murdoch (vying with
Eleanor Summerfield and Isobel Barnett).

Petticoat Line, 1968: l. to r. Rita Markelis, Marjorie Proops, Anona Winn,
Isobel Barnett, Renée Houston.

(Above) *One Minute Please*, rejigged: *Just a Minute* in 1969 with (l. to r.)
Clement Freud, myself, Derek Nimmo, Nicholas Parsons, Kenneth Williams.
(Below) My grandson James Beaumont, co-inventor of *Steal*, with me on the set
in September 1989.

chaplain, who had telephoned the Archbishop of Canterbury who *could* issue a special licence. 'We might even get a licence by Tuesday.'

On that Saturday morning at about eleven-thirty, verbal permission for us to marry came through. I called on the vicar of St Barnabas, Woodside Park, and he said he could marry us in his church on the following Tuesday at midday, but only provided we could produce the special licence in time.

With some misgivings, I told him that the Archbishop knew all about it and was probably signing the licence even as we spoke.

Winnie Winston was magnificent: she would hold the reception in her house, she declared. She called her brother and ordered him to come over and be best man.

By coincidence, Enid's mother and my mother had both got their wedding cakes from the same shop (now extinct), called Buzzard's, who had built up a great reputation as the world's best wedding, birthday, christmas and christening cake makers. We caught the bus to their emporium in Oxford Street. On the way there, I asked Enid what she had done to get her mother's permission.

Her answer was brief and simple. 'I told her that if she didn't give it, we were going to live together anyway.' Today, as we approach the year 2000, that may not seem at all outrageous; but in 1944 it was unthinkable, economically dangerous and anti-social. It worked; and poor, shocked Mrs Senior wrote the necessary letter. What she hadn't worked out was that, if she had not written that letter, Enid would not have changed guardians; therefore she would have been whisked away to foreign parts, and we would not have been able to marry.

Because of sugar and other rationing Buzzard's cake was a sad joke. It was a lump of indefinable brown substance, covered with a white cardboard lid which at a distance looked like icing. The icing 'flowers' were made of plaster of paris; we still have them. As there was no delivery service, we carried this curio back to Woodside Park on the underground.

By this time, the special licence had also arrived, its huge red Canterbury Seal depending from the bottom contrasting greatly with the commercial imprint at the top, which read, 'Ten Shillings'.

It was very impressive (except for the financial demand for ten shillings) as it began in Gothic script:

William by divine providence
ARCHBISHOP OF CANTERBURY,
Primate of all England
and Metropolitan, by the
Authority of Parliament
lawfully empowered for the

purposes herein written:
To Our well-beloved in
Christ . . .

After all that ecclesiastical preamble, it was a little disappointing not to find the document signed by the Primate of All England, who at that time would have been called William Cantuar; it was signed by a Mr H. T. A. Dashwood – no doubt an admirable man. We just hoped he had mentioned us to the Archbishop.

There were few at our wedding because it was a last-minute affair; because of this, several friends thought Enid must be pregnant. We'll never know how many were disappointed as they counted the nine months away and nothing happened.

A train took us to Dudley after the ceremony. Father was very ill, but he forced himself to dress for dinner that evening, and Mother had seen to it that the dining-room table was weighed down with some family silver, which for once I did not find ostentatious. Champagne was resurrected from the cellar, but Enid and I were so naïve that we told each other quietly afterwards that we would rather have had ginger beer.

Dinner over, we sat, rather upright and uncomfortable, in the drawing-room, drinking Father's best brandy and, unseen by anyone, Enid tipped hers into a potted plant; this did not flop over as in comedy films but survived splendidly on it for days.

When bedtime came, we both felt embarrassed at saying, 'Good night,' and said futile but truthful things like, 'We must be going up now as we've had a long and tiring day.' We had, but it was difficult to say.

We slept in a large double room with two single beds. Mother had been slightly silly, bless her, because she had separated the two beds by a large mahogany commode, which turned into a bedside table, with a decanter of water and a glass on top. I suggested that we get the commode out of the way because it was rather wide and neither of us was likely to use it in the night, nor would we suddenly want a drink of water for no reason at all. The house had polished board floors with rugs on them so, when I started to move it, the commode made a dreadful racket, juddering across the floor, with the decanter and glass sounding like a fire-alarm bell.

Enid said I had better stop doing that, as Mother was likely to come in to see what all the noise was about. The thing was now about two feet from the wall and even more of an obstruction. It had to be pushed back or it would look funny. Bit by bit, we juddered and jingled it back to the wall.

On reflection, I often wonder how my sister and I ever came to be born, because Mother made no secret of what she called, ' . . . all the nasty bed part of marriage.'

Poor Father.

Poor Father, indeed. Next morning at about half-past seven, without tapping on the door, he came straight into the room, humming 'The Skater's Waltz' and carrying a tray with a teapot, milk, sugar and two cups and saucers, which he put carefully down on the commode, saying he hoped we'd slept well. Because we were staying there, he was making a tremendous effort to hide the effects of his failing heart.

Our one-week honeymoon, spent walking round Dudley Zoo, was soon over.

Father gave us £50, which made us think we were rich enough to stay in a hotel. Once back in London, we headed for the Rembrandt Hotel near Harrods and booked in. Enid got a job as secretary to the director of the Imperial Tobacco Company for £6 a week, while I went back to putting records on and changing needles at the BBC for £2.50 a week in the happy dungeons of 200 Oxford Street.

On my third day, there was a funny and frightening moment when I had to go down to the BBC at Bush House to fetch something or other; as I left the building with Gerry Wilmot on our way back, we started walking up a longish stone corridor from the reception desk to the revolving doors which would let us out into the Aldwych.

Without any warning (because they never gave any), a V-2, the silent flying telegraph-pole bomb, fell at great speed from the stratosphere and landed at the Bush House end of Kingsway, destroying a building on the south side. Just as Gerry Wilmot was putting his hand out to give the revolving doors a shove, the bomb blew the doors in, knocking us both down with considerable force. We both fell over backwards and slid on the seats of our pants, sitting upright, the full length of the polished stone corridor, until we bumped, comparatively gently, against the reception desk we had just left.

Gerry dusted himself down and, as if nothing had happened, said, 'That was a wasted journey. Let's try again.' To which he added as we walked along the corridor again, 'Christ! It feels as if my bum's on fire. Is it?' I looked at his trousers, which were undamaged; my bum also seemed to be on fire. Next day we informed each other that we had been badly blistered from the friction.

Each day I read the BBC noticeboard, looking for a better job and somewhere to live. Our money was lasting very well; we were living as well as anyone in the UK, but even with Enid's relatively large salary we could not go on living in a hotel for ever.

By luck, I came across two good things on the same day: one was an advertisement from a woman who lived in Oakwood Close, Southgate, and who wanted to let her flat to 'a reliable BBC employee'; the other was an advertisement for the job of 'Producer, Variety Department, theatrical experience an advantage'.

Life changed. We took the flat before all the £50 had gone, and I was given an appointment to be seen by the board of the BBC Variety Department at 3 pm the following Wednesday at the Aeolian Hall in Bond Street, which was then the Variety Headquarters.

I was at a slight disadvantage, because we neither of us had enough money to buy a radio. They were relatively expensive things in those days. So there was no way of finding out what sorts of things the BBC Variety Department did.

The board assembled slightly after 3 pm because of the public house licensing hours, and the Masons Arms being about five minutes' walk away. The board was made up of happy smiling John Watt, a showman to his fingertips and an admirable Head of Variety Department; his second-in-command, Mike Meehan, ex-Indian Army colonel, producer of 'In Town Tonight'; and Leslie Bridgmont, the stout perspiring producer of endless good comedy half-hours. All three later became good friends.

Being showmen and in no sense businessmen, they had no idea what questions to ask, and I was no help to them as I didn't know what to say, and anyway had trouble saying anything.

The bowling was opened by John Watt with his lined, humorous, tanned, kindly face. He came straight to the point with, 'Why do you want to join this department as a producer?'

'Because I used to be a conjuror.'

This *non sequitur* produced a mumble from Mike Meehan, which sounded like, 'Well, I suppose that's as good a reason as any.'

They all nodded in agreement.

Each of the three had a piece of paper and a pencil in front of him, and they were all doodling, not making notes of any kind; it was easy for me to see, as it was a small table – so small it was apparent that one of them had spelled my name wrong.

I had a dread that someone might ask what my favourite radio show was.

Leslie Bridgmont pulled out a handkerchief and mopped his sweating brow before asking what I had been good at at school.

I said something about History, English and Maths, before being interrupted by John Watt, who said it didn't really matter because if anyone had asked him what he did best at school he would never have been made Head of Variety. The other two laughed and nodded.

John Watt asked the name of the best theatre I had conjured at and I lied, saying, the Palace Theatre, Birmingham.

'Really, now that's very interesting. The Palace Theatre, Birmingham? I must remember that.'

I had a feeling that I had said the wrong thing.

Mike Meehan pulled out a piece of paper, which must have been my

BBC record, and, much to my relief, said I had a good timekeeping record; then he asked me about a Hindi disc show in which I had played all the wrong announcements to the discs. After he realised it was true, they all laughed again and he asked, 'Do you speak Hindi?'

'No, sir.'

'I don't think I'd have got 'em right either,' he said, 'and I'm supposed to know a bit of the damned language. Hindi's difficult. Not even all Indians know it. Spent years out there. Quite pleasant in the summer if get up into the hills. Only way to keep cool.'

John Watt put a stop to that by raising his hand a few inches above the desk.

Leslie Bridgmont asked, 'Why did they put you on to a Hindi show if you can't speak it?'

'I don't know, sir.'

'Damned stupid!' said John Watt, looking directly at me. He asked a few more questions and then told me to go down to his office and wait there. 'Anyone will tell you where it is.'

I knew I hadn't got the job, but I'd had a go at it; and I felt very silly because I had not made any inquiries about the different variety shows, at the same time being thankful *they* hadn't asked *me* about them.

Someone showed me into John Watt's office and I stood there for about fifteen minutes, looking out of the window at Sotheby's front door opposite in Bond Street.

He breezed in. 'Ian,' he said.

'Yes, Mr Watt.'

'Look, you're Ian, I'm John. We don't stand on ceremony here. We're going to put you on six months' trial at no extra pay, if you'd like that. You can start on Monday, the week after next.'

'Oh, thank you.' It was both a shock and a surprise.

You'll follow other producers around, watching and listening to what they're doing. You will also spend some days at the BBC training school opposite Madame Tussaud's learning about production and studio engineering techniques. The rest of the time you will be assisting our producers. At the end of six months we'll have another chat about it and see how it goes.' He stuck out his hand to shake mine.

As we shook hands he said quietly, 'You really wanted this job, didn't you? You wanted it badly enough to invent a theatre.' I looked down at the floor. 'If you ever played Birmingham, it was most likely to have been the Hippodrome. Birmingham has no Palace Theatre.'

'Oh.'

'Were you ever a conjuror?'

'Oh yes. I really was.'

'Any good at it?'

'No.'

'Splendid! Most radio producers are failed actors, comedians or writers. We've never had a failed conjuror before, so perhaps you will bring something new into the world of British broadcasting. Did you ever tell the authorities that you could speak Hindi?'

'No. Why?'

'I don't suppose now I'll ever know why they put you on to a Hindi disc show.'

(Those aren't the exact words, but that was the note on which we parted.)

At the BBC training school I learned about acoustics, balancing microphones, programme structure, the internal workings of the various departments of the BBC, how a pair of half-coconuts can be made to imitate horses' hoofs, how dried peas tipped from side to side in a box would sound like the sea breaking on shingle, how scrunching cellophane sounds like a fire blazing, how in sound no one can tell the difference between fire, heavy rain and frying, and even how a railway train imitated with a roller skate sounds more like a railway train than a recording of the real thing.

The famous announcer, Stuart Hibberd, lectured us on news reading. He said that if he could not check the pronunciation of, say, 'mithridatism', having never seen the word before and having it shoved in front of him at the last minute, the best way was not to hesitate but to pronounce it with authority. If wrong, no one would ring in or write in. 'Hesitate,' he said 'and you're lost, even if you're right, and you get swamped with insulting letters.'

We were also told about how the research into the popularity of programmes worked. The BBC system at the time was largely developed by a man called Silvey; his research team would stop people in the street to ask them about the programmes. The interviewers were divided into classes: the lower (D and E), being the majority, were asked more often than the upper (A and B) classes. They were asked what they had heard the day before – any further back would be inaccurate; even answers about 'yesterday' were sometimes inaccurate. (This was revealed by the simple process of showing the people a list of Home Service programmes which they had to tick. Next, and so on a different sheet, were the Light Programme shows, also to be ticked. Many people claimed to have heard two shows at the same time because they liked to say they had listened to more 'up market' shows than they really had. Many sheets showed religious services, which the interviewed often pretended to have had heard in order to impress the interviewer.)

Another form of research was conducted, to find out what the listener thought of the programme; it ran from marking an A plus for a really good show, through A and A minus, down to the dregs at C minus. At first this was presented as a vertical drawing rather like a thermometer; however, Silvey soon noticed that on hot days people gave more value to the A bracket at the top, whereas on cold days the C bracket at the bottom was marked. He then designed the scale horizontally, which eliminated this inaccuracy. Another curiosity of audience research was that people exaggerated their views. Many would either be over the moon about a show, or they would hate it fiercely. There were very few moderate opinions.

We also learned that a radio switched on is not necessarily one being listened to. People would turn a show on and then go into another room, or play cards, say, with the radio on in the background.

Silvey also used the diary system; several hundred people were given diaries in which to write their opinion of shows for a very limited time. A new diary owner would listen to more programmes than a normal person and would fill the pages with extreme views. After a few weeks the views would be moderated, as would the listening. In the last section, the diary owner would have grown bored and would forget to fill it in. For that reason, the research specialists would ignore all but the middle section.

Silvey's conclusions as he gave them to us are almost certainly true of television today. He told us to ignore figures that purported to give the audience in thousands but to watch for increases or decreases. Those differences were the only sure guide as to a series gaining or losing popularity.

By 1945 it was evident that there were different grades of radio producers. At the top were the few producers who would create, write, administer and afterwards edit a show. Then there were those who could neither write nor improve a line but who were casting experts. I soon noticed how they went about this most difficult job: they would first ask the creator of the show for his or her views. Once the star was chosen, they would also ask the star whom he or she would like in the show. They listened closely and chose from the best of the advice. Weaker producers would never ask because they wanted to be thought of as strong men, and the way to keep someone out of a weak producer's show was to recommend them. There were other producers who were fine administrators but creatively incapable.

Today, with the advent of tape that can be edited, there is yet another form of contributing producer: one who will cast and record the show without comment, before diving in with scissors to find a polished diamond at the end of his work.

At the bottom were the majority of producers with no administrative, creative, editing or casting skills, but who attracted talent because they sat in the honeypot which was the BBC itself. The honeypot drew outside show people, who needed broadcasting to express themselves as writers, actors, comics, singers, musicians or whatever. That last type of producer had little to do except to delegate to his secretary or personal assistant the business of booking the studio, making sure tickets were issued, if it was an audience show, and time the rehearsals so that cuts or additions could be made.

It has been said of many brilliant shows that they stayed at the top in spite of the producer. Two very well-known writers once assured me that the cast had to be urged at the rehearsal read-through of the script not to laugh in case the producer roused himself to look for the dirty meaning, thus spoiling a good line if it was suspect or wasting valuable time if it was not suspect.

I was lucky in that I trained under two fine producers, Henry Reed and Leslie Bridgmont. Henry taught me how to produce a variety show with music, starting with a series called 'All Join In', which was made up of well-known popular musical songs, sung by a different star each week. The intention of the show was to get the studio audience singing some of them, with the listener at home joining in as well. The last part never worked as far as research showed. In retrospect, it was really unlikely that Mrs Bloggins at home doing her ironing on her own would suddenly burst into song just because we, in the studio, were singing 'June Is Bustin' Out All Over' from *Carousel*.

Henry said the trick was to begin noisily and end noisily, to put something sentimental in the middle and all the other stuff either side of the centre. Always let the artist have one song he or she really wanted, even if it didn't fit the show, because the artist's goodwill was essential. Out of that bunch there had to be at least three numbers Mrs Bloggins could hum.

We'd produced one with Vera Lynn (who later most deservedly became Dame Vera). I had sat in silent awe in Henry's office while he talked to the star, asking her opinion about which songs would be popular, which ones she would like to sing because they were new, and which would be suitable for the audience to sing with her. The script was written out of this interview, and Henry was good at interviewing her skilfully, to draw out relevant points for the announcer to read between the numbers.

Today, if this sort of show came back, instead of an announcer, chosen for his melodious voice to read Henry's script, there would probably be an interviewer, carefully briefed to ask penetrating and interesting questions.

One of the UK's greatest singing musical-show stage stars at the beginning of 1945 was Harry Welchman, a star on both sides of the Atlantic and the lead in the immensely successful *Desert Song*, which was packed out for every performance. Getting a seat for that show then was as difficult as getting a seat to see Jason Donovan or Kylie Minogue today. The ticket touts had managed to scoop most of them, and queues stretched round the theatre.

Henry had booked Harry Welchman to record an 'All Join In' at the Paris Theatre in Lower Regent Street on a Sunday, the only day the singer was free from performances of *The Desert Song*. I had heard of the show and of Harry Welchman, but had never seen either and knew none of the songs from the show. Enid and I could never have afforded to go to the theatre, and as we had no radio we were supremely out of touch with show business.

To plan the show meant agreeing the music with the great star, seeing that the musical arrangements were suitable, that the orchestra was composed of the right players (something the conductor always did), deciding on any vocal backing group (again usually done in conjunction with the conductor), seeing to all the administrative items, including the script, and keeping to the budget.

Our meeting with THE GREAT MAN Himself was booked for 2.30 on the Thursday, ten days before the Sunday when the show would go out live and be recorded, for a repeat later that week.

Henry went to the Masons Arms, as was his lunch-time custom; as I could not afford this luxury on my £2.10s.0d a week, I sat in his office and ate my sandwich – because, on that money, even the admirable BBC canteen was too expensive.

At 2.15 the telephone rang.

'Hello.'

'This is reception, Mr Reed . . . '

'This is Ian Messiter. Mr Reed's – er – at the – out keeping an appointment.'

'Oh, I have Mr Welchman here. He has an appointment to see Mr Reed.'

'Keep him down there. He'll be back soon and Mr Welchman will see him as he comes in through the hall door.'

'I can't, sir. Mr Welchman said he was in a hurry and he knew where Mr Reed's office was, I think he's waiting for the lift, and he'll soon be on his way up.'

It was impossible to see the lift from the reception desk at the Aeolian Hall. The huge lift was originally built for moving grand pianos it was quicker to walk; and the office was on the fourth floor, I had plenty of time to panic.

I tidied the place up as best I could and took the teacups off the piano and hid them in a filing cabinet with a couple of beer bottles.

Soon there was a knock at the door. I said, 'Come in,' and a strange chap walked in. It was a relief to be sure this was not THE GREAT MAN himself; I had seen him on posters, plastered all round London, and this was not the least like him. Posters, like television today, make people look bigger than they really are.

'I'm so sorry,' I said, being very anxious to give the great star the welcome he would expect on his arrival, 'but could you come back in about two hours, as I'm expecting to meet . . . '

'Certainly not!' said the stranger. 'I haven't got two hours. I'm ten minutes early because I'm very busy. Where's Henry Reed?'

The penny still hadn't dropped. 'If you go round to the Masons Arms in Maddox Street,' I blundered on, 'you'll probably meet him coming back. He has a meeting here in ten minutes.'

'He certainly has! It's with me!'

'Oh dear. Then you must be Mr Welchman's manager.' An excusable mistake, since he looked so small.

'I AM Harry Welchman!' This was said pompously, pretentiously and rudely. What really upset him was that I, unlike everyone else in the world, was not in a state of the vapours at meeting a star of the first magnitude and, worse, did not even recognise him. Pride can withstand hammer-blows, but not minor irritations.

I prayed for Henry to come back as I offered the star a seat. 'Now then,' I said meaninglessly, 'we're going to do a show on Sunday week, so you'd better tell me a few things about yourself so that we can write a script.'

This was more than he could endure. 'All you need to know about me can be had from my agent, who has copies of all my press cuttings, including the latest press release. Surely you can find those!'

I opened the top drawer hopefully but could find only a collection of beer mats and two bottle-openers. Shutting the drawer quickly, I said a second prayer for the return of Henry, but God was busy doing something more important. 'No, your agent doesn't seem to have sent anything.'

'Well, I've no more time to waste here,' said the star and, in the words of the well-known theatrical cliché, swep' out.

At half-past four Henry came back. After he had heard my tale of woe he said, 'Oh, Hell! I'd forgotten all about him. Ring his agent; think of an excuse. Apologise and set up another meeting. Tell them I was in a taxi that hit another taxi.'

'Were you?'

'Of course not, but I could have been and . . . '

The conversation was interrupted by a huge explosion nearby, followed by the roar of the arrival of a flying telegraph-pole, a V-2. We stood at the window of that office on the fourth floor of the Aeolian Hall watching the plume of smoke saluting the dead and dying as we silently, selfishly thanked God it had fallen on someone else. We stood, motionless.

Eventually he turned slowly to me and said quietly, 'Oh Christ!' He was silent for a few seconds before going on, 'And only a minute ago I thought missing an appointment with Harry Welchman was important.'

That must have been in February 1945, because the last of over a thousand V-2s fell on London on 28 March of that year.

After a short time with Henry Reed, I found myself working for Leslie Bridgmont, the fat and energetic producer of solid comedy, who had been on my appointments board. He was a contributor, in the sense that, if a line didn't seem funny at rehearsal, he was quite capable of rewriting it and improving it. He could put shows together from scratch knowing by instinct where there should be musical bridges (musical chords) from one scene to another, how long each 'scene' should be, where to cut duff material and extend the music to make up the time if necessary. He could and did sometimes rewrite the music. His casting was impeccable.

He taught me never to correct an actor by reading the line to him. 'If the actor's any good, he'll only imitate you. If he's not good, he shouldn't be there anyway.'

Instead he would take endless trouble with a badly spoken line, explaining patiently and unpatronisingly what the actor should be thinking when saying the line. He was very firm with this part of production, even when time was short.

He also showed me how to be lazy in spite of his built-in energies. His philosophy for producing a series (which would usually appear in bursts of thirteen or twenty-six) was to get a good idea, a good script, a good lead and a perfect supporting cast. Those four goals are hard to achieve. However, once he had done that and had put great energy into the first three or four shows, he said he could spend the rest of the rehearsals having a quiet snooze in the back of the stalls. He usually did.

He was also a listener in that, if the star made a suggestion, he would check carefully. 'Too many producers' he said, 'have a little circle of competent friends, and through idleness they stick to them. This thinking produces no new talent, which is the fertiliser on which entertainment grows.'

John Watt, Head of Variety, took it for granted that I could read music when he gave me my own series to produce. I did not deceive him into thinking I was a musician; he just never asked me. The show was simple, and it didn't stop me working with Leslie Bridgmont because there was so little to do.

Called 'Starlight', it was a show without a studio audience which went out live from the basement of Broadcasting House from three to three-fifteen in the afternoon. In an era before car radios, I often wondered if anyone heard it. Mother didn't listen because, as she put it, 'It's not proper music.' I thought Phyllis Robins singing 'Daddy wouldn't buy me a bow-wow' was splendid, even though I knew it wasn't Mozart.

Each week we presented a different musical artist to sing or play, with a pianist and an announcer, for whom I would write the linking material. One week it was a pianist alone, the brilliant Ivor Dennis, who had rehearsed and timed his material on his own, some days before, so all I had to do was welcome him to the studio and take a final run-through with the announcer, remembering to start my stopwatch at the beginning and stop it at the end. A fifteen-minute show had to run for fourteen minutes and thirty seconds, to allow for the continuity studio to link into the next programme.

I felt very important on these weekly occasions and wore my stopwatch on a black silk ribbon round my neck, rather in the way a young doctor will keep his stethoscope on even when it isn't needed. This was the only outward sign that I was a producer – or so I thought, until one day I was stopped in the corridor and asked 'Are you the chap that comes round to check the studio clocks, we think ours is slow?'

The run-through with Ivor Dennis was perfect. The programme engineer was satisfied with the balance of the announcer's microphone and the piano microphone. We waited for the red light. Ivor rubbed his hands together and clicked his knuckles to flex his fingers.

The red light was on. The announcer waited for the green. It was going out live. The announcer opened the programme and introduced Ivor, who was seated at the Steinway which only just fitted into the tiny studio.

He was about halfway through the first piece when the studio door was shoved noisily open and one of the studio cleaners (called 'Brown-coats' because of their brown dust coats) pushed a large vacuum-cleaner in, ignored the piano, plugged in his cleaner and switched it on. I've never moved so fast in my life, as I dived in best Sherborne rugby-tackle form and pulled the plug out. Without speaking, I pointed to the announcer's microphone and then at the red light, hoping the brown-coat would realise we were broadcasting live.

Shaking his head from side to side, he pulled a piece of paper from his pocket, placed it slowly on the flat of his hand and jabbed fiercely at it with his unsavoury right thumb as he said, 'Look, I got me instructions 'ere. In writing.'

I whispered that there must be some mistake, that we were on the air live.

'Oh well,' he said with no attempt to keep his voice down, 'somebody got it wrong.'

While I was trying to get the vacuum-cleaner out, I found myself on the opposite side of the announcer's microphone to the brown-coat who now, in a slightly aggrieved and louder voice, said directly into it, 'Too much bloody broadcasting going on 'ere!'

13
The incredible misters

A DISTINCTION should be made between a panel game, which is played between professional broadcasters, and a quiz game, which is played between amateurs for prizes, or, paraphrasing Andy Warhol, 'their fifteen minutes of fame'.

The first ever panel game was broadcast by the BBC in 1937 and it was a spelling-bee with a cast of well-known theatricals.

The first panel game I produced was another series of that same spelling-bee in about 1946 and the cast was Claude Dampier, Kathleen Harrison, John Clements, Leslie Mitchell, and the duty announcer as chairman. We broadcast it from another of those small studios in Broadcasting House, with two microphones, one for the announcer who read the script and one for the team who stood round it, as this was the easiest way for four people to use one microphone. The announcer read from a script in this fashion: 'Claude Dampier, spell a word meaning relating to quality. It is QUALITATIVE.'

If he got it right, he scored a point, which my secretary would mark on a paper next to the announcer. If he spelled it wrong, no point was awarded and the announcer continued: 'Kathleen Harrison, spell QUALITAT-IVE.' And so on . . . a very boring idea, made worse by the lack of a studio audience. On second thoughts, an audience might have slept through it. It was an idea handed down by someone in authority, possibly with the BBC's charter in mind – which emphasises that one of the functions of British broadcasting is to 'educate'.

It is impossible to say why this programme had run for so many years, except that these were relatively early days of broadcasting, and it was the duty, the pleasure and the luxury of this public service to try anything.

As it is a service which is not leaned on by advertisers to get good audience figures it has the enormous advantage of being able to try . . . fail, try . . . fail, try again . . . and then succeed, with no one in the wings shouting, 'Boo!' after every failure, thus discouraging experiment.

One of the greatest of all comedy shows, ITMA, which ran throughout the war, gained little but complaints during its first six broadcasts, but the BBC bravely said it must be kept on because it might acquire an audience. The ITMA figures slowly climbed as the listeners grew accustomed to this new form of humour. The BBC was right to keep it going, as the following years proved. Every family 'funny man' would come out with the catch phrases, 'This is Funf speaking,' or, 'Don't forget the diver,' or, 'I don't mind if I do,' at the slightest excuse. Most of the credit for the show must go to the writer, Ted Kavanagh, a man with a huge fund of original humour.

I had the honour of producing this giant of radio shows for the first time under the most frightening circumstances. The producer, Francis Worsley, had been taken ill and the Head of Variety sent for me. Not too much could have been known against, me as he asked – or, rather, told – me to produce the show while Francis was away.

Father never had the radio on and he disliked it so much that, if he heard the six pips time-signal by mistake, he would look at his watch and complain that the BBC was still two or three minutes out; furthermore, Enid and I were too poor to afford a radio; so at that time I had never heard of ITMA.

Towards the end of the day other producers were beginning to show me uncommon respect, and it seemed that to produce ITMA was the peak of ambition. I started to get alarmed as the fame of the show filtered through to me by inference. But there was no one I knew well enough to ask about it. I didn't know what to do.

I telephoned Enid. 'What's ITMA?'

'The greatest radio show ever produced anywhere, and it goes out all over the world. Why?'

'I have to produce it.' Silence. 'Did you hear me?'

Enid was too overawed to reply at once. Slowly she described it to me. My terror increased. I had never heard of Tommy Handley and she spoke his name only in reverential tones.

When I met Tommy Handley, my knees were shaking. He immediately put me at my ease, saying, 'Don't worry. Just time the run-through. Allow four minutes for laughter and applause. When we're on the air, signal to me three minutes from the end. I will wind up in time for the closing announcements and the signature tune.'

That's exactly what I did. That performance originated from the Criterion Theatre at Piccadilly Circus. I have no idea what it was about or why anyone laughed: I was too scared to listen.

There was sheer luxury in radio production in those days. We may not have had the editing ability which tape gives us today, but we had two days' rehearsal for ITMA. On the day of the show we had two audiences: one audience saw the dress rehearsal, which allowed us to discover the dead wood, the blank spots and the gags that died, so that they could be weeded out. The next audience saw the live show on transmission when we knew that all the gags left in would get laughs. On that show the audience was in hysterics.

Head of Variety, John Watt, stopped me in a corridor of the Aeolian Hall next morning. 'Well done!'

All I'd done was make sure my stopwatch was wound up. I did more ITMAs after that until Francis was better.

While ITMA was running successfully I was still working with Leslie Bridgmont on 'Stand Easy', starring Cheerful Charlie Chester and Arthur Haynes, on 'Merry-Go-Round', which included a quiz run by Harold Warrender, and on 'Waterlogged Spa' with Eric Barker, Pearl Hackney and Jon Pertwee, for which Eric Barker wrote the script.

On more than one occasion the then Queen Mother, Queen Mary, would turn up, unannounced, with a tightly corseted equerry at the Paris Theatre, where we did so many shows, including that one. She would stand or sit quietly in the control room with Leslie and me to watch the rehearsal. She was either a little stage-struck, or it could have been the disciplined informality of show people that appealed to her.

One day Leslie Bridgmont entered his office at the Aeolian Hall, looking very embarrassed and mopping his perspiring face with a hand-kerchief because it was a hot day. Leslie always had a face like a hot day even in the winter. He had been taking a short walk in St James's Park when he saw a dignified lady whom he recognised walking with a man he'd met before but could not place. He knew the woman well by sight and there was something very familiar about her hat which made her look taller than she really was, he told me later. He remembered that she had a remarkable son, but he could not recall either who she was or what the son was noted for. The tall lady said, 'Well, Mr Bridgmont, what a pleasant surprise to see you here.'

'Isn't it a lovely day?' said Leslie, his mind churning trying to remember who the tall elderly lady might be. So he took a stab at it, hoping it would give him a clue. 'And what is your most successful son doing now?'

And of George VI, Queen Mary most charmingly replied, 'He's still the king.'

A permanent involvement with broadcasting is inclined to give one a strange view of the people who are the audience at home.

There was a sketch which Eric Barker wrote for 'Waterlogged Spa' and which was played by his wife, Pearl Hackney, as a nurse, and himself as a patient in a wheelchair with a bandaged leg sticking out in front. The sketch involved Pearl letting the chair go at the top of a steep hill, so that it ran down, in and out of the traffic, with Eric yelling all the way, and ended up in a pond with a great scream and a splash.

This was done in the usual way, with one microphone for Eric and

Pearl, who stood in the centre of the stage at the Paris Theatre, another microphone for the thumps and splash – which on that occasion soaked the sound-effects girl as she dropped half a paving-slab into a large tub of water – and the noise of the traffic came from the discs of recorded traffic played from the control-room. It was all very convincing and Eric's sharply written lines drew laughs from the studio audience all the way.

A few days after the show we had a number of letters from people who were convinced that we had put an invalid into a wheelchair and risked his life in order to get people to laugh at the cruel spectacle of his dangerous descent through traffic, to fall into a filthy pool. Some letters were quite abusive and threatening.

As my week was by no means filled, and I now had an office and a secretary, I remembered the success H. G. Wells had had with his *War of the Worlds* and *The Invisible Man*, fantasies in which the central or sympathetic character was usually a little man of plain thought, no pretensions and as much a physical coward as most of us.

My first venture into this world was to invent a little man who discovers, via parish church records and historical coincidence, that he is descended from King Midas, and wishes he could turn things to gold – but only with his left elbow. In my play, *Mister Midas*, he did just that, immediately making his pint of bitter solid and undrinkable. From there the story took off.

Before taking the play to the head of the department and risking rejection and the unintended snub that must accompany it, I wrote more plays in this vein. *Mister Parrot* was about a little man who owned an intellectual parrot with a great command of English. The parrot, having read and memorised all Shakespeare, managed to get the lead in *King Lear* at Stratford.

Mister Jericho was about a little man who sprayed his sore throat with insecticide, mistaking it for medicine, and as a result his voice broke windows every time he spoke.

Part of the reason I wrote a number of these fantasy-comedies was that the BBC programme planners liked to book a series of similar shows in order to build up an audience. When I had a quantity, I took them, fearful of being laughed at rather than laughed with, to Michael Standing, who had replaced John Watt as Head of Variety.

I will never forget his comment as I handed him the results of many weeks of day, night and weekend work: 'Thank you, but give them to my secretary.' I hardly slept because of the echoing silence from that office.

I often found myself sharing the same lift with Mr Standing – and he was very much 'Mister' and not 'Michael'. He would acknowledge me politely but never mentioned that pile of plays in his outer office. The days of silence turned to weeks and the weeks to months, so I began worrying about the security of my job, fearing that the high-ups of BBC Variety must consider that anyone calling himself a producer who could write such rubbish must be asked to resign.

One Friday morning, after I'd given up all hope of ever hearing from Mr Standing and had even thought of throwing away my own copies, the phone rang. A girl's voice said, 'Mr Standing would like to see you in his office. Will you make an appointment?'

'I'll come down now.'

'He's at a meeting. His first free half-hour is next Monday afternoon at three.'

'I'll be there.' The rest of the day seemed interminable. I went home that evening and told Enid what was happening and that she could expect me to be fired for writing rubbish.

The dreaded Monday dawned, and all I could think of as I went off on the underground was that at three in the afternoon I had that appointment with Mr Michael Standing, who would either fire me or send me back to being a Recorded Programmes Assistant because my plays were so silly. From habit I went to the canteen for lunch, but contented myself with a penny cup of tea; my appetite was gone, lost in the prospect of meeting Mr Standing.

At three o'clock precisely, wearing my only suit, which Enid had neatly pressed, the shirt without the frayed cuffs and a muted tie and well-polished black shoes, I tapped on the door to Mr Standing's secretary's office. She asked me in. I was almost as frightened of her as I was of him; I reminded her of my appointment and was asked to wait, as he had someone with him.

She offered me a cup of tea which I did not accept, realising at once that I need not have wasted a penny on the canteen cup of tea. I spent the next two or three minutes wondering if my tie was straight and if my flies were properly done up; while the secretary was making polite conversation, I could finger my tie and reassure myself on *that* score, but fiddling with my flies in front of her was out of the question; I would just have to trust to luck.

Eventually I was admitted to Mr Standing's office. To my astonishment, he smiled at me; he had always frowned at me before, and I had assumed it was because I had been given my job by his predecessor, John Watt. He was suspicious of my qualifications, if any. I think he was an Oxford man himself; my university had been places like the Queen's Poplar, and the army. In his world, a background of public school and varsity were essentials. I had had the former, but I didn't suppose anyone had noted it.

He tapped the pile of plays in front of him. I recognised them only too well. 'They've been through our plans board,' he said, and then he paused as he clasped his hands, put them behind his head and leaned back in his chair. This was unpardonable: he didn't know what he was doing to my ulcer. The 'plans board' was a group of senior producers who vetted all new ideas and scripts so that the head of the department could go before the programme planners, who usually broadcast what the department recommended. 'We have suggested that the Home Service give you a series. They have accepted our suggestion. They want all these plays produced at weekly intervals.'

The Home Service was roughly equivalent in content to Radio Four today. But at the time there were only two networks, the Home Service and the Light Programme, and television had only twelve thousand viewers, most of whom watched cards which read

NORMAL SERVICE
WILL BE RESUMED
AS SOON AS POSSIBLE

This today would be equivalent to being told that well over half the adult population of the country would be listening. They were booked for once a week at 8 pm, peak time. With the exception of those tuned in to the Light Programme (and Father, as he didn't like the 'damned wireless') every listener in the land would hear these plays.

I was also to produce them myself, with no strings attached and with no senior producer breathing down my neck. I felt like a second-rate garage mechanic who had won the world's most powerful racing car.

I was still sitting opposite Mr Standing and feeling very conscious of the enormous power of radio. If the plays were successful, there was no saying where the future would lead. Nothing in my life had ever been properly successful – certainly nothing where my ambitions lay – so I was forewarned of disaster. There had to be a trip-wire somewhere; there had to be a disaster, since this sort of thing didn't happen to uncertain people like me with my stutter and with Father's threat echoing out of the past, 'When you realise how useless you are, we can discuss some proper career and, failing that, there's always the army or the church.' (I was delighted that the army could not now be in the running: but I knew I would make a rotten vicar.)

I was very surprised when Mr Standing brought the interview to a close, because I thought he would be giving me a whole sheaf of notes, cuts and corrections to make in the plays. He gave me none. Instead, he wished me luck.

Gladys Young was the greatest radio actress of the day, and I had to nerve myself to telephone her. The very idea, the cheek, the presumption of insignificant, unaccomplished me telephoning her and offering the great actress a part was unthinkable. But in each play there was a woman of her uncertain age. She had a great talent and ability to change her character or her voice, or both. She also attracted publicity, so it was logical to ask if she would like to read through them all; with luck, she might choose one.

I picked up the telephone as soon as I was back in my office and dialled the artists' booking section and asked for Gladys Young's telephone number and address.

'Who wants her?' asked a bored-sounding girl at the other end. I told her my name. 'Who?' I repeated it. 'Are you a member of the staff?' I said I was. 'Spell it.' I spelled it. 'What do you do?'

'I'm a producer, I've written some plays and I want Miss Young to read them. They're going out as a series. Not a serial, as they're all different. They'll be a series and . . . '

'What department are you in?'

'Variety.'

'Plays come from Drama Department. What did you say your name was? Spell it.' I spelled it again . . . And so on.

She wisely double-checked on me and called me back with the secret, ex-directory number.

I grew to know Gladys Young well. I liked her as a person and I had respect for her talent. During my telephone call she was charming and agreed to read the plays, keeping a special eye for the middle-aged wife of most of the 'Incredible Misters'. Each was different, each a suburban housewife, each to be appalled by her husband's ability, either to break glass with his voice, or turn Buckingham Palace's railings to gold with his left elbow, or own a duck that suddenly took to laying uranium eggs, or invent a pill that gave the taker the power to dominate any person he spoke to, and lots more.

I said I couldn't let her have them at once, probably not for a month, because, the minute I knew she was going to read them – and this in itself frightened me – I knew that her part in each play not only had to be rewritten but also should be longer. Every spare minute was used, scribbling and revising the plays. She might like to be in all of them.

Weeks went by, the advance schedules showed the plays were placed, so I hurried, sweated, hurried some more and sweated some more.

I took the rewritten plays round to Miss Young and left them with her. This was proceeding backwards, as I had not yet cast the lead in any of them, and I should have done that first since, as soon as she saw the generic title, 'The Incredible Misters', she knew that a man must be playing the lead in each of them.

Gladys Young liked the plays and even liked her part in each of them, so I moved on to the next stage, which was to get the people I wanted and the studio I needed, all at the same time; This proved to be a complex matter of living on the telephone, dodging theatrical agents and generally playing hard for some to find, while being as available as possible to the people needed.

While this was going on, the film producer, Jay Lewis, who was to become famed for producing *Morning Departure*, *The Gift Horse* and many other films, somehow got to hear about one of my (as yet unproduced) plays, called *Mister Quack*, about a duck laying an atomic egg and upsetting the balance of world power. He telephoned, asking me to meet him anywhere I thought fit or to come over to his office in London's Wardour Street. My BBC office was as small as my curiosity was big concerning the lifestyle of important film producers. We would meet in his office.

Enid, who had only recently pressed my suit for seeing Gladys Young, pressed it again for Jay Lewis, while I polished my shoes again, found the unfrayed shirt and the muted tie, in all of which I wandered up Wardour Street, looking for the great man's office. No, there was no trace of a swagger in my step, because the plays had not yet been out, the press could sometimes be merciless, and I was prepared for them to eat me alive.

From the start, Jay and I got on well. He was a smiling, sociable man but, physically, he was everything he hated.

'Look what happened to me,' he said. 'Other film producers have an eye for a pretty girl, like I have, and most of them are tall, easy-going and confident. Here am I, short, bald, fat, nervous, and everything girls don't go for.' Poor pink, podgy Jay was just that; but he had charm, not the switched-on and-off sort but empathy, and an excellent brain. He had a great wit, loved comedy and, as with all creative humorists, he concealed an underlying deep sadness.

'I want to film *Mister Quack*. It's very funny and it needs expanding. You've missed a lot of possibilities for humour by keeping it too short. With radio you have to grab them or they'll switch off; I understand that, so I know why you jumped quickly into the plot. With cinema you can afford to spread the opening, because the customers are in their seats, they've paid. As long as the middle and the end are worth while, they'll stay seated. And the end must be good, so they tell their friends. You've got a winner there, but for the cinema we shall have to spread the beginning.'

'I can't.' I explained that the BBC had already accepted it. After further explanation he told me that the BBC had accepted a series of plays called 'The Incredible Misters' and that this was only one of the series.

'Surely, if you withdraw *Mister Quack*, you can write another to put in its place?'

And so that's what happened. Jay and I would meet as often as possible in his office, while at the same time I was writing a new play called *Mister Pumphrett*, to replace the one we were expanding.

Jay always appeared to be in some sort of financial trouble. One of his greatest inventions was his extraordinary office. After a good lunch at the original Ley On's in Wardour Street, he was emboldened to let me into his strange secret.

We went into his office, where his desk and chair crowned a semi-circular rostrum. 'Now, Ian, look. Let's put this bottle of champagne on the desk. Put your script there with it and choose a few books from that case at the back of my chair to put with them.'

We did all that and then went into his secretary's office, which was also his outer office and waiting-room. He told her to 'do the magic', whatever that meant, and she pressed a very ordinary bell-push. After a few seconds' delay Jay took me back into his office. The books were back on the bookshelf; my scripts, papers and briefcase, which I had left leaning against his desk, had vanished, with the champagne.

'Good, isn't it?' said Jay, beaming from ear to ear. 'By far my best trick.'

'There's someone else in here,' I guessed as I looked in his coat cupboard – to find nothing.

'Even if there were someone else here,' he said, 'he couldn't possibly have done all that in the time. Come outside again.'

We went back into his secretary's office, and she 'did the magic' again. We walked straight back into Jay's office, to see the books out again on the desk, just where I had put them before. The script, papers and briefcase were as before, with the champagne.

Then he showed me how it was done. The semi-circular rostrum was the visible half of a revolving circular rostrum. A duplicate chair, desk and bookcase were on the other side of the circle. The contraption was driven by an electric motor. The whole thing had been rigged up for him by a friendly special-effects film man.

'You see, Ian, when you are in films, sooner or later creditors will want to find you – or, worse, artists' agents start to besiege you when they get wind of a casting session. So I had this done. When someone I don't want to see comes into the outer office, Pat presses the button. Round I go, and I can get on with my work at the back of all this. I just have to remember not to use the phone or to sneeze.'

Jay was a better friend than I realised at the time because, shortly after buying the film rights of *Mister Quack*, he went into one of his 'broke' periods. We had just had a sumptuous meal and he was standing at the kerb, trying to hail a taxi, when he told me he was broke. I said, 'Then at least catch the bus if you're only going to the station – and I'm paying you back for that wonderful meal.'

'Certainly not. When I go broke, I do it in style.'

'Then I'll pay you back the advance you gave me on the film.'

'No. That's going to make money for you.'

'But you can't make it now if you have no money.'

'I know that. It makes me very sad. But wait a while; you have a surprise coming.' With that, a taxi drew up and Jay vanished.

I discovered what the surprise was, a couple of weeks later. Jay had sold the film rights to Eros Films, and he made sure all the money was paid to me. The film was made, with Douglas Fairbanks Jr in the lead, produced by Daniel Angel and directed by the brilliant writer/director, Val Guest. It was now called *Mister Drake's Duck* and was given its premiere at the Prince of Wales Theatre in the West End of London.

In the meantime I produced all the other 'Incredible Misters' with wonderful casts. Bernard Miles (now Lord Miles) was in one or two of them.

Leslie Bridgmont's advice about getting the best cast possible and asking others for casting advice now proved its value. We did not get one adverse press criticism.

Enid and I wanted a break, so we went up to Dudley to see my mother and father. Father was still an invalid but had good days when he was up and about.

'The Incredible Misters', which had all been recorded on those funny old Watts discs, was still running on Tuesday evenings at 8 pm. On the first Tuesday after we arrived, I asked Mother if we could have dinner at nine, so we could hear *Mister Will*; we all have our vanities, and I assumed she would want to hear it with Father.

'Oh no,' she said, 'we can't mess up the evening to listen to the wireless. Dinner is always at eight.'

Father said, as I had written and produced it, I must know all about it and what was in it, so he couldn't see any reason for my wanting to hear it yet again.

14

Conversations with rules

THIS WAS NOW THE BEGINNING OF 1946, and Enid said with some glee and a little apprehension that she was pregnant.

Mother's reaction was strange. I telephoned the good news to her, to which she simply said, 'Oh Lor'! You'd better tell your father.' Father was delighted.

We had moved from our flat in Southgate to a place in Mill Lane, West Hampstead, and we could not stand it because it was so scruffy. Our local doctor said that Enid was not pregnant; he kept up this attitude for so long that, when he finally did confirm her pregnancy, no hospital bed was available, and the only bed we could find for her was at his private clinic; this was what he had intended all along because, knowing my name and not realising that the BBC paid their staff so little, he assumed I could afford it. We had to turn his clinic down as being too expensive but at least we could afford to move from Mill Lane.

By chance, I had become a friend of a brilliant comedian and magician called Peter Waring, who was earning fabulous sums from theatre and cabaret work, all of which fell into his lap because he was always broadcasting. (On radio, he was a fine raconteur – not a magician, for obvious reasons.)

In those days the BBC was parsimonious with all their artists. They well knew that broadcasting made names, and big names could always top the bill for a large fee at some theatre or other. To a performer of any kind, a broadcast was like water in the desert. On the billing, it was vital for many to put 'BBC STAR', and that would guarantee them a busy box-office. There was no need therefore for the BBC to pay artists huge (or even relatively small) sums. Tiny sums would do.

Peter lived in a £50-a-week flat in Devonshire Mews, London W1; in those days, a good six-room West End flat cost about £10 a week. Our place in Mill Lane had been expensive at £2 a week, because it was in a scruffy area in West Hampstead.

Peter Waring had a woman cleaner who cooked and shopped for him every day except Sunday. He also had a valet to take care of his many suits and run errands for him. Under his suave exterior and exquisite superficial manners, ebullient with sophisticated humour unknown for a long time to most, lay a liar, a cheat, a fraud, a thief and a cold man with no vestige of a conscience. He claimed his knighted father was Chief Constable of Dorset; it turned out that his mother was an office cleaner and his father a bus driver. Psychologists would later find this fixation with powerful policemen most interesting. Most of his education had been at the expense of HM Government at Borstal and, later, in various prisons, where he learned his entertainment skills by practising on the inmates with whom he lived.

Peter knew of our circumstances and, as his valet's wife was an estate agent, at his command she immediately found us a first-floor flat with four large rooms, a decent kitchen, bathroom and lavatory for only £2.10s.0d a week; it was number 30c Upper Montagu Street, just off Baker Street, London. On a fine day I could walk to my office in Bond Street or to the studios at Marble Arch. Estate agents today might call the flat 'elegantly situated'.

No one could say that Peter did this for us simply because I was now making my name as a radio producer, since he had all the shows he needed, from guest appearances to his own series. He never appeared in a show of mine. Our friendship developed partly because he had found the impossible for us, the flat; but mainly because we were both fascinated by magic, at which he had a great skill.

There was a slight catch in his interest in us, but this took a while to surface.

It didn't occur to Enid or to me that the spacious flat, so 'elegantly situated', close to Regent's Park and to shopping in Oxford Street, was suspiciously cheap; nor did we wonder why we paid our rent straight to Peter and not to the agent, a Mrs Gilbert. Once or twice she telephoned to ask about the rent, and I told her I had paid it to Peter Waring. She would always react by saying, 'I see. Er – yes, I suppose that will do.' She sounded very flat when she said it. It puzzled me.

The fact that his valet was Mrs Gilbert's husband, whom he employed at £8 a week, might have made us suspicious – except that we didn't know; Peter never told us, and later we found that he was keeping the flat money for himself while Mrs Gilbert was paying the real (and higher) rent, not wanting to jeopardise her husband's overpaid job as valet.

Peter called him Gilbert, a normal Christian name; as I didn't realise that this was his surname, there was nothing to make me link Gilbert with Mrs Gilbert.

But Enid and I had another problem. As the crooked doctor had made us too late to book into a local hospital and we were so late in asking for a bed, the local prenatal clinic found one for us in Wisbech, Cambridge-shire. Filled with apprehension, I had to put Enid on the appropriate train with twenty to thirty loud, foul-mouthed women from the East End, all

pregnant but none married, except Enid. The maternity home turned out
to be a horror of a place: it was badly run and dirty, and served poor food.

The first intimation I had that there was something strange about Peter
was while Enid was up in Wisbech, about to give birth to our daughter,
Susan Jennifer. Three days running he introduced me to his fiancée . . .
fine – but each was a different pretty girl, and each proudly showed me a
different ring that Peter had bought for her.

This was show business. I was broad minded so I thought, 'What the
hell? It's nothing to do with me anyway,' and forgot it.

Peter Waring usually either came round for his rent on a Saturday
morning, or I would walk round to his place and pay him. It was always
cash, and on my first and only request for a receipt he laughed and said,
'Don't be silly, I shan't forget you've paid.' He never forgot and he never
tried to get the rent twice.

One Saturday, while Enid was still in Wisbech, two things happened to
make me wonder about Peter, but only to the extent of questioning his
sanity. I was walking round to his place when we met in Baker Street, as he
was on his way to see me. I gave him the rent money, and we thought we'd
mooch together along Oxford Street. His photograph was often in the
papers and magazines, and he loved being asked for his autograph. There
were plenty of girls around to accost him for just that reason; girls adored
him and he was frequently mobbed.

Still in Baker Street, we wandered into a sweet shop, where I produced
my ration book so I could buy a quarter of a pound of peppermints. The
shop girl was obviously excited at having Peter Waring in her shop, so she
wasn't paying much attention to me; but we both couldn't help noticing
that Peter was filling his pockets with wrapped barley-sugar sticks.

'Wait a minute, Mr Waring!' said the girl, distinctly embarrassed, 'I
haven't weighed those.'

Peter, in his slow Oxford drawl, said, 'There's no need to weigh these,
I'm not paying, and I never bother with coupons.' He strolled nonchalantly out into the street, his pockets bulging with barley sugar.

After I had paid for my peppermints and handed over my coupons, I
told the girl I would try to get him to come back. I caught up with him – he
wasn't hurrying – and I said he mustn't do things like that. He refused to
discuss the matter and gave me a stick of barley sugar.

He was top of the bill at either the Hippodrome or the Palladium at the
time and he asked me round to his place for the following evening, the
Sunday, telling me that he had a wonderful invention to show me. 'It's
quite brilliant,' he said. Enid was still in Wisbech and I had no programme to work on that day, so I went. We had a decent supper, probably
from the black market, swilled down with endless cups of tea. He was
teetotal but was obsessive about tea, which was also rationed.

After supper he opened a small cardboard box and produced what looked to me exactly like an iron for ironing clothes, and that's what it was. I don't know whether this was one of the first that had a little light which goes out when the iron is hot enough, but it was obviously the first he had ever seen. It fascinated him beyond any normal person's fascination with such a simple gadget.

He switched it on. We sat and looked at the little red light for ages until it went out. 'There!' he said. 'Now watch. It's a miracle.' He was quite serious.

He switched it off and stood it in a soup plate, filled with cold water. Taking it out of the water, he dried it carefully and switched it on again, turning it up to maximum, so that there was a long delay before the light went out again.

We had had supper, and a little woman had cleared away by about eight; but at half-past midnight Peter was still demonstrating his new toy. When I said I ought to go home, he said, 'I think you're bored by this. Don't you understand the ingenuity behind it?'

I went home and, next morning, I telephoned a well-known girl singing star. As she is still, as I write, broadcasting occasionally, I will not give her name; she knew Peter well and I knew she had had, or was having, an affair with him. I told her about the extraordinary evening.

The gist of what she said in reply was, 'That's odd. He came to dinner at my place last Sunday, and when I was doing the washing up after he'd gone home I missed a large carving dish. Not one of any value, it's one of those willow pattern blue-and-white things. I searched everywhere for it and was forced to conclude that Peter must have broken it by mistake and hidden the pieces out of embarrassment.'

Our first child, Susan Jennifer, was born on 10 June, two years to the day after the landing on Omaha beach. There was no one with Enid at the time of the birth because the midwife had told her she was not in labour, possibly because it was a Bank Holiday weekend. Enid was sitting on an unmade bed in the home calling for help when Susan was born. Immediately after the totally unaided birth, Enid was offered nothing to eat except a soused herring. As soon as she came home, she wrote to the Minister of Health and had the so-called maternity home closed.

On their first Saturday at home, Peter Waring came round to get his £2.10s.0d and was very jovial and happy for us about the new baby whom we showed to him with natural pride; Susan was an exceptionally pretty and twinkling baby. We asked Peter to dinner, one Sunday evening about two weeks later.

Dinner was a normal affair and, given how everything was rationed then, it was probably more like supper. It was a pleasant enough evening, during which Peter and I exchanged conjuring tricks. I showed him several he didn't know, and his dazzling sleight of hand was almost mesmerising when he showed us a few card tricks.

When it was time to go, he asked if he might use the telephone to call a taxi. The telephone was in our bedroom; he used it, then came out, wearing his raincoat which he had previously left on the bed. He went straight out through the front door, having said thank you with his customary good manners, adding that the taxi would be with him at once.

Just after he had gone, Enid said to me, 'Did you notice an extraordinary bulge under his coat?'

'No. Why?'

'It looked odd, that's all. I wonder what it was.'

Suddenly I remembered the missing plate from the singer's flat and his curious behaviour when he openly stole sweets from a shop. Rather than worry Enid by telling her this, I wandered round the flat, under the pretext of checking the windows and looking in on baby Susan, inspecting our bedroom in particular, the only place where he had been on his own. Nothing seemed wrong to me or out of place.

Bedtime came. We undressed and climbed into bed. Just as I was about to turn out the main light from the switch near the door, I asked Enid to put on the bedside lamp; it was a cheap lamp with a large shade.

'Oh,' she said, 'that's odd. It isn't here. Where have you put it?'

Then I told her about Peter's curious behaviour while she was in Wisbech. The lamp had gone, and there had been the big bulge under his raincoat when he left.

At about this time I was producing 'Twenty Questions', and the team was Richard Dimbleby, Anona Winn, Jack Train and Daphne Padel. Jack Train told me another strange story about the rich Peter Waring. In company with other stars, they had apparently gone down to Portsmouth to entertain some sailors on a battleship. Peter had let it be known for some months that he had been a naval commander, invalided out after being torpedoed. Jack remembered this and, while being introduced to the commander on the battleship, had said, grabbing Peter's arm, 'Then you two should have a lot to talk about. I'd like you to meet Peter Waring, an ex-commander.'

'Really?' said the commander, glad to meet someone with common ground. 'Where did you serve?'

Peter named an area. Pressed, he named a ship. The commander mentioned that that ship had never been in that area to his knowledge. 'Who was in command of the fleet?'

Peter was scuppered. It soon emerged that Peter had joined the army once briefly and had been discharged on health grounds; he had never been in the navy. The company was acutely embarrassed and the subject was immediately changed.

Anona Winn later told me that when they went ashore that same evening they were put up in a very pleasant boarding house, where they were well fed and cared for. It was there that Peter suggested they all made a contribution for the landlady, ' . . . to show our appreciation of the way she has looked after us.'

To back his words with example, he produced a pound note and said, 'Let's start here.' (A pound was then a considerable sum of money.) He went round the entire company, collecting money from each of them. It was a company of stars, who had money too: there were singers, comedians, musicians, and all star names. When the total amount, which was considerable, was in his hand, he called for the landlady to make the presentation. She was very touched and thanked them all as she put it carefully into a pocket in her overall.

Peter said, 'Now that's not a very safe place to keep it. I, as you know, am a magician, so may I come to your room to find you a really safe place to hide the money so that no one can ever find it, except you?'

The story may as well stop here, because you must have guessed the end. The first out of that boarding house the next morning with a much fatter wallet was Peter Waring, cool, suave, polite, sophisticated and, as always, charming.

The terrible death of Peter Waring is described later in this book.

Producing 'Twenty Questions' was enormous fun. The entire team was a good happy company. It was a very popular show with astonishingly high ratings. History says that the game had been invented by Lord Palmerston, who played it with Queen Victoria. The theme, as you know, is simple: an object, say a billiard ball, is divulged to the listeners and to the chairman, but not to the team, who have to guess what it is within twenty or fewer questions.

Played before a studio audience, it went out live and was simultaneously recorded, for a later broadcast. The show ran for years and had at least three chairmen, the first of whom was Stewart Macpherson, a Canadian with a sharp wit and a good command of words.

Part of my job as the producer was to think up the objects, and that was fun, too. There were little tricks, like having the same object twice in the same show or making the object 'The one sitting next to me', which of course is different each time the questioning moves to a different person.

Here's an example of how that sort of 'object' can get a big laugh. The team then was sitting in the order: Jack Train, Anona Winn, Richard Dimbleby, Daphne Padel. (Old fans with good memories will know that this order was later changed.)

JACK	(*sitting next to Anona*): Is this person male or female?
STEWART	Female.
DAPHNE	Is she well known? (*the one next to her was now Richard Dimbleby.*)
STEWART	You'll have to rephrase that question.
DAPHNE	Surely you can answer that with a yes or no?
STEWART	No I can't, and no.
DAPHNE	No what? You can't answer?
STEWART	Both. If you are asking if she is well known as a woman, the answer has to be no.

And from that point chaos reigned, to the audience's delight until Anona finally saw through the trick. People often said that Anona was psychic, as she had astonishing intuition; while the game was really played for laughs, Anona would get the right answer more often than any of the others.

People often asked whether it was rigged; did we for instance give the team any hints in advance? The answer to that is, 'Yes, once.' Not in a broadcast, but on stage. We had rigged the show with gags, and the result was terrible; it flopped. That game can only be played straight.

I grew to know Richard Dimbleby very well and soon discovered why he was so respected: he was never rude by mistake and was never late for anything. He did once forget a live Thursday night 'Twenty Questions', however. As he always arrived half an hour before the show, I started to worry when we had only ten minutes left. By chance I had his telephone number on me, so I rang his home in Hampshire, and Richard answered. He was shocked that he had totally forgotten. He made no excuses; he owned up and was profuse in his apologies. I said he need not worry, as I would soon find someone in the audience, and we could make publicity capital out of it.

We did – but not quite in the way it should have been. Running back to the studio, I jumped on to the stage and said, 'It's sad for me to have to tell you that Richard Dimbleby can't be here this evening. He makes no excuse but says he just plain forgot. Give him a round of applause for telling the truth and not saying his car broke down.' They did. 'Now we are one short for the team. There must be somebody here in the audience who has sat at home thinking, 'I can do that as well as them.' Well, now is your chance. Who is brave enough to take Richard Dimbleby's seat and join us to play "Twenty Questions"? Any volunteers?' There were only two minutes to go. 'While I introduce the team – think about joining us for half an hour.' I introduced the team and added, 'Now, who feels brave enough?'

A man left his seat and came up to join me, centre stage. I asked him his name; he gave it. I could smell whisky and he was swaying slightly. What now? I couldn't say to him, 'I think you've had one drink too many and may spoil the show.' There were no other volunteers, so I couldn't make the seat the prize for answering a quick question. There was a minute left before the red light.

I looked at Jack Train, Daphne Padel and Anona Winn. They all smiled blandly back at me. I turned and looked at Stewart Macpherson; he was fiddling with his headphones.

There was half a minute to go. Taking a chance, I let the man take the spare seat, and I prayed.

Luck favoured the show. The man was so dazed he hardly spoke. The team were aware of his condition and spoke over him on the rare occasions when he did open his mouth, and he didn't slur his words. The press never noticed; the show was given the extra publicity, and no damage was done.

Radio in those days was often big news. With almost every entertainment show came publicity, which showed a side of the press I never suspected.

Newspaper reporters would waylay producers from time to time in order to get a story. In contrast to tales we hear today, the reporters were absolutely trustworthy. If X of some newspaper rang and said, 'Is it true that Miss Y is being auditioned for your new show?' it was always possible to say it was or was not true, but 'Please don't print it yet, the time isn't ripe.' These requests were honoured.

Even my simple task in 'Twenty Questions' got me into trouble. I had to check that no objects were chosen which had the possibility of double meanings, which could lead to a buzz of dirty sniggers from the audience.

It was really stupid of me on one show to choose a sporran and follow it with a fig leaf. This was done deliberately to give the show a bit of a lift, but in those days it was disgraceful. The juxtaposition of these objects led to a hullabaloo.

I was sent for by Mr Standing; he took my name off the show, told me to continue producing it, but insisted that he or his second-in-command, the friendly, bumbling, white-haired ex-Indian Army major Mike Meehan, should vet every list. Vetting with Mike was always done in the Masons Arms; vetting with Mr Standing was done in my absence: I had to present the list to his secretary, who would invariably return it with some items crossed out. I have never found out why he crossed out 'a civil servant'. Even now, all these years later, I still wonder what he could have taken exception to with that, unless it was that people in show business sometimes make fun of them.

One year, just before Christmas, the command came from King George VI for us all to play 'Twenty Questions' at Windsor Castle. A letter to my parents, which I have edited, tells most of what occurred.

A very merry Christmas to you both. Busier than ever at the office
and in the studios with 20 Qs and planning the new Piddington
telepathy series for Jan. 16, 23 and 30 or would have written
before. Windsor Castle was an experience.

It all went well there. Among those present were the King,
Queen and Margaret Rose. Elizabeth was away in Malta as you
know and I don't envy her a bit, as it is cold and damp there this
time of year.

The three Royals enjoyed the show very much. It showed on
their faces and they said so afterwards. The King made it clear
that it was his choice and that's why he enjoyed it so. When you
remember the rubbish that is often forced on the Royals, this
must have been a change for him.

I wrote the objects on a blackboard so the audience could see
them but the team couldn't. This meant standing in front of the
foot-high platform and near to the King who kept thinking up
objects for the team to guess and whispering them to me so I
could write them on the board. Some were funny such as 'a dirty
knight' - and he didn't have to tell me how to spell 'knight'. I
could see what he meant from his expression. As a stutterer
myself I noticed that he too does not stutter when he whispers.

After the show we went to the King's private drawing-room and
we, that is the team and Maurice Winnick who has some sort of
ownership of the show and was responsible for the evening's
music, were formally presented. This was the only boring bit of
the evening and pointless too as we had all been chatting earlier.

When that was over we went back to the Waterloo Chamber
with the Royal family and spent the next three hours chatting and
dancing to Maurice Winnick's band.

I was down to dance with Margaret Rose but at the time the
Queen was talking to me about a play we had both seen on
television so I missed the dance. The King was great fun and had
a stock of spicy jokes which the Queen said she had heard before.

Windsor Castle is a most impressive building and the King's
equerry had shown me over much of it during the afternoon. He
told me what a draughty place it was and how hard it is to heat it
properly during the winter.

The King, between two dances, asked Maurice if 'waving a
stick to make the men play is all you do?' Maurice replied, 'Yes,
sir, but there's a lot more to it than appears on the surface.' To
which the King replied with a smile and his inevitable stutter,
'Rather like being a king.'

Not mentioned in that letter was a small and revealing conversation, the lead in to which I have completely forgotten; but somehow the King was talking quietly to me about endless parade inspections, when he suddenly said that he enjoyed them except for one thing. Politely I asked what that was. 'I-i-i-if the p-p-parade is in the morning, I can have nothing to drink with my b-b-b-b-breakfast. Because no one thinks a King ever has to pee.'

During the dancing we carried toy balloons with lucky numbers on them which a singer drew from a hat. Stewart, who was about to leave 'Twenty Questions' to go back to Canada, said he would like to take one of the prizes home with him; the King, hearing this, popped Stewart's balloon with his cigarette, grabbed the remaining shreds of rubber so he could identify the number and, by what was virtually a royal command, 'fiddled' a prize for Stewart.

When Stewart Macpherson left the show to run his own sports stadium in Canada, he was replaced at first by the great, irascible broadcaster, Gilbert Harding, who seldom spoke well of anyone. Some of his extra-ordinary, bad-tempered, abrasive behaviour was due to his being an impotent homosexual, or so I'm told. Some of it, I knew, was due to drink.

He was one of the strangest people I met in my world peopled with strange characters. On one occasion we were sharing a cab to a studio when we found ourselves in Trafalgar Square with policemen holding back the crowds who were waiting to see the Queen pass by on her way from Buckingham Palace to the Mansion House.

'Drive on!' Gilbert shouted to the cabby, who opened his sliding glass panel and apologised, saying it was impossible because of the police and the people.

'Who,' asked Gilbert, having now left the cab and addressing the multitude, 'do these Royals think they are that they can impede innocent citizens going about their lawful business?' He waved his umbrella and, at the top of his most considerable voice, shouted, 'Out of my way! Let me pass!' He was remonstrating with all those nearest to him. One or two had to duck out of the way of his aggressive umbrella. This tirade continued, building up to a crescendo as he grew redder, louder, more breathless and more impossible with every passing second. I noticed two policemen looking at us and discreetly edging our way.

From the other side of the square came the sound of cheering as we caught a glimpse of the Royal coach. The cheering grew louder as the coach approached.

Suddenly, using his umbrella, Gilbert struck the shoulder of a man in front of us with his hat still on. 'What do you think you're doing with that silly hat on?' he demanded and went on, 'Take it off! Wave it! Cheer! There is our dear Queen! Have you no respect for Royalty? Come on, everyone. Cheer! We have the only decent Royal Family left. Cheer her Majesty!' And he cheered with all his might. The cabby took his cap off, looked at me with a puzzled expression and scratched his head.

We arrived in good time at the Playhouse Theatre at the bottom of Northumberland Avenue, to perform one of my first 'inventions', as I like to call them; it was named 'False Evidence'. I had wanted to call it 'Spot the Liar!' but Mr Standing said the word 'liar' was unpleasant and 'not really BBC'. The show asked three people to tell a story about themselves, two of them true and one a fabrication. The jury of twelve from the audience had to vote as to which was lying. Mr Standing changed that line to 'which has been giving false evidence'.

We did this show on radio for some weeks, with Franklin Engleman defending each speaker, Leslie Mitchell prosecuting, and Gilbert Harding as the judge to sum up. We never briefed them in advance as to the identity of the liar.

We also performed it on television with outside broadcast cameras in the Playhouse, a theatre then not really suited to the cumbersome machinery needed. For those television occasions, Gilbert wore a full-bottomed wig and gown, which was technically wrong but which looked impressive on the screen.

Leslie, Franklin and I had met in secret, some days before, and I had decided that, knowing Gilbert to have such an uncontrollable temper, it would be fun to challenge almost every ruling that he, as the judge, made. This would be sure to produce fireworks; he would lose his temper, and we would get newspaper headlines.

After three weeks of this, and with Gilbert Harding getting quieter and quieter instead of the reverse, I asked him tentatively if there was anything really wrong.

'Yes,' he said meekly – and when he was meek he was very, very meek – 'I have a feeling that those two really don't like me, so I'm probably wrong for the show.'

The splendid plot had backfired. But I never really believed Gilbert, and I still don't. The real problem was that in any show he had to be the giant, the Colossus, the star. Both Leslie and Franklin were great stars in their own right, so Gilbert was in fact having a little sulk by refusing to play with people of his own stature.

It was a great disappointment to find 'False Evidence', in a different form but with the same underlying principle, imported from the USA under a different title, many years later. I have since changed my original game and have simplified it, while keeping to the same theme of three people, one of whom is lying. It is now excellently produced by one of the BBC's top sound producers, Edward Taylor, on Radio Four with Tim Brooke-Taylor in the chair and re-christened 'Hoax!'

But that same Gilbert Harding was a weekly triumph in 'Twenty Questions'. He made the show, with his petulance and irritability with the team, the audience, me, the objects and even the Mystery Voice. Since the show was live, and the audience knew it, they also knew there was no controlling Gilbert. To say that I produced the show would be a joke. I just made sure it got on the air and hoped simultaneously for the best and the worst.

Listening figures rocketed as people tuned in just to hear this human Stromboli erupt. They were seldom disappointed, and his anger was always real.

The most memorable evening started when Gilbert asked me to meet him at the Savage Club in Carlton House Terrace before the show. This is a club, founded in 1857 mainly for successful actors, artists, writers and comedians, which once took a pride in being a little outrageous. I had no idea how long he had been there before I arrived. I myself have a rather priggish attitude to drink; I'll drink like a fish after the work is done but never touch a drop before, however small my own contribution to the show.

This goodie-goodie attitude irritated Gilbert, who kindly bought me a triple gin-and-tonic. As the tonic was already in it, there was no way of pouring it back into the bottle. I suggested that it be put in the fridge until later. No risks could be taken on any show, let alone a live one.

Gilbert was angry at this and downed the triple gin rather than waste it, on top of whatever else he may already have had. He was noted for his alcoholic capacity, so I thought little of it. The fuss over the drink was no minor fuss to Gilbert; no fuss was ever small to him. He blew it up, saying that refusing his hospitality was a major insult. I explained that we had a show to do. He said that, as far as he was concerned, I might as well sleep through it, for all the contribution I made to 'Twenty Questions'. 'As you do nothing for the show, I have no idea why you're being so stupid,' he said with scornful contempt. This conversation was making us late, so we took a taxi to the Paris Theatre, arriving with two minutes and forty-five seconds to go. It was a cold night.

Gilbert seemed to be angry but perfectly sober as we went down the stairs to the studio, so I dashed on to the stage to introduce Richard Dimbleby to the audience; in turn, with great speed and professionalism, he appeared not to hurry, although he was very conscious that we were late as he introduced the team.

A moment before the second hand of the clock clicked up to eight-thirty, when the studio became live, Richard said ' . . . and here is our chairman, Gilbert Harding!'

Gilbert entered, to applause from a packed studio, and sat down to pick up his headphones so that he could hear the Mystery Voice.

I was standing to the left and close to his chair (in order to signal to the man who held up the object cards to show the audience what the team had to guess), so I saw at once that something was wrong. Gilbert had his headphone leads in a tangle; the warmth of the studio, compared to the cold outside, had made the alcohol take effect on his brain. His mind was as muddled as the cords to the headphones.

Listeners heard grunting, spluttering, thumping and curious words – certainly not swearing, for Gilbert never swore. In the midst of trying to unravel the cords, which were now getting entangled with the microphone cable, he could be heard complaining about his introduction. 'I dislike,' he said, 'being introduced as some variety act.'

The announcer from the continuity studio, back at Broadcasting House, who had put us on the air snatched us back and said, 'They do not seem to be quite ready for us to go over to "Twenty Questions".'

A few seconds passed and we were back on the air again, as the green light signalled Gilbert to begin. He was about to erupt. The first object went by reasonably, even though in the middle of it he crossed swords with Richard Dimbleby whom he called 'the BBC's sacred cow'. The audience didn't laugh because there was a great, almost national affection for Richard.

The second object was 'a peony' and Jack Train hit on it at about the seventh question. Gilbert said, 'No,' the audience made plaintive noises, and the team, knowing better, went on, to be counted out at the twentieth question. Gilbert named it. Jack complained. The audience muttered.

Gilbert took off his headphones, turned and beckoned me over to his chair. There was really no need for me to have gone to him because, at the top of his voice, he asked, 'Ian, what's the matter with those idiotic people in the audience?' I told him that Jack got it right at number seven. 'Serves them right,' said Gilbert, 'they shouldn't take this silly game so seriously. Let's get on to the next object.'

This time he crossed swords with Joy Adamson (who had since replaced Daphne Padel). I don't remember what the difference of opinion was about, but Gilbert said, 'You're wrong; like being Joy by name, but not by nature.'

He finished the programme some three minutes too early because, as he put it, 'I'm fed up with this idiotic game; and as for the score, if you've been listening you won't need it, if you haven't, you won't want it. I'm going home.'

In those days the BBC was full of people who were looking for errors which they could turn into a hangman's rope. Mr Standing rang me himself next morning and said the Director General, Sir William Haley, would like to see me at eleven. I presented myself at Broadcasting House in my usual state of abject terror. It was generally assumed that the Director saw no one. Ever.

I was ushered into his hushed imposing office on the third floor. He didn't look up when I came in, so I stood like a schoolboy in front of his desk. In time and without hurry he finished what he was writing. He blotted it carefully, before laying his pen on one side and looking up slowly.

Messiter?'

'Yes, sir.'

'How did you let Harding broadcast when he was so obviously drunk?'

I explained that he didn't appear to be drunk when he first came into the studio, and that it must have been the warmth that had brought out his behaviour.

'That programme,' went on the DG, 'is down for a recorded repeat next Monday. Cancel it.'

I spoke up stutteringly, astonished at my own bravery. 'Last night's show might make a paragraph in some papers on about page four, near the bottom. If we stop the repeat, it will make page one in most papers.'

'There's no question of making a show with a drunk as the chairman. Cancel it.'

'I . . . ' I wanted to suggest that it might be more in the BBC's interests to put in an old 'Twenty Questions' with the minimum of explanation, but the words stuck again.

'I said cancel it.'

So I did, and, being the show with the highest ratings at the time and with no television to speak of, it was to become front page news.

Back in my office, I rang Mr Standing to tell him what had happened. He said he already knew, and would I please send for Gilbert and fire him from the show. Meanwhile would I let him have a list of possible chairmen; he would make the choice. This was their decision , but I had been ordered to wield the axe.

I rang Gilbert's number, but he was out. He was out because he was on his way to see me. Late that afternoon, he entered, my office and burst into tears. I told him what I had been ordered to do. He said he would go to see the Pope because as a recent convert to Roman Catholicism this would help his soul. Sure enough, he went to Rome a few weeks later.

Meanwhile, the BBC did not take him off any others of his several weekly shows.

It is impossible to discover the logic of his being banned from 'Twenty Questions' alone.

Gilbert Harding was replaced by Kenneth Horne, who was one of the few men who spoke ill of no one. Kenneth's success was due to his being everybody's uncle; he was always good company and never appeared depressed. Being a comedy writer, he would study the objects for the show very carefully for some time; this gave him the opportunity to think up one or two smiles which they might otherwise not have earned. He was also a businessman of considerable acumen and earned himself a place on the boards of Triplex, Ronseal and Chad Valley Toys.

I had to defend Kenneth to Mr Standing once over something he had said during the programme. It wasn't a grubby gag but some political joke, which Mr Standing had heard and had not liked. The conversation ended with Mr Standing saying that Kenneth must be a bit of a fool. It surprised me to hear the Head of the Department falling into the common error of thinking that a man who is partly a professional comedian, making laugh-provoking remarks, must also be a fool. Most of us know that the funnier the 'fool', the more brains he conceals.

As I sat looking at the Head of the Department and thinking of Kenneth with his alert mind, good directorships, writing ability and broadcasting wit, I wondered how this unapproachable man had managed to become Head of a Department dealing in humour.

However, there was one memorable exception, when he showed his humorous side at my expense, and it was worth it.

Every Thursday morning from 10 am until midday, the Variety Department held a meeting in the Aeolian Hall, Studio 2. There we freely discussed and criticised, blamed and praised one another's shows. It was usually a productive session, attended by all the producers who were not recording or broadcasting at the time. We asked questions, such as: why were studio audiences often kept queueing in the rain at the whim of some peak-capped commissionaire, when rehearsals were already over and they could therefore be housed, drier and happier, inside?

My question one Thursday went like this: 'Mr Standing, I hung my raincoat up in the cloakroom at Broadcasting House yesterday and saw the cloakroom attendant listening to a radio supplied by the BBC. I don't have a radio in my office; in order to keep in touch with programmes, I would find it an advantage. How can I get one?'

With one of his rare smiles, Mr Standing replied at once: 'Ian, stay with us long enough and you may yet have a BBC radio when we promote you to cloakroom attendant.'

I was fascinated by the theory that game-shows were not being fully exploited. It was like looking over the edge of a cliff at something so obvious, I wondered why no one had ever spotted it before. There must be hundreds of ways of producing shows which were really nothing more than conversations with rules. The cost of a game-show, which has virtually no rehearsal, is minimal compared to that of rehearsed show.

Developing the thought further, I remembered the Sherborne master who had told me to talk for sixty seconds without hesitation or deviation. It was not long before the extra rule concerning repetition came along. Unlike the traditional location for new ideas, the bathroom, this arrived one September when I was on top of a number 13 bus.

So that whacking had moved from my behind into my head, and I thought I could see the germ of an idea for a show in it. It happened quite suddenly and with the curious cartoon sparkle that I often imagine when a good idea strikes. There was most certainly a show there. The few unscripted game-shows at that time were based on a questions-and-answers format. My idea was a total break from the expected. In the entertainment world, the audience will accept progress that moves gently from one idea to another, but they might not accept a total break from the form to which they were accustomed. However, it was worth a go. The possibilities seemed endless.

An appointment was made for me to see Mr Standing so that I could put forward the idea, which I wanted to call 'Just A Minute'.

The familiar fear of those in command welled up. We met at three o'clock one afternoon, by which time the project was all neatly typed out and included a breakdown of costs. I explained it to him with care but, being a rotten salesman and possibly inhibited by the stutter, I could not convince him that it was even worth a trial. He said it was much too complicated for our listeners to follow, and he rejected it. Unfortunately, when I wanted to go back the next day and talk a little more about it, he had been taken ill.

The following day at a quarter past six in the evening when I was again near his office I bumped into the second-in-command, white-haired, crinkly-faced, friendly Mike Meehan, who made his name creating 'In Town Tonight'.

We thought it not inappropriate to toddle up to the Masons Arms, where we bought a few pints. I was careful to buy, but not to drink more than a duty sip, as selling the one-minute talk-show was all-important and I knew, liked and respected Mike.

He was a truly creative producer, but his weak point was his memory. After he had downed a pint and settled into his usual chair, I put the idea of 'Just a Minute' to him. He asked me to enlarge on it, and he ended up by liking it. Asked if the department would use its allocation of pilot programme money on an experimental bash, he hesitated. (Test programmes are called 'pilots'.) We talked a little more, and his hesitation started to dissolve like a snowflake in summer.

By now Mike, bless him, was jovial and receptive. I asked him again if it was worth a bash. Again he hesitated before asking thoughtfully, 'What'll a pilot cost?'

I was ready with the answer, which today would be pathetically little. He mulled it over and asked who I had in mind for it.

I suggested Yvonne Arnaud, Valerie Hobson and Nan Kenway versus Gilbert Harding and Kenneth Horne . . . and I deliberately left the last name out so I could ask him who he thought would be right. He came up with Reggie Purdell. That was a good name; now that he contributed to the idea, as far as I was concerned he was helping and would therefore continue to help.

He suggested Roy (Desert Island Discs) Plomley in the chair, with me beside him, armed with a stopwatch, a gong and a hooter . . . it was not quite the show it is today.

The minute he said, 'Go ahead, it sounds as if it might work,' I finished my pint, made an excuse and ran back to my office, where I laboriously typed a memo with two fingers to Mike, confirming that he had agreed to £X for a pilot of 'Just A Minute', with the team as suggested, and thanking him for his suggestions, cunningly adding a couple I had thought of, because I knew he'd never remember that much detail mixed in with the truth.

After four or five attempts at typing it (all the secretaries having gone home), I produced a professional-looking memo and whizzed down to his office to plonk it on his desk so that (I hoped) he would remember what had transpired in the pub.

Whatever it was that the Assistant Head of Variety had to do to get a pilot allocation, he did. This enabled a studio to be booked, and every artist wanted was, by remarkable luck, available.

Mr Standing came back from his sick leave to discover the pilot a foregone conclusion. He sent for me to say that the title 'Just A Minute' sounded slick and therefore cheap. 'Wouldn't it be more dignified', he asked, 'to call it "One minute, Please"?' This was not really a question, it was an order; so the title was changed. This suited me well. Now that the Head of Variety had added his two penn'orth, he was by definition backing it. He added that he wished us luck, but the show couldn't possibly succeed as there were no proper rules. That was and, over forty years later, still is part of the fun of the game. It is why the chairman takes so much stick, and why today's chairman, Nicholas Parsons, who deliberately draws fire from the team on to himself, has helped to make such a success of it.

Rehearsal was difficult because all the artists, being accustomed to the quiz format, took a while to realise they were not being asked questions.

In the middle of the afternoon rehearsal, using subjects that would not be used on the show, Yvonne Arnaud stood up and said in her gorgeous French accent: 'Ziss is ze rubbish. However can ziss game be played?' She looked at me and asked, 'Oo is ze idiot oo says that we play such a stupid game?'

I owned up at once; there was no option. She was extremely embarrassed, having thought that the show was some import from America, as some of them were then. She had naturally thought I was just the producer, not the inventor. She came over and kissed me, and the positions were reversed, because now I was having to cheer her up, so appalled was she at her accidental lack of manners. It seemed she'd never snap out of it.

It was a terrible blow that one of our greatest artists had denounced the show in front of the others before it had ever been heard by an audience. Snubbing me in the studio was no worry. If you stick your neck out in show business, someone who has never stuck his neck out will try to chop through it. But this is known to everyone in show business and we are all volunteers. The worry was that perhaps she was right and that the press would pillory us.

Kenneth Horne, friend and avuncular performer, made it worse by trying to heal the wound. He told me not to worry, as they'd all do their very best to make something out of it. Such open patronage made me feel he didn't believe in it either.

Roy Plomley did believe in it and, without a trace of patronage, told me so. Roy was already a star through his weekly show, 'Desert Island Discs'. In later years our two families were to become great friends. He was a kind, thoughtful man and, away from the microphone, did not appear to be a showman.

That evening, with cumbersome teams of three men versus three women, we played to a full house at the Paris Theatre. It was the collection of star names that drew them, and they loved it. It is seldom that a pilot goes out on the air, but this one did.

It soon became clear that this was an ideal way of trying out new people. With six people on the teams, anyone less than good was soon forgotten, and if they did not speak well and were boring, someone else would literally save the show and buzz. Roy always knew what to do: if he too thought the performer no good, he awarded the point to the better speaker, making plausible excuses for doing so. A few listeners noticed this and, taking the game seriously, wrote their usual rude letters.

We ran like that for two or three years, getting a good press, thanks to the strong ones like Kenneth Horne, Valerie Hobson and Yvonne Arnaud. Chairman Roy Plomley showed great wit; Gilbert Harding found plenty to complain about, especially if points were awarded against him.

I held auditions every week and made some worthwhile finds. Among them was Jack Sherry, who spoke so fast that no one could ever buzz him; I have never heard a faster speaker, with such clear diction. Then there was the day I auditioned the whole of the chorus of the then Windmill Theatre in two shifts. Since I auditioned in sixes, the time came at the end of the day when we were down to five. No one had so far come up to the show's standard. One girl, I noticed, had not come up on to the stage. I invited her up; she said no, because she wouldn't be any good and she'd only come to give her friend courage. The other girls finally persuaded her to sit in the sixth chair.

For the purpose of auditions I didn't bother Roy Plomley; I took the chair myself. The girl's name was Margot Holden.

'Miss Holden, please talk for one minute without deviation, hesitation or repetition on BOOKS.'

Margot opened her eyes very wide and in her eight-year-old's voice (although she was about twenty), she said, 'I can't really, because I've never read a whole one.'

That did it. The theatre was full of chorus girls, their boy-friends and the usual hangers-on; they laughed. She broke them up. Part of the success of the show lay in finding contrasting voices. That voice alone was enough. Added to it was the attitude of the original dumb blonde.

During the shows she did everything, from pretending she'd forgotten the rules, asking the meaning of any word of more than two syllables, offering to resign because she thought Roy was being 'horrid' to her, calling upon the audience to side with her against the other team, to walking halfway off the stage because Gilbert was rude to her. He frequently *was* genuinely rude, because he hated what he thought of as a dumb blonde.

She played it beautifully; no one ever knew that her hobbies were English History and Astronomy. She was about as dumb as Marilyn Monroe – in other words, she successfully concealed a sharp intellect.

It was during this search for outrageous characters with unusual voices that the extraordinary Gerard Hoffnung appeared.

15
Gerard Hoffnung

THIS STORY OF THE ASTONISHING GERARD HOFFNUNG starts in the waiting-room of a dentist, who had the unlikely name of Pulham. It began with my finding a magazine there. Yet another coincidence was about to take place. (My present dentist is a most competent man with the equally unlikely name of Payne, which has nothing to do with the story. Nevertheless, another coincidence; and it was September again.) The story started while I was looking at a remarkable caterpillar in carpet slippers, one for each foot – and that made quite a lot of carpet slippers; Freeman, Hardy & Willis would have aimed their advertising at caterpillars if those insects could have been persuaded to wear shoes.

All this was taking place in Mr Pulham's waiting-room. The caterpillar was not a patient, waiting for a filling or a drilling; it was a delightful double-paged colour spread in the now extinct *Lilliput* magazine. That creature had an artful, sly, knowing appearance – and yet the bedroom slippers gave it a cosy, cuddly, endearingly benevolent look. That an insect should have this aura was remarkable. The cartoon was signed 'Gerard Hoffnung', at that time an almost unknown name. It can't be said that he was totally unknown, because presumably the editor of *Lilliput*, observant man, knew him, and so, it turned out, did his housekeeper and his cat.

Dentistry in 1949 was not as advanced as it is now, and it can be assumed that spectacles were equally crude, as Mr Pulham first drilled the wrong tooth then filled it and finally drilled the right tooth. (He charged for the correct one only.)

That was the year when our son, Malcolm, was born. The great comedian and friend, Tommy Handley of ITMA, died. Anthony Asquith made a film of my distant cousin, Terence Rattigan's play, *The Winslow Boy*. The Russian blockade of Berlin was lifted. Many people heard the zither for the first time when it was used for the Harry Lime theme music in *The Third Man*.

With a sore face after the dentist's ministrations, I did not go straight to my office at the BBC but to a BBC exhibition in Piccadilly, where Pan American have their offices now. Coincidence again! Blacking in vast areas of a large mural was a man perched on top of a ladder. The painting was in black and white and was of a supposed BBC orchestra, peopled with strange characters. They all reminded me strongly of the caterpillar in bedroom slippers. This mural had the same style and was possibly by the same artist, so I asked the chap at the top of the ladder if he knew Mr Hoffnung.

'Oh yes,' he said, without turning round, 'I know him slightly.'

'I've just been admiring a picture by him, of a caterpillar in slippers. Have you seen it?'

'Yes. Not very good, is it?' he said as he slapped more black paint on to a drawing of a man in a black suit crashing a pair of cymbals together.

'I thought it was great.'

'Few people agree with me,' he sighed.

'What's he like?'

'Who?'

'What's Mr Hoffnung like?'

' 'Orrible!' He slammed more black paint on to the suit of the cymbalist in silence before saying, 'And I can't talk to you down there and get on with my work up here at the same time. Mr Hoffnung's very mean and doesn't pay me by the hour. Come on up here so I can see you.'

I told him there wasn't room on the ladder for the two of us.

'In that case I'll come down, because I want to stop for lunch and you obviously won't go away. So I must warn you.'

He came down, frowning as he contemplated what to say next. He was short with a stocky, heavy, muscular frame and a shiny pink face. He wore a white overall covering his brown Harris tweed suit. His shoes were brown and beautifully polished.

'Yes. Now I see you,' he went on breathlessly as he took of his overall, 'I must warn you. Never get involved with that two-timing, disgraceful creature Hoffnung.' He dropped his voice as if he wanted to avoid being overheard. He hunched his shoulders, did a lightning impersonation of the Hunchback of Notre Dame, complete with one bulging eye, and half put his hand over his mouth. 'You know what artists are,' he hissed, 'and you must have read books about the shenanigans on the Left Bank of the Seine.' His voice dropped further and became even more malignant. 'He's just like the worst of that disgraceful lot. Drink! Drugs! Humph! Women!' He stopped and stared at me to see how I would react, before adding, 'Even sex! He paused again, staring at me to be sure that the awfulness of the word 'sex' had had its full effect on me, before going on, 'All that sort of thing and more! Dreadful! Wouldn't be quite so bad if he had talent. He has none. And worse: he's been known to take other people's pictures and sign them as his own.' He straightened up suddenly and asked in a loud voice, 'And why are you asking so many questions about him? Are you from the police?'

I assured him I was not. His was an interesting voice, which ranged up and down the scale from squeaks to squawks to grunts.

'If you're not from the police, what *are* you from? Everybody comes from somewhere.' He looked over the top of his spectacles, raised his eyebrows and added in a sinister low voice, 'Everybody: but there's a possible exception in that man Hoffnung.' There was a long pause while his face went through various contortions of smile, frown, surprise, puzzlement, wonder, expectancy and another quick flash of the Hunchback. 'Yes,' he said slowly, 'and what are you?'

I told him I was radio producer.

'Ah!' he exclaimed. 'That's different. There's a pub down the road called The Yorkshire Grey. I am Gerard Hoffnung. How do you do, and how old do you think I am?' The last sentence was a curious *non sequitur*. From his voice, his balding head and his eccentric gesticulating, he seemed to be about sixty-five.

He gave no opportunity for a reply – which was just as well – as he added, 'I'm happy to say, I'm twenty-five.'

And he was. This was 1949; he had been born in Berlin in 1925. He was five years younger than I.

We went for a beer and a sandwich at the pub, where he told me that at Highgate School he was so backward that his mother had arranged for him to have a coach. The coaching was very boring, so he would go armed with a violin and play it just to annoy the coach, who was trying to teach him geography. If he wasn't fiddling about in order to avoid being coached, he was drawing cartoons embellished with Gothic complexity.

A great deal of this curious conversation was overheard by the others in the pub, who were becoming aware that this was no ordinary man; they put their glasses down and turned to look at him. It wasn't a conversation so much as a monologue.

Meeting the extraordinary Hoffnung at that moment was a matter of great good fortune, as it was exactly when an outstandingly different voice was needed. He was obviously right for the show, as he was a splendid and unusual extrovert. I mentioned the show. Not only had he heard *of* it, he had heard it and liked it. I gently eased the conversation around to his appearing in it; this had to be done with the greatest possible diplomacy, since in those days, as now, all bookings were done by way of the booking section or department, who understood contracts and all those complicated matters, including the impossibility of filling in forms.

'Are you aware,' he asked, 'that there is considerable fear involved, not knowing what to expect?'

I told him that, being new to the show, he would get at least a small hint concerning the first subject he would have to speak on; that should help his first-night nerves and calm his fears.

He looked hurt. 'Fears? My fears? I'm not afraid. Certainly not! I'm concerned about people. All those people who have queued up outside the theatre in all innocence being let in and suddenly, through no fault of their own, they are confronted with me. They might start fainting all over the place. It'll be very untidy of them. I'd be banned and struck off the RSPCA.

Back in the office, armed with his name, address and telephone number, I thought it wise to ring the Contracts Department. Those admirable, overworked people who, because of their responsibilities, were trained to dot every 'i' and cross every 't' were a little suspicious of me. Perhaps someone had warned them that I seldom obeyed rules, skated on thin ice, took chances, and did all those things which are anathema to the civil service minds that the BBC administrators had in those early days.

Whoever took my request to book Gerard Hoffnung must also have taken the precaution of ringing the head of my department, Mr Michael Standing.

In his office, where he always seemed to be speaking through a sheet of plate-glass, he inquired politely who Hoffnung was. I told him he was a cartoonist.

'Does that make him a good broadcaster?'

'No. But I'm sure he is.'

Mr Standing was a wizard with words. He had made his name as a broadcaster and could and did conduct the most penetrating interviews. He was much older than I; from my point of view, he was the schoolmaster while I was the pupil.

I left his office, filled with terror. Mr Michael Standing had not ordered me not to book him, but he had made it clear that Mr Hoffnung had better be good; my reputation would be at stake and, by implication, so would his. To give him his due, he could have played for safety and stopped me. The Contracts Department could easily have been telephoned, since no contract had at that moment been issued, and asked to book any one of the many top names of the day. I rang Contracts Department and asked them to confirm Hoffnung's contract.

The BBC booked him for the following week's edition of the show. Even that, rumour has it, was not straightforward. They offered him the beginner's fee of about four guineas (£4.20) or whatever it was at that time. Gerard Hoffnung thought he would enjoy himself and, being an artist and not a broadcaster, he did not expect a fee and so declined. It was not until the contracts' lady had reached sixteen guineas (£16.80) that he accepted . . . At least, that's the story he told, some years later.

His appearance on the show was the first of many. The audience loved him. The press loved him.

It was at one of these shows that he asked me to forgo the fun of talking to the audience and explaining to them what they were about to hear. This traditional introduction, called the 'warm-up', is usually done by the producer, and it takes place at all audience shows before the recording or live presentation. I asked him why, and he told me that he had an interesting cutting from the trade paper aimed at builders. Looking at the paper he was waving in front of me, but not reading it, I made the mistake of suggesting it would be highly unsuitable as a 'warm-up' for a comedy panel-game. He told me that it was about a builder explaining why he wanted sick leave, having had an accident while trying to haul a barrel-load of bricks up to the top of a building with a pulley.

A serious letter about sick leave would be entirely the wrong mood for such a moment, I declared. Gerard said it would be in the right mood for such a moment. I disagreed. Without further ado, he pushed me to one side and stood, centre stage, looking at the audience in silence and pulling faces at them, while they gazed back at him.

He said, 'Well!' The audience went on staring silently at this odd figure. To this opening remark he added, 'I – er – oh.' At that time he was not well known; perhaps they thought he was an engineer come to look at the microphone, which he tapped a couple of times to check that it was all right. He blew into it and suddenly asked, 'Why are you all behaving like this? Don't you usually applaud anyone who comes out here?'

They applauded politely and a little uncertainly. He waved the paper at them. 'This is a trade paper for builders.' He said it as if expecting more applause, but they just looked blankly back at him. He started to read the letter as he went on, the audience clearly approved.

From then on he would read this letter before every 'One Minute, Please' show. After each reading he would mark it meticulously, adding a word here, removing a word there, shortening and lengthening pauses from time to time, until it was the polished performance famed in every English-speaking country in the world as 'The Bricklayer Story'. The version most people know was recorded at the Oxford Union. It is a shame there was no video recording in those days, as to see him do it made it even funnier. His widow, Annetta, recently told me that the bricklayer story had its origins in about 1926.

Enid and I got to know Gerard very well. He came to supper on many occasions, but the first was the most memorable. At that time we were living in Worcester Park and our address was number 1 Perry How. Gerard was due at about seven. At five, the telephone rang. Enid had not met him. I was out; she answered the phone.

'This is Gerard Hoffnung here.'

'We're looking forward to seeing you this evening.'

'Yes, but I have been looking in my atlas to find a map of Europe and discovered that where I live in Thornton Way is very distant from where you live. And what is a How?'

'A what?'

'A How. You live at One, Perry How. I know what one means, I know what Perry is; but what's a Perry How?'

Enid explained to him that it wasn't a pear drink but a road. He grasped the idea but continued, 'I'm still not sure I can come unless . . . ' He stopped and made one of his curious high-pitched squeaks.

'Unless what?'

'Will it be worth while? I mean, if you're having something worth eating, I'll be there.'

We were, so he arrived bearing a huge tuba.

'I've er, brought my tuba,' he explained unnecessarily.

'Good,' said Enid, without much idea of what she was meant to say. 'It'll be all right in the hall.'

'Certainly not. It's house-trained. I take it everywhere with me.'

We had supper with the tuba on its own chair.

Gerard later turned the radio on full blast to listen to *Faust*; like a swordsman unsheathing his sword, he pulled Enid's knitting needle out of her knitting, losing all her stitches, and conducted the whole work with it. That done, and because I had fallen asleep, he gave us a tuba recital, which nearly shook the apples off the tree in the garden.

He was also a prison visitor until pressure of work just before his death forced him to give it up. His unconventional behaviour endeared him to the prisoners and, eventually, to the authorities.

A typical meeting between a group of prison visitors and those running the jail would be dominated by Gerard's demands that the prison rules he did not approve of had to be abolished or changed to suit him. One rule is that a prison visitor must not know what crime the inmate had committed. 'Why not?' asked Gerard.

'Because it's the rules.'

'Then how shall I know if the prisoner is telling me the truth?'

'You won't. You're not here to talk to the prisoners about what they have done wrong.'

'As I'm not here to tell them they've been very naughty, because they already know that, then why should I not know what they did?'

'Because it's in the rulebook.'

'Then get a new rulebook.' And so on.

He would give prisoners his home address (a practice not encouraged by the Home Office), and ask them to meals when they came out, which Annetta, his wife, would cook. They would both allow and encourage the old lags to play with their children. As far as is known, the ex-prisoners respected these invitations, for there is no record of any of them stealing from him or abusing his hospitality.

One one occasion I asked him to lunch with me at Verrey's in Regent Street. I arrived first, went downstairs and was having a drink at the bar when I realised that he was very late. This was most unlike him; he always had good if off-beat manners.

The commissionaire came quietly down the stairs to speak to me. 'There's a gentleman outside who says he knows you and that you have asked him to lunch.'

'That'd be Mr Gerard Hoffnung.'

His name was now well known and the commissionaire asked 'THE Mr Hoffnung? Mr Gerard Hoffnung? Oh dear.' He looked ill-at-ease and it seemed reasonable, knowing my guest, that there had been some sort of misunderstanding which I prayed had not caused a crowd to form in the road.

I followed the man up the stairs into the street, and there was Gerard, a little red in the face.

The commissionaire, acutely embarrassed, spoke before I could get a word in. 'Mr Hoffnung, I am sorry, I didn't know who you were. Of course you can come in.'

Gerard said, 'I most certainly will not. If you pay me I will not come into your restaurant. I will never come into your restaurant. If you bring my lunch to me right here in Regent Street to eat on the pavement I will not so much as touch it.' He looked beyond the man at me. 'Aaah! Ian, my dear boy, I understand that I am not allowed in this restaurant because I am wearing an open-neck shirt and no tie. We will find somewhere else to eat. This man,' he said, pointing to the commissionaire, 'Says that no one comes in without a tie. He obviously wants me to find a lorry-driver's pull-in, and some of them are very good. Now he finds out who I am and says I *can* come in! This is the height of snobbery.'

'He's only doing his job. I'm certain he didn't make the rule up.' (This was in the days when good restaurants demanded that male customers wore ties.) 'He's just doing as he's been instructed.'

'Well, I don't want to eat in a place that has such silly rules.'

There was nothing for it but to go. We went.

He loved the macabre; for instance, he drew an empty hearse with a notice on the back reading 'JUST BURIED'. He had no respect for the pompous, even in art: at an art school, he drew a grotesque picture of a nude from life; no one could talk him out of drawing a wasp on her behind.

It was his love of the macabre and the grotesque that led us both one evening to visit the South Bank cinema during its season of horror films, to see the 1920 classic version of *The Cabinet of Dr Caligari.*

We travelled eventfully from Golders Green station. After the train had entered the tunnel, a cat started miaowing piteously. I looked around at the other passengers but could not see a cat. Gerard also gazed around, making quite a performance of his looking. There was another '*miaow*'.

'Pardon my asking you,' he inquired, without a trace of pardon in his voice, 'but are you being exceptionally cruel to some creature such as a cat in a handbag? Madam!' He was addressing a harmless-looking woman nursing a very large bag. 'What's in your bag? Is it a cat?' She looked alarmed and opened her bag for his inspection. 'Then it's not you,' he said. 'You can close it now.'

He went up to a man in a pin-stripe suit and a Guards tie. 'Sir, have you put a cat down your trousers?' The man stood up; the train was drawing into Mornington Crescent station. He made no reply and left the train when the doors opened. 'He,' said Gerard, 'doesn't look as if he lives at Mornington Crescent. Nobody lives at Mornington Crescent.'

There was another loud, pitiful *miaow* as the doors closed. Without the background sound of the train, I knew for sure what I suspected earlier: the cat was Gerard. When he sat down he said quietly, 'I'm not sure whether that was a pussington or possibly a pussinger. What do you think?'

'A pussinger – yes. Called Gerard?'

'You could be right. I'm inclined to agree.'

There was worse, and then much worse, to come that evening. I had no idea what Gerard had in his brown, hairy, tweedy right-hand jacket pocket.

We were sitting on seats facing the direction of the train; I was next to the window, he had a gangway seat. The middle-aged man opposite him had arrived after the 'pussinger' episode so, if he noticed Gerard at all, he probably thought of him as a respectable old buffer.

Gerard leaned forward as if to speak to the man opposite. The man reacted by leaning forward to hear what Gerard was about to say. Gerard then settled back in his seat without speaking. Another station came and went. Gerard leaned forward again as if to speak to the man. Again the man reacted as most people would. Again Gerard leaned back in his seat in silence as the train pulled up at another station. As we drew out of the station, Gerard leaned forward for a third time, with the same result. This time Gerard spoke. 'Were you about to ask me something?'

'No,' said the man.

'Then don't keep leaning forward. I find it most distracting.'

Eventually we went into the National Film Theatre on the South Bank. The classic 1920 horror film started without interruption from Gerard at first, except for one outcry loud enough for the projectionist to hear: he wanted the film stopped when the subtitles came on. 'They're not on long enough to read!' he said, and he said it so loud that people turned around to see who was making the fuss.

In a whisper, mainly from embarrassment, I said, 'Never mind. Everybody knows the story.'

I wished I had kept my mouth shut. 'I shouldn't think for a minute, Ian, that everybody knows the story.' Gerard was not a man to whisper.

'Well, most of them probably do.'

'That's not the same thing at all. You can't just sit there and say they 'probably' know the story. I'll bet that most of them have no idea what it's all about. Just look at them! Do they look as if they know the story? For instance, do you know the story?'

'Yes.' The embarrassment was increasing.

'Tell it to me.'

By now the audience was making very audible shushing noises.

'Not now. I'll tell it to you afterwards.'

'Ridiculous! It'll be too late then.' He paused and I foolishly thought the episode was over. He pointed at the screen. 'He's the villain, isn't he?' I thought the question rhetorical so not in need of a reply. 'Well, is he the villain or isn't he?'

'I don't know.'

'There you are! You've no idea what it's all about.'

He was right. I hadn't the least idea of the story.

'Watch this!' said Gerard as he leaned forward and tapped the shoulder of the woman in front of him.

'Madam, d'you know the story of this film?' She kept still, faced the front and made no reply. 'You see,' he said rather loudly, 'that lady doesn't know the story. I didn't think she did.'

We were in the back row and Gerard had the gangway on his right, so I didn't notice him fiddling with something in his jacket pocket. I had no idea what was happening, even after a girl, about three rows in front of us on the other side of the gangway, screamed.

'Oh dear,' Gerard said to me, 'this is a terrifying film. Would you like some?'

'Some?'

'Yes. I've brought you your own kit,' he whispered. 'Here it is.' And out of his pocket he pulled a sponge-bag, full of wet seaweed he had got from a fishmonger. The seaweed was tied to a string, which in turn was suspended from a collapsible broken radio aerial. It turned out that he had taken this out and dangled it over the face of that poor girl, making her scream.

The usherette saw what was happening and asked us to leave. Gerard said that if we could be allowed to stay she could have all the seaweed. She let us stay.

On the way out Gerard thanked her, apologised and told her that the seaweed would be quite nice, warmed up for her supper, 'with a little pepper and tomato ketchup.'

This was in 1952, the year in which Paddington Road Safety Week organisers asked me to stage 'One Minute, Please', which was billed by them as a 'new form of quiz now on the radio every Friday'. This tied in with their slogan: 'Think for One Minute, Please. It may save your life.' First, I rang Roy Plomley: he was free that night. Next, I rang Gerard Hoffnung: he was free . . . and so on, until I had a complete team.

The whole evening was a rumbustious débâcle because, in the interests of road safety, the tickets for the show had been distributed round the local newsagents and given away; this meant that all the children in the neighbourhood got hold of them, and they were our only audience. Five-year-olds raced up and down the aisles and ten-year-olds hurled ice-cream cups, orange peel, paper darts and any loose objects they could lay their hands on. These objects were not thrown at us on the stage – although some did find their way there accidentally after the curtain rose, because it appeared that the children didn't fully realise there was anyone on the stage.

We gazed out at a seething tumult of yelling, shouting, screaming, kicking children, who had not the slightest idea of what we were about to do.

Fifteen-year-olds at the back fought with chairs and some of them made their way purposefully on to the stage, possibly because the light was better there.

Half the audience was facing the wrong way as they fought off the assault from the darkness behind them. White-coated attendants walked among the children, shouting, 'Shut up!' at the tops of their voices. I remember slipping a note to Roy Plomley to ask Hoffnung to speak for a minute without deviation, hesitation or repetition on the subject of children. Given the subject, he stood on his chair and shouted 'SHUT UP!' This seemed to work. The children were silent for a moment while they looked at the extraordinary figure on the chair. As he sat down he said, 'And I should jolly well think so.'

Whereupon the noise started all over again, and a cheeky twelve-year-old boy walked up to him and asked, 'What you supposed to be, mister?'

Hoffnung came over to me later and said, 'Look!' pointing out a small boy who was quite casually peeing against the wall.

Long before our allotted time was up, we all agreed we had had enough, the curtain was brought down and we ran from the place in abject defeat, with Hoffnung fighting a rearguard action while he muttered, 'Quite astonishing! Humph! Quite astonishing!'

At what point does any one of us ask, 'Are these our last moments, our last hours, days, months?'

Some of Gerard's last moments were spent dining with his dear Annetta at our flat, just off the Finchley Road. He was not quite his normal self, except that before dinner he asked Enid if there would be a pudding. She told him there would be a chocolate soufflé.

'And will there be soup?'

'No,' she said, 'we're starting with a prawn cocktail.'

'In that case' said Gerard, 'I will start with a bar of chocolate, then I'll have the chocolate soufflé and,' he hesitated, 'what's the main course?'

'Roast duck.'

'Roast duck? Duck? Only one? Just the one duck? And there're six of us.' He was told that there were in fact three ducks. 'Then why didn't you say so at once? Are you ashamed of them? No, no,' he protested, raising his hand to stop Enid explaining, 'I know I shall get my share now. But three ducks for six people's a bit extravagant . . . ' He caught Annetta's reproving eye and changed the subject. 'After that, I'll finish with prawn cocktail.'

And he did. His behaviour up to that moment was true to his own curious ways. He often asked for a bar of chocolate, so we kept some for just such an occasion; this was normal. It was shortly before he left that he started searching his pockets.

'Ian, you have stolen my tobacco pouch and pipe.'

'You must have left them on your chair.'

'No. You've taken them, and I can't go home without them. Hand them back.'

This was not normal; something was wrong. I saw a bulge in his jacket pocket, tapped it – and it turned out to be the missing objects. His mind was beginning to play tricks.

He and Annetta left. It had been a very happy evening. The awkward moment was forgotten temporarily.

He died the next day in hospital at about lunchtime, after collapsing at his drawing board that morning.

Meeting his doctor, we discovered that the tobacco pouch and pipe incident was typical of someone starting a brain haemorrhage.

He was thirty-four years old.

The old go to meet death, but death has to stalk the young.

16
Flying High

SHOW BUSINESS MEANT LONG HOURS as more and more programmes were undertaken; however, the hours were no problem because the work and the people were fun. The shows were never taken for granted: just as they had all appeared, so they could all disappear just as miraculously.

It was early in 1949 that Mr Standing, who was in the control room at the Paris Theatre at the same time as I was producing a musical show there, by chance discovered that I couldn't read a note of music. The conversation in his office next morning, when I again expected to be fired, went something like this.

'Ian, you never said you couldn't read music.'

'I'm sorry, but no one asked me if I could.'

'Then, given a musical show to produce, it must surely have made you realise that . . .'

'I checked up in the schedules, I have produced over two hundred musical shows, if you include those little fifteen minute "Starlight" shows.'

'Well?'

'There have been no complaints, possibly because not being able to read music has prevented me from interfering with the decisions of the conductor. And surely it is the conductor who is most in control in the studio where the subject of the show is music. The producer's job on those occasions is to smooth the way, so he can look after the orchestra with the minimum of irritation . . .'

'Ian, with respect,' said Mr Standing, 'I don't think it is your job to tell me what the producer's job is.'

I still pride myself on not saying that he hardly ever came to the studio and that I had produced far more shows than he had. 'There can be no kudos,' I persisted, 'in being able to tell the conductor that middle C on the piano is the note over the key-hole. What's more, that great composer Irving Berlin can't read a note. To change key, he has a special piano so that all the strings shift when he pulls a lever.'

Mr Standing said that that was rubbish and of course Berlin could read music. How else, he asked, could he write it? Still disbelieving me, he finally understood that just because I could not press the talk-back key to reprimand the first violin for playing an A in place of an A sharp did not mean that I could not put a musical together. Rather impertinently, I added that the great West End stage musical producer of the day, C. B. Cochran, would look strange dancing in tights with a feather fan; such a deficiency did not stop him producing great shows with girls doing just that.

Later, passing me in the corridor, he was gracious enough to stop and apologise because, as he said, he had just found out that indeed Irving Berlin could not read a note. It didn't stop him looking puzzled.

Variety Department held auditions every week, on the principle that, as the BBC was then a monopoly, we had no right to turn anyone away unheard. Producers were on a rota to attend auditions; most hated them. I was always searching; to me, they were like dipping your hand into the bran-tub at a fair: mostly a waste of time, but you never knew what might come up.

A lady, about forty-five years old, turned up to sing at one of these auditions; after asking her name, I ushered her into the studio. She said she didn't need the staff pianist, as she would accompany her own singing herself. Opening a huge suitcase, she spread out her music all over the place. It was apparent that she would take longer than the ten minutes she had been allocated as she had not even made up her mind what she would like to sing. Knowing how nervous artists can be, I coaxed her along with pleasant platitudes, at which she smiled condescendingly. Finally she was all set to play. I went back into the control-room and sat down next to the engineer, awaiting her song.

Suddenly she said, 'What's this?' She was pointing at the microphone.
'It's the microphone.'

She stood up as if insulted. 'I,' she said with great emphasis, 'am an opera singer. Mine is a trained voice. I have sung in Italy.' She did not mention La Scala, Milan, but the implication was there. 'I do not need one of these modern microphone inventions.'

I tried to explain to her that we were in a sound-proof room, separated from the studio by two sheets of glass, and that therefore the only way we would ever be able to hear her would be by the aid of the microphone.

'I,' she said, gathering up her music, 'have never sung into one of those things – and I am certainly not going to start now!'

Another ten minutes went by as we helped her get her music back into the suitcase.

At another audition, a comedian of some promise (I'll call him Mr X) who had done a few shows on stage, some of them with me in the past, and whose name was known to several producers gave a passable performance and was about to be offered a spot in a radio variety show when he called me into a corner and said 'Look, Ian, you put me in a show and into your "One Minute, Please" and I can fix it for your wife to have as many nylon stockings as she wants – ' nylon stockings were like gold-dust then ' – and I'll get you a couple of new tailored suits.'

This was a stupid man. I said, 'That's wonderful. I'll send a memo to the head of the department, copied to all producers, telling them of your wonderful terms.'

His face fell. 'You don't understand,' he said. I told him I did understand. 'Then you must be joking.' I told him that it was a very sad joke.

Next day, the memo went out with a copy to Mr X 'for information and to file'. To my knowledge, he never broadcast; no one dared book him, for fear that others would think money or other favours had changed hands.

Thinking in terms of new voices for 'One Minute, Please', I asked the then Head of Drama Department if I might attend his auditions. He most kindly sent me the dates of the next six auditions.

Boys and girls came and went with what I, with youthful lack of respect, in those days called Sixth Form Drama Voices, trained in some first-or second-rate drama schools, each having been their school's equivalent of the 'Student of the Year'.

When the numbers of drama schools are added up, and it is remembered that each one has a 'Student of the Year', it seems cruel to raise youngsters' hopes of stardom in this way. Each one was also considered by its mother – those dreadful pushy mothers – to be everything the theatre has waited decades for. Poor young things, they were mostly rubbish as performers.

I learned quickly that you do not have to 'know someone' in order to be a theatrical success, nor is a RADA training a passport to fame. Talent is so rare that, when it does appear, it radiates like a blinding light: it shows in the way the entrance is made and in the artist's command of the audience. Both of these, sometimes even before the voice, can tell the onlooker that here is a star.

The bimbo who gets the part because she slept with the producer will fail. The producer will remember, make a note in his book and look for the next bedworthy actress. The bimbo who sleeps with the producer and who also has talent should have more self-respect and confidence than to demean herself in that way; such behaviour is prostitution, no less and no more.

It was in one of these drama auditions that two Canadians, Bernard Braden and his wife, Barbara Kelly, appeared, reading bits from Shakespeare, Shaw, Wilde and Rattigan. When Bernie finished, Barbara started to tell him savagely what he'd done wrong. She then read some *Saint Joan* and a couple of other things while Bernie kept interrupting her in order to put her right.

As there was no studio audience to laugh, my straight-faced drama colleagues up in the control box with me took it all seriously, while I creased myself, watching each of them put the couple down as useless. One of them asked 'Why are you laughing, Ian? I see nothing funny in these two young people spending all that money, coming all this way from Canada, just for this.'

'But they are funny. They are comedians.'

The straight drama producers all looked at me and shook their heads sadly as I slid through the door and almost ran back to the Aeolian Hall in Bond Street. By now Mr Standing was trusting me, as I had had several successes. He, bless him, trusted me again this time. Yes, I could have an allocation for a pilot.

The show was called 'Leave Your Name and Number', and the theme was that of Bernie and Barbara continuously going to auditions and being turned down.

The excellent script was written by Eric Nichol, who was, I think, a Canadian professor of English. He was a fine writer, with the art of verbal economy which in turn made his gags funnier. His attitude to the show was unusual: he would deliver the script each week, saying that, whatever we might think of it, *he* would not rewrite anything; but *we* could change whatever we liked, as he was going home to write the next week's show. He was so professional that few alterations were needed.

I was carpeted in the middle of the series for allowing a doubtful gag through. Mr Standing sent for me in the middle of the series because, within the plot, Bernie and Barbara had to go to see a farmer, played by Norman Shelley.

'Can we see the piglets?' Barbara asked.

'Not just yet,' replied the 'farmer', 'because it's their teat time.'

That, according to Mr Standing was '. . . vulgar, tasteless and not what is expected from the BBC. Any more jokes like that, and you will be taken off the show. You will write a letter to Mr Nichol, telling him to clean his ideas up.'

I telephoned Eric, told him to swill his mouth out with salt water and wash his typewriter in sulphuric acid, and we had a good laugh.

We all knew Peter Waring was odd, living in a world of his own imaginings where there was no morality, no conscience, no concern for others. There were odd exceptions to this; for instance, he had found us that flat and asked nothing in return. He had given money one or twice to charities and he had willingly given his services as a performer to causes he genuinely believed in. No one is wholly good or wholly bad.

So it came as a shock to read in all the national papers that Peter John Roderick-Mainwaring, otherwise known as Peter Waring, star of radio and stage, had been bailed to appear at Lambeth Magistrates' court on a charge of non-payment of a maintenance order made in favour of his wife, Leita. Until then it hadn't been generally known that Peter was married.

And worse was to come. The clerk of the court revealed that Peter was already on bail to appear at another court the following week on serious criminal charges.

The goodwill generated by Peter's hard work in good causes was swiftly becoming worthless.

All this was going on at a time when I met two very clever young people, Sidney Piddington and Lesley Pope, his wife. They called their act 'The Piddingtons', and it seemed that they could read each other's minds. Certainly they didn't use any corny old-fashioned word-code, such as 'What is this?', in which the word 'what' stood for 'watch' and so on.

This was the only programme ever to make the front page of nearly every national newspaper almost every week. Never once did the Piddingtons claim they could read minds – other people claimed that for them. They were scrupulously careful to finish each show with words such as: 'Telepathy or not telepathy? You are the judge.' This, as well as their turning down suggestions from scientists that they be subjected to controlled experiments, must tell you that the act was not what it appeared.

We called these thought-reading tests 'experiments'; and for one experiment I wanted to have a submarine under the English Channel with Lesley in it, while Sidney was in the studio. The Royal Navy couldn't cope with a submarine, but the admiral I spoke to suggested that perhaps a firm specialising in diving equipment might come up with an answer. The firm Siebe Gorman, based in Surbiton, were happy to suggest that we used a diving bell.

To have some idea of what that entailed, imagine an up-turned empty tumbler being pushed into a bowl of water. The air keeps the water low in the glass; the further down the glass is pushed, the further the water comes up on the inside and the higher the pressure grows. A diving bell is just that, only with a grid to stand on that lets the water in.

A set of tubes at the top pumps fresh air in to raise the pressure and keep the water out, and to help the inhabitants breathe. As the bell sinks deeper, so the water rises; for that reason a waterproof rubber suit, which came up to but not beyond the armpits, was worn.

Lesley, Sidney and I thought we'd better have a good look at it all before committing ourselves to the show, as a thought-reading broadcast must be live, since recordings can allow for all sorts of juggling. Once committed, there could be no turning back.

The chairman of the diving-equipment manufacturers introduced us to the head diver, Stanley Mearns, and I impulsively volunteered to test it all for Lesley.

Stanley Mearns showed me how to get into the rubber suit, telling me that the pressure down there would be great enough to hurt if I had any coins or other hard objects in my pockets. I took off my jacket, took the comb out of my back pocket and coins from my trouser pockets.

We sank slowly down to what seemed a great depth, with Stanley in his rubber combinations working the controls, able by air pressure alone to control the speed of descent and eventually ascent. Twenty feet down the pressure was tangible, and I felt a pain in my left thigh but thought nothing of it. All the way down Lesley on the intercom was asking what it was like. 'Terrific,' I said, my voice ringing with confidence so that I shouldn't put her off. 'Wouldn't have missed it for anything.'

After spending five minutes on the bottom of the tank chatting to Lesley and Sidney, we came back up very slowly and Stanley Mearns explained 'the bends' to me. While Lesley was putting on her rubber trousers for her practice dive, I took mine off in a small room to the side and managed to look at the place that had hurt: there at the top of my left thigh was a clear impression of my latch key. The impression took two days to disappear.

Lesley too enjoyed her trial; on the way back to London, she told me that she suffered slightly from claustrophobia but that it wasn't bad enough to stop the broadcast.

In the studio at Sidney's end of the business, in addition to the press, we always had two or three famous guests who were beyond reproach and who would never knowingly take part in any kind of trickery. We called them the judges, and they were all the calibre of Kingsley Martin, then editor of the *New Statesman*.

As an ex-magician, albeit a bad one, I have no intention even now of giving away what was a damned fine act, carefully planned and painstakingly executed; but the fun at Sidney's end on that night made me nearly ill with fear.

Kingsley Martin was given a pack of cards and asked to shuffle them before spreading them out, face down, on a table. He was then asked to pick one and show it silently to Sidney, who looked at it without speaking.

From twenty or so feet under the water in Surbiton came Lesley's voice as she announced the card: 'It is the seven of diamonds.' It was.

That pack was not all it seemed. What a scoop for a paper to expose the Piddingtons! There had been many attempts to do this and none had succeeded. Kingsley Martin sensed that the trick had something to do with the pack and, before I could clear them away, in a split second he scooped them up and put them in his jacket pocket, where they remained for the last twenty minutes of the show. Because he was too busy 'helping' for the rest of the time, Kingsley never had a chance to look at them – and I made sure he was kept occupied.

At the end of the show a man jumped up from the front row of the audience. 'I'm from the *Mirror*' he said. 'May I look at those cards?'

Kingsley Martin said, 'Yes,' holding on to them tightly, 'but if they are some sort of fake, let us print the story first.'

'Of course,' said the man from the *Mirror*.' 'Let's look at them together.' At that, he grabbed the pack and ran through the back exit and out of the theatre.

He was not from the *Mirror*. He is very much alive today, which is why I am not putting his name in print. He is highly respected in another walk of life altogether. He was and still is, as far as I know, a friend of the Piddingtons.

Late that night Lesley, Sidney and I met to hear her end of the story. She had spent only five minutes under water during the original test; but for the broadcast, which was from 7.30 pm to 8 pm, she had had to stay submerged from 7.15 until well after 8 because of coming up slowly. She was a wonderful actress, so her voice never gave away the strain her claustrophobia had put her under.

On another occasion when we had a near miss it was even more frightening. Lesley was always scared of performing and was inclined to throw up from fright, about ten minutes before a show. On this occasion she had good reason to be very frightened. We had a gimmick – never mind what is was, but it would allow her to be locked in another very small studio and name, without hearing a word from Sidney or the studio, the objects the studio audience were giving him.

Unfortunately, the gimmick failed us during the afternoon rehearsal. The room Lesley had to be locked in would be examined in her absence, before the show by the press. To catch the Piddingtons was now the fox-hunt of Fleet Street.

We three sat in a tight triangle – we had to: all fakery was a secret from the BBC, the announcer, the commentator, the programme engineers and the other staff. I was wondering if the broadcast would have to be scrapped due to Lesley's sudden 'illness', which made her suggest that Sidney should fall off the stage and break a leg. Then certainly we wouldn't be able to broadcast.

Sidney had an idea. 'This,' he said, 'is a live broadcast. So if it is live, every radio in the country will be able to receive it.'

'Yes,' said Lesley rather glumly.

'That's the whole point,' added Sidney. 'Here we are, bewailing the failure of our gizmo, when all we need is a radio set.'

In those days radios were much bigger than they are now; concealing one, easily done today, was next to impossible then. We went into the little studio where, in great fear of being caught, Sidney and I pulled up the carpet – only to find that the floor was of concrete; there were no floorboards, as we had hoped.

It was Lesley who thought of putting a screw hook under the table and hanging the radio from it, dead centre. This meant that, to avoid what is known as a howl-back, when the sound from the speaker gets back to the microphone and so goes round and round, Lesley had to ensure that she never had the radio on when her microphone was live. This was going to mean a certain amount of ducking and dodging about for her.

It was half-past five and the shops were shutting. We had no radio and no good strong hook. Sidney and Lesley were too well-known to be seen buying a radio, and anyway autograph-hunters would waylay them.

Thank God for Enid. Because of the children, she didn't come to broadcasts, but she was with us then, and she shot out to get both the radio and a hook. (We still have that hook, after all these years.) Meanwhile I bought three packs of cards to put on the table, together with a pepper mill, a ferret's cage and one of those Chinese boxes that are difficult to open. These odd items were to sidetrack the press into examining them, since none of them was even remotely connected to the show.

Returning, Enid screwed the hook under the table and hung the radio from it.

Lesley went outside and threw up.

The audience arrived. The commissionaire informed me that my six Fleet Street guests, from the six national newspapers, were at the reception desk. I gave them a drink and took as long as possible over it, so there would be little time left to examine the studio, where I took them as close to 'On Air' time as possible. I sat on the table, quaking with fright. The rubbish I had bought worked; it was there to distract them, and that's what it did. They opened and shuffled all the cards; they tried and succeeded in opening the little magic box; they examined the cage with care; they even unscrewed the pepper mill.

Panic. Some peppercorns fell out and rolled on the floor. One of the journalists stooped down and picked up a few. Luckily, he had his back to the table, so all was well. He didn't look under it. I told him not to bother with the other peppercorns as the studio would be vacuumed out later.

(My expense sheet was queried later by Mr Standing for the cost of these odd items. I could not give him a satisfactory explanation, and I had no intention of giving my friends away. So I told him that he must take my word for it that they were bought in the interests of the BBC. By now he had learnt to trust me, but I noticed a funny look on his face as I left his office.)

Eventually the members of the press took up their places outside the cubicle studio door to make sure that no one except Lesley got in or out.

There was one further drama that night. The narrator was a first-class man when sober; it was his job to introduce the pair, and earlier in the day I had had a word with him about drinking. He solemnly swore he would not drink until the show was over. During the crisis of buying the radio and the distraction gimmicks he vanished. I had too much to worry about without thinking of him.

At 7.25 I went on stage to talk to the audience and in order to build up the usual suspense feeling, told them not to expect every 'experiment' to work. (Radios were not as reliable then as now, so this was the truth.) Wondering where on earth the commentator was, I introduced him at 7.29. It was a relief to see him make his entry. He bowed to the audience and they applauded splendidly. As he straightened up from his bow he seemed a little unsteady – but perhaps it was only my imagination.

The red light came on. 'Ladies and gentlemen,' announced the commentator, 'this is the Home Service. We present – The Pissingtons.'

I didn't have to have the ability to read minds or look into the future to foresee trouble over the name 'Pissingtons'. As producer, I was responsible for letting another drunk reach the microphone. I could see the sack coming.

But at least we were on the air, and fortunately there were no other disasters that night. I was expecting to be carpeted, possibly fired, and was therefore not at all surprised to receive a call next day, not this time, from the Director General but from the secretary of the Chairman of the BBC, Lord Simon of Wythenshaw. Could I spare the time to see his lordship at once?

I thought this was going a bit far. Surely Lord Simon could delegate my exit from the BBC to the Head of our Department? There wasn't even time to clear my desk, nor was I wearing a decent suit as I raced up to Broadcasting House and told the receptionist that Lord Simon was expecting me. I was very tired from the show, the night before, and my chest was hurting again.

For Lord Simon I had an escort. One of the commissionaires, an ex-sergeant major, accompanied me from the reception desk to the lift and thence to an office. Did the BBC really shoot people? He knocked on the secretary's door for me.

I whispered, 'Thank you.'

A girl's voice said, 'Come in.'

The commissionaire opened the door for me and announced, 'Mr Messiter.' Before making his exit.

The secretary knocked on the Chairman's door.

'Come in.'

She opened the door for me and announced, 'Mr Messiter,' and ushered me in.

Lord Simon stood up, came over and shook my hand. 'Glass of sherry, Messiter?'

'Oh, thank you.'

He opened a little cupboard and produced a ship's decanter and two glasses. 'Please sit down.' I sat. 'Cigarette?' I smoked then, so I took one from the huge silver box on the desk. He leaned over and lit it for me. I was old enough to know that excessive politeness is often the prelude to a punch in the mouth. I felt wretched.

Pouring himself a glass of sherry, he asked, 'Now tell me: the Piddingtons. How's it done?'

So that was it. What a relief!

'I've worked with them for some time now, and – I'm sorry – I really don't know.'

'No idea?'

'None. I'm too close. I can't see the wood for the trees.' I know he knew that I was protecting my friends, and the rest of the conversation was about the broader aspects of broadcasting. He realised he mustn't press me, and we parted on very good terms.

One week, we thought it would be a great idea to put Lesley in a balloon – until we discovered that they are virtually uncontrollable and are so dependent on the wind that any sort of planning was out of the question. The engineer and broadcast equipment in those days would anyway have been too heavy.

Next I tried to hire a helicopter. It was expensive but worth it. Every programme had to have a budget, or the whole of broadcasting would be out of control. The BBC is respected for never being in the red at the end of the year, and that is something still owed to Lord Reith's original administrative guidelines. No, there would not be enough money for the helicopter.

I telephoned British Overseas Airways Corporation (which later became British Airways). Making a name may not please your friends as much as it infuriates your enemies, but it has its uses. There was no question of writing to BOAC. I telephoned the Chairman who, having heard of me, later discussed the whole thing with me over a very good lunch.

The glamour plane of the day was the Stratocruiser. It would be wonderful to get hold of one: for instance, all those seats could be filled with the ladies and gentlemen of the press.

'BOAC,' he explained, 'is government controlled. I can't just lend you an aeroplane, or there'll be questions asked in the house.'

I suggested that such a stunt might have good advertising value.

He smiled and told me not to worry, as he had thought of a way round it. Back in his office after lunch, he called up the man in charge of training pilots. That was it. He checked there was nothing in the rulebook to prevent passengers being carried during training, as long as they were not paying passengers. It was going from good to better.

We could have a Stratocruiser, and it would be flown out over the Atlantic while keeping in touch with the BBC. There would be room for a BBC engineer and his equipment.

There would also be room for a commentator. I chose a very well-known man, who said the Piddingtons were just Kiddingtons and all rubbish. He was a man who loathed anything of that nature. He had already told me they were a couple of fakes, and anyone but a half-wit would see how it was done, provided he was standing next to either of them. This almost violent conversation about how dreadful the Piddingtons were had taken place in a pub. The speaker: Gilbert Harding.

I asked him if he would agree to go on the plane with Lesley Piddington and be the commentator. I was playing with fire again: With the hospitality of the airline, Gilbert might get drunk again and muck up the whole thing.

'Can I say what I like?' he asked with his normal arrogance, wiping away what could only have been surplus gin from his watery, red-rimmed, bloodshot eyes.

'Nobody's ever stopped you yet.'

'I'd better warn you that, when I see through it, I shall have no hesitation in broadcasting the truth.'

'Then I'll ring Talks Booking Department and see you get a contract.'

'Ian . . . ?' He leaned backwards, as he frequently did when about to be difficult and pompous at the same time.

'Yes, Gilbert?'

'I just want you to be sure you know what you're letting yourself and your faking friends in for.'

'I do.' I reckoned that, even if he did rumble them, which was unlikely, it would still be first-class show business. It would make headlines, whichever way it went.

That was that. Next on the list was to ring round Fleet Street and fill the remaining fifty-five seats on the Stratocruiser with journalists from the top papers and magazines. By the standards of the day, it was a huge aeroplane. The plane was to fly from Filton, near Bristol. When all the seats were filled, Lesley was searched by two stewardesses to make sure she was carrying no form of receiver. It would not have mattered if she had been, because the metal shell of the Stratocruiser would have stopped all radio waves except those through the pilot's receiver.

When the day of the live broadcast arrived, we had already had more advance publicity than any show of the age. This was splendid; we could not have asked for more. But it did make us very nervous: we were going to be watched by the press as we had never been watched before; we were going to be heard by almost everyone with a radio. The show would hit the highest listening figure ever dreamed of in the UK.

I was in the London studio with Sidney. We were very tense. We knew the appalling risks we were all taking. We both knew Gilbert would do everything in his power to expose the show, both because of his inborn sense of theatre and for his own ego. If he succeeded, it would make him even more impossible – and even more of a national anti-hero.

We were to go on the air, live, at seven-thirty as usual. With ten minutes to go before the red light was due to come on, I received a message to say that the weather was unfavourable and that the pilot refused to take off. The decision to take off must and always will be that of the pilot alone. This one didn't want to go: weather reports showed too much turbulence.

Enid will vouch that I can be grumpy sometimes, and I can even be cross – but I never raise my voice or throw things about. This occasion was and still is the only exception. I picked up a studio chair and hurled it across the floor, smashing it to pieces against the wall.

I took a phone-call from Filton. 'Wouldn't it come to the same thing if they did the show with the plane on the ground?'

'No, it wouldn't. The show must be cancelled.'

Meanwhile Gilbert Harding and the reporters in the plane on the ground at Filton raised such a hell of a protest that, astonishingly, the pilot changed his mind. They were in the air a few minutes before the steady red light showed in the studio.

Conditions in the air were terrible: wind and cloud were wretched, making the flight bumpy and alarming, and seat-belts were essential, as it was like a roller-coaster ride. Many people were ill and most were very frightened. Lesley threw up twice, once on the ground from nerves and the second time from airsickness.

This was to be the most remarkable in a series of remarkable broadcasts.

We had a studio audience of a hundred and fifty people, each with a clearly numbered envelope and a piece of blank paper. They were asked to write down anything they liked on the piece of paper or, if they preferred, to seal something small in the envelope.

One of the four judges (all of whom were well known to the audience and therefore, above suspicion) was asked to call out two numbers between 1 and 150. The pilot from the plane then said he would deliberately cut off the plane's communication with our show until the control tower told him we were again ready for him.

The numbers chosen were 33 and 88. After the numbers had been called out, the pilot was asked if he had received anything from the studio. He had not.

Gladys Young, the star of many radio plays, asked the owners of those numbers to come up on to the stage. She kept one envelope for herself and she handed the other to Hugh Williams, the film star. She opened hers and, without speaking, passed the contents to Sidney who, again without speaking, looked at it.

From the plane came Lesley's uncertain voice. She said, 'Hail to thee, blithe spirit, bird thou never wert.' Sidney gave the paper back to Gladys Young, who confirmed that those were the very words written on the paper.

In Hugh Williams's envelope was a partly-filled-in crossword puzzle from the *News Chronicle*, a popular paper of the day. Not only did Lesley give the words already filled in but corrected some wrong words.

It was a sensational broadcast. Again, I give nothing away by saying that Enid, sitting at home listening, nearly panicked. The night before, we had been to Fleet Street, where you could usually buy tomorrow's paper from about 11 pm onwards. There I bought a copy of the *News Chronicle*. We worked on a few clues of the crossword. Immediately after the broadcast, a *News Chronicle* reporter telephoned Enid and, not naming the paper he was from, except to say that he was a reporter, mentioned the crossword. 'You mean,' said Enid in an unguarded moment, 'the one from the *News Chronicle*.' She could have bitten her tongue off, but she recovered immediately before the man suspected something was wrong.

'As nobody in the broadcast mentioned the *News Chronicle*, how did you know which paper it was?' he asked.

'Because we take that paper every day and I always do the crossword.' (Except for that one, she's never done a crossword in her life.)

He asked the name of our newsagent, which he was given. We later checked to find that he had in fact telephoned the newsagent's.

That was too close for comfort. The truth was that we *did* take the *News Chronicle*. The lie was that Enid actually can't stand crosswords. That's possibly the reason why so little of it was filled in right.

After their giant success on the air, the Piddingtons were offered huge sums to appear at the London Palladium and other top theatres round the country. We got on well, partly because we shared a common secret and partly because we were the same ages. Enid and I would often meet them when they were back in town. Because of his stutter I couldn't ask Sidney to appear on 'One Minute, Please', but I asked Lesley.

She did well, so well that people wrote to the BBC to say that it wasn't fair having her on the show as she could read the mind of Roy Plomley (then the chairman) and so always knew her subject in advance and would also know precisely when she might be interrupted.

All the professional magicians knew the couple were skilled per-formers, and there was a natural fear that it might come out that Sidney had been a conjurer in the past and that his wife was a trained actress. Had that got out, the game might have been up. So it was surprising to read many po-faced letters to various papers from people who believed in telepathy, making idiotic suggestions such as getting the pair to sit outside the Kremlin during the Berlin airlift in order to read Stalin's mind.

'What a waste,' wrote a Colonel Grey of Wimbledon, 'that two such brilliant minds should be trifling with the rubbishy people of show business. What valuable assistance these two could give to the board of a reputable company, or to . . . ' and so on.

That was one of the few letters I replied to. I said that the Colonel should be ashamed of himself for suggesting industrial espionage. I came to regret sending that letter for, while he did not have our telephone number at Worcester Park, the Colonel could and did keep ringing me at the BBC; my formidable secretary, Maggie Stratton, kindly but politely kept him at bay as often as possible, but not often enough. I also learned never to reply to fan letters on headed writing paper. If you do, the fan has your address, and the correspondence becomes tediously timeconsuming.

When we had realised there was something wrong with Peter Waring I am ashamed to admit we no longer asked him around and we refused his invitations. In retrospect, this was wrong: a friend should remain a friend, whatever he had done wrong. He was still very much the big star and was still regularly mobbed, so it came as a shock to read that he had been remanded in custody on fraud charges involving thousands of pounds. This was incomprehensible. He never earned less than £200 a week – a small sum today, but worth at least ten times that amount in 1949.

He was just thirty years old when he appeared at Marylebone accused of obtaining money under false pretences and obtaining credit without disclosing that he was an undischarged bankrupt.

A Doctor Woodard of Harley Street said that Peter had helped organise a concert for and at the Middlesex Hospital; shortly afterwards he had asked if he could borrow two sums of money, for both of which he gave cheques. The cheques bounced. Peter had told Doctor Woodard that the BBC owed him thousands of pounds. That was a stupid remark as, in those days the BBC didn't pay thousands. He then wrote more cheques in favour of the landlord of his flat; they, too, bounced. All this took place within four days of the trouble over the maintenance for his wife and two children.

It all came out. He could not help spending money; he even gave it away. But, knowing him as I did, I am certain that generosity was not his motive. It was vanity.

If the papers were accurate about his being engaged to ten girls at the same time, that must have been very costly. Add that to the high rent of his flat, and he must have had a problem getting by, even on his earnings. It was already known that he gave lavish parties at expensive restaurants sending, hire cars for his guests, and occasionally hiring aeroplanes if they had to come from a long way away. The papers also added that he borrowed large sums from each of his fiancées. None of it made sense.

He had recently become engaged to a pretty girl; this time, however, he did intend to marry her – don't ask me how, because he had not been divorced by his first wife. The new finacée's father had rumbled his future son-in-law, first by discovering that he had not divorced his first wife, next by being landed with a dud cheque. He talked his daughter, Sheila, out of the marriage.

Peter claimed that this was done out of pure snobbery, because his future father-in-law had discovered that Peter's father had been a bus driver, not the Chief of the Dorset Police with a knighthood. This was typical of Peter; he could never face facts.

I dug a little deeper into his past. When he left school at fourteen, he had joined the Royal Sussex Regiment, to be later discharged because a packing case damaged his wrist. When he had shown his damaged wrist to Enid and me, he had said it was the result of being torpedoed.

He went to live with his parents in Catford; however, he thought the extra burden of himself on his father's wages was unfair, so he walked to Southampton and stowed away on the *Ile de France*, hoping to reach Canada; but he was arrested at Cherbourg and sent home, to serve twenty-eight days for stowing away.

He thought he'd try films so, rather than do it the conventional way (if there is one), he broke into the house of film and stage star, Sonnie Hale, the husband of Jessie Matthews. He didn't go there to steal, because he brazenly knocked on the study door and there found Sonnie's secretary, who gave him a pound and suggested he tried Shepherd's Bush Studios.

Again he showed an unhinged mind by breaking into the studios – not to steal but just to sleep. Sleeping was how the night watchman found him, and again he was arrested. He appeared before the magistrate next morning and was discharged.

In 1935, when he was sixteen, he had been sentenced to Borstal for stealing a cigarette case. Again his unhinged mind showed clearly, because he stole it from Lord Sysonsby, who had employed him as a footman. He never opened the case but the jeweller to whom he tried to sell it looked inside and saw the engraved words: 'To Lord Sysonsby from King George V'. The jeweller rang the police and Peter was given three years in Borstal.

When he was twenty, he was given six months for false pretences. It was in jail, in front of what can truly be called a captive audience, that he discovered his talent for magic and comedy. He came out of jail to a job in the BBC's accounts department. Knowing the trouble the BBC take vetting applicants for any job, even the tea ladies, this was surprising, and it was doubly surprising when it is remembered that it was in the accounts department where money was about.

Now, on 9 July 1949, he faced a string of charges for various kinds of fraud. Before he was sentenced he stood in the dock, tears streaming down his face, as he said he had worked hard to get where he was and that it was unfair to kick him, now that he was on his knees. Never, he said, would he he able to rise out of the gutter again. In this he was telling the truth, perhaps for the first time. What he could not see was how he had affected other people, how he had robbed and conned innocent men and girls. Enid and I were lucky to have lost only a bedroom lamp and the singer to have lost only her willow-pattern carving dish.

Peter was sentenced that afternoon to nine months, and was driven away to Pentonville Jail. That evening, to try to cheer him we sent him a telegram which was simply his own comedy catch-phrase, 'Press on regardless.'

Enid and I never knew whether he got it because, at 5.45 am on Saturday 10 July he found some mailbag rope in his cell and hanged himself from the bars of his window.

In July 1952, shows were crowding in on me, and there seemed to be no let-up. As we now had two children, with one at a nursery school, I started to realise that my love of broadcasting was a little selfish because it didn't pay – and seemingly never would, unless I did something about it.

Nobody likes talking about money; least of all do we like asking for more. My upbringing prevented me from even considering a state education for our children; my snobbery was deeply and shamefully ingrained. Nevertheless something had to be done, so I went to see Mr Standing.

'Please sir, I want more money,' was the gist of the conversation. I was earning it: I had invented a new games, written fresh plays, and had not been paid extra for them and had received good press reviews all round.

I discussed it with the brilliant writer/producer in the same department, Charles Chilton, because he was one of the few who really created shows from nothing. His attitude was idealistic. 'What do you want to go bothering with money for? It's the job that's fun. It it's money you want, why not drive a lorry? There's lots of jobs like that with more money, but the people who take them must be very boring. You'd go crackers. Try sitting next to your bank manager for a morning and find out what he does, and you'll see then how lucky you are.'

Just the same, there I was on the first floor of the Aeolian Hall, sitting opposite Mr Standing whom I respected but, for reasons I've never understood, was in awe of.

'I'm not Father Christmas,' said Mr Standing, 'I can't conjure money out of the air.' And as we talked I noticed his shirt-sleeves: the cuffs were frayed. It wasn't snobbery this time that brought me down to earth. Here was the Head of the Department, and he was hard up. There was no future for me in that building any more. I didn't even want to be Head of Variety because it would stop me inventing and writing. Administration is too skilled an occupation for someone like me. Mr Standing was excellent at his job.

There was therefore no reason for me to poison his coffee. Even if I had, the BBC in those days ran on civil service lines, so that, unless the next in command had been taking bribes and openly sleeping with actresses or actors, and provided he had never bounced a cheque, he would automatically take the top seat. I had no way of guessing that Independent TV was round the corner and that it would affect BBC salaries. Later, Independent Radio would affect them even more.

All this was forgotten for a while, because my mother and sister had both rung me on several occasions to say that Father was dying. On each occasion I had to tell the Head of the Department and get leave to go home. He always gave it to me. I always went. Father didn't die then.
It is one of life's continuous tragedies that sometimes false alarms are real.

There was yet another call from my sister to say again that Father was dying. It was the day of a big show, I forget now which it was; but I said I'd come up the next day.

Next morning, the telephone rang again. Father had died. I felt, and still feel, terribly guilty that I was not there and had put a show before filial duty.

Shortly after this I was asked to do a revival of the Piddington broadcast – not in the sense of reviving them, they didn't need it. They were still top of the bill everywhere they went, and they had returned from a very successful tour of South Africa.

We did a show from the Paris Theatre; after it was over, Sidney introduced me to an American friend of his who had been sitting in the audience. He lived in South Africa and was the big radio star out there. His real name was Ralph Boffard but his radio name was Bob Ford. In Johannesburg he had presented the Piddingtons.

He was a blunt and persuasive speaker. He said, 'Ian . . . '
'Yes, Mr Boffard.'
'What's this MISTER Boffard crap?' he asked, laughing as he added, 'Call me Bob. MISTER Boffard's for my timber business. I'm going to open a radio studio of my own in Johannesburg and I need you to run it. I like your style. Think about it tonight. Lunch with me tomorrow,' and so on.

Sidney called me later that evening and told me that Ralph Boffard was a timber millionaire and at the same time a competent broadcaster.

He was not in fact a timber millionaire . . . but he was a most competent broadcaster. He was an American and had been in the US navy, when his ship lay at anchor off Durban, South Africa; that was when and how he had come to marry the pretty daughter of a timber millionaire. They lived in Lower Houghton, the upper-crust part of Johannesburg – if any white person, living well and in comfort on the disastrous fascist regime of South Africa, can be considered upper crust. Scum floats to the top too. I knew nothing of South African politics then. I do now, and if it is true that all parties eventually die of swallowing their own lies, South Africa is showing remarkable vigour in its death-throes.

In my mind's eye I could see Mr Standing's frayed cuffs. I met Boffard next day for lunch and liked the money he had offered. He said I could do all the programmes I liked and invent all the games I wanted to, I could have free artistic licence to do what I liked.

I already had this enviable licence within the walls of the BBC, but I forgot this under the pressure of Boffard's persuasive salesmanship. There was more money to do it with, as his studio would supply Springbok, the commercial side of the South African Broadcasting Corporation, the government broadcasting system.

I didn't get the full implication of the expression '*government* broadcasting system'. I'm not sure that I even heard it at lunch – and if I had, I wouldn't have really understood its significance. It is necessary to experience it to understand what it means.

17

Natives are not allowed to learn new skills

BECAUSE I WAS BEING PAID MONTHLY, it was necessary to give the BBC a month's notice; but I gave them more, because it seemed proper. Mr Standing was surprised and puzzled, even after I had pointed out that, if I could be creative inside the BBC with no addition to my salary, it seemed reasonable to suppose that, unless the well of inspiration suddenly dried up, I could be equally creative outside the BBC and get paid for it.

As tactfully as possible I mentioned that Producer X, who created his own shows, cast them, improved the script and so on, was being paid the same as Producer Y, whose secretary held the stopwatch and told him when the show in rehearsal had either over or under-run, so that the writers and cast could adjust it to length.

It wasn't so much the logic of the argument which upset him as the vulgarity of making it a money issue that surprised him.

The ghost of Mrs Johns flitted about, saying, 'A gentleman never mentions, let alone discusses, money.' And she, like my mother, would have recognised Mr Standing as a gentleman, even though he was in show business.

It was early summer. By coincidence, my resignation took effect on 1 September – September again. It was a sad occasion, made doubly so when I discovered that the staff of the BBC at the Aeolian Hall – producers, secretaries, commissionaires, lift girl, musicians, artists, and performers had had a whip-round and bought me a wonderful set of luggage. Comedian Eric Barker said they'd bought luggage to make sure that I went.

In those days, flying was for the very rich; people did not jump on and off planes as we do today, so my flight to Johannesburg was very special. It was on the first commercial jet airliner in the world, the Comet, which had been in operation for five months only. Cooped up for eighteen hours in one small plane, I quickly got to know the cabin staff – so it came as a great shock to read that, a couple of flights later, the same plane exploded, because of metal fatigue, over the Mediterranean.

The press welcome at Johannesburg was overwhelming and almost everything I said was printed but misquoted; fortunately, there was nothing damaging. The carelessness of newspapers was something I had already experienced in England, but South African papers were far worse.

'Ian Messiter,' read one, 'top Hollywood film producer is about to take over South Africa's Springbok radio station.'

I telephoned the paper to say that I have never been to Hollywood, had never produced a film, and was in South Africa only as an ideas man, hoping to produce a few programmes to contribute to Springbok Radio. Then I wrote a letter repeating the corrected detail. The correction was never printed. Springbok Radio, the government commercial service, did not telephone me or take any action at all. When I met the head of the service later, he said he'd seen the story but he never took any notice of what the papers printed.

Bob Ford, radio star (alias Ralph Boffard), was at the airport to meet me, and together we enjoyed the press interviews. Bob was good about the photographers, insisting that he should never be in the same picture with me. He didn't play the old trick of putting a hand on my shoulder or pointing a finger into my chest so that the papers' editor could not cut him out. Unless you have been part of show business, you may not understand that a showman likes to be in every picture, so this was a genuine sacrifice on his part.

Bob and I went to his studio the next day. The electronic equipment, which he had picked up in the USA, was good – as far as I could judge; but I knew then (and still know now) nothing technical.

Large rooms usually echo, so the studio had been lined with sound-deadening material. Snag one: someone, in order to cheer up the place, had had it painted with gloss paint, which reflected the sound. A great deal of money had therefore been wasted. As Bob was so proud of his studio I never mentioned this.

Snag two: there were no sound-effects discs. This would make it impossible to put in backgrounds: traffic, thunder, horses, crowds cheer-ing, church bells, animal noises or anything at all.

Snag three: the engineer, Cornelius, predictably nicknamed Corny, did not know how to edit tape. Nor did I, so I found out how and did all the editing myself.

I met the studio sweeper-out, errand-boy and general factotum; he was a very pleasant tall, young Zulu called Timothy, and I shook hands with him, as I had with Corny. Bob later told me quietly that it wasn't necessary to shake hands with kaffirs.

Bob's wife, Nesta, in whose house I stayed for the first week, spent ten minutes explaining this appalling distinction to me. In those ten minutes, the seeds for the return journey were sown. But I was there, Enid and the children were going to join me later; and I thought it sensible to find out more about this beautiful country, twisted though it is with a lunatic, dangerous, pointless, vicious internal political system. It is a volcano with a lid on; the more firmly that lid is held down, the greater will be the explosion when it comes. It is a matter of time only.

After I had found out how to cut and splice sound tape, I called the Zulu, Timothy, into the control-room and started to teach him editing, as I knew I was to be the administrator, producer, writer and everything else, since Bob would be spending his days at the Hillman Timber offices owned by his father-in-law. I told Timothy that his pathetically low wages would improve enormously when he could edit; he would even be able to help and occasionally take over from Corny on the control panel and balance the microphones. During one of these lessons, I learned two things: the first was how it all worked, and the second was that Timothy was exceedingly bright and willing to learn. He never forgot anything.

One day just before lunch, Bob breezed in. 'Hi, Ian! Everything OK?'

'Fine.'

'Come out for a quick bite. I have about forty minutes.'

I went. He said, 'I hear you're teaching Timothy some of the skills of the studio.'

'He's very good.'

'You must not do that.'

'Why?'

'Kaffirs are not allowed to learn skills.'

It was as abrupt and unsympathetic as that.

I found out later that natives were allowed, say, to carry bricks in hods but not to learn the skills of bricklaying They are not allowed to learn anything that may put them on equal footing with the white man.

Our studio income came from our clients. We had several panel games; one was a sort of 'What's My Line?' for the General Tire (*sic*) and Rubber Company. It was fun. Bob was the chairman and made a good show of it. Another was 'One Minute, Please' which I now called 'Just A Minute'. (I forget who sponsored that.) Another show was a letter-writing competition, sponsored by Basildon Bond.

The business of having no skilled engineer worried me and so did the absence of sound-effects discs. However, both could be obtained in London so, after a consultation with Bob in his palatial timber office, he gave the all-clear to my asking an ex-BBC engineer (who will be called Bill Dagwood for the purposes of this book, in case he is still alive). I didn't know then that the BBC had sacked him but there is no point and nothing to be gained by raising an old ghost after he has paid for his errors.

Bill was to buy some two hundred and fifty sound-effects records, which we needed so badly, and to fly out on 1 November, with his wife and adult daughter following him later by boat.

The day after he arrived, he borrowed £75 from me because, as he said, he didn't have the money to pay for his wife and daughter's passage out. If I didn't lend this money to him, he would go back to the BBC. I didn't know it then, but this was something he could not do; however, not knowing he had been fired, I believed him. It was only after I had handed the money over to him that I found out that Bob Ford had already given Bill the money for the fares out.

I was still not on my guard. When I tackled Bill about this, he said there had been other expenses in connection with bringing his dependents out; I was not to worry, I would get my money back in a couple of months. Needless to say, I never saw the money again.

Production became simpler. Bill operated the controls in the control-room very well. The sound-effects records allowed us to produce little plays and a kind of soap-opera. We now also had a weekly comedy show, starring a local comic called Al Debbo. I wrote the scripts which, with all my other duties, I now admit nearly killed me. But not one of those shows died on us; this was largely due to Al's talent and partly due to the use of sound-effects. After we'd recorded the first with no sponsor, we asked one possible client in to hear it; it was sold and a series booked within twenty-four hours.

We also had collections of listeners' dreams, which I dramatised and then asked some psychoanalyst to explain. This drew a huge mail, mainly from nutters who believed in that kind of rubbish.

I did not buy a house; I rented one, because I already had a feeling of impermanence. It was at 59 Kelvin Road, Bramley, a suburb of Johannesburg about two miles from Alexandra Township, that still disastrously filthy, rat-ridden slum, with other infestations, where the natives were allowed to 'live'. Stupidly and in ignorance, risking life and limb, one day I went down there to see how they really lived. You don't need this book to describe what it looked like, because there have been many TV films since then, which show that in the townships there is no drainage and no sewers, people really do live in sheds made of cardboard three-ply wood, and he is a lucky man who finds a piece of corrugated iron which he can use as a roof. So you know what it looked like. Without going there, however, it is impossible to guess what it smelled like. Yet the white South Africans say they are religious people and those descended from the original Boers claim to be especially religious. They call themselves Christians, or so I heard . . .

Enid joined me in Bramley with the children just before Christmas, which is very hot in Johannesburg.

We had a houseboy called Wilfred, who was up to no good. In retrospect I do not blame him; from his point of view, we were millionaires and he was just an underpaid houseboy. We also had a cook-girl called Paulina, who was a delight. She really loved our children and made a great fuss of them.

One afternoon we saw that *King Kong* was on at our local drive-in cinema. Paulina said she had heard that it was a great film. Enid said it was and that she should see it. The problem was this: natives were not allowed in the drive-in. We found a way round that one by lending Paulina some white gloves, powdering her face with flour and giving her a large hat to wear. We also thought the disguise would be helped if little Malcolm sat on her lap and with Susan on her right, which was the side where the man selling the tickets on the way in would be.

All the way there in the car, Paulina was talking about how she could go to jail if she were caught, and how we would be heavily fined. Like us, she still felt a certain thrill at outwitting those Afrikaners.

Mentally screwed up with apprehension, we drove through the gates. The man at the ticket office looked into the car to see how many we were and to make sure we had no other children hidden on the floor who would thus get in free. It was a very nerve-straining moment. We were all terrified he would see through the disguise, because Pauline's head and face were different from that of a 'European'. (White South Africans stupidly called themselves Europeans, when most of them have never been to Europe.)

After successfully buying five tickets, we were in. The original *King Kong* has always been a good film, but it's even better when seen on an outsize screen out of doors with an adjustable amplifier in the car. Paulina loved the film; the only other nervous moment was when the 'boy' came round, going from car to car selling hot-dogs, ice-creams and drinks. The word 'boy' applied to what was usually a man is a deliberate white man's slur to lower the status of that native from the dignity of manhood. The 'boy' tapped on my window and looked inside. We bought five ice-creams – and once again we had got away with it.

We giggled all the way home.

Paulina was not allowed to sleep in our house, but in a shed at the bottom of the garden. Her lavatory and shower was a single cubicle with a hole in the middle of the floor.

We knew this was all wrong; the full impact of apartheid came home to us one night when Enid heard someone at the front door. When we opened it, a black man fell into the house with a knife sticking out of his back. We pulled it out. He was still alive, so we wrapped him in blankets, to stop him going cold from shock, and telephoned for an ambulance. After twenty minutes the ambulance arrived. They wouldn't move him because he was black. They told me to telephone the police, which I did. This made it impossible not to tell them he was black, because the same rigmarole would only happen all over again.

The police took their time about arriving, and of course there was no ambulance. We had said he was a stretcher-case, since moving him would cause him to lose even more blood. Two policemen picked him up under the arms and dragged him into the car, almost throwing him into the back seat.

The senior man was in the house. I asked him if that was the way to treat anyone.

'Look, man,' he said, 'I can tell from your accent that you're from England. You're all like this when you first come out. That kaffir's probably on drugs and may have been in a township fight. You're number fifty nine Kelvin Road, the first house he'd find. Don't stand any nonsense from them.'

When I telephoned the police station the next morning to see how he was, no one could tell me. 'Well, you see, man, we don't keep records of every bloody kaffir that causes trouble.'

I should have checked more carefully on the engineer we flew out from London. It's easy to be wise after the event but 'Bill' was a petty crook. A disreputable competing Johannesburg studio suddenly decided to entertain Bill richly; two weeks later, all our valuable sound-effects discs vanished. It didn't take Bob and me long to find out that Bill had sold them to the other studio. Foolishly, he had made us less competitive, while making himself only a relatively small sum.

Bob and I laid a trap. In his timber office, we planted a small microphone inside the desk lampshade; under the desk was a recording machine. I managed to get Bill round to that office at two o'clock one memorable afternoon, and together Bob and I interviewed him.

We were scrupulously careful not to browbeat him in any way, just in case the tape had to be played in open court. We even said we knew he did not have much money and that the temptation must therefore have been that much greater.

After twenty minutes, he owned up. (That tape still exists.) The lines in which he admits the theft and the sale of the discs sound somewhat arrogant.

Bill was thrown out on the spot. The only satisfaction we had was to hear from Studio X that Bill had applied there later for a job and been turned down.

It goes without saying that, even under the conditions of apartheid, there existed some black comic talent – and plenty of black musical talent of a very high standard. However, we were not allowed to broadcast it; this was very frustrating, as I saw it as a possible way of pulling down some of the apartheid barriers. I was told I was being impractical: most whites did not, and still do not want these barriers pulled down.

It was also a well-kept secret that Paulina's son, Lucas, often played with our son, Malcolm, who was the same age. Those two three-year-old boys had a lot of fun together.

We knew our stay in Africa had to be limited because of the appalling social conditions. But it came to an end rather more suddenly than even we expected. Little six-year-old Susan was the cause. One day Enid heard her saying to Paulina in the kitchen, 'But I ordered you last night to clean my tennis shoes. Why haven't you done them?'

Enid told Susan that no one must ever be spoken to like that. Poor little Susan was made, rightly, to apologise to Paulina. It turned out that the children next door spoke to their servants like that, and that was where she had picked it up. If this was to be the influence on the children, then the sooner we got out of that country, the better for everyone.

Enid, Susan and Malcolm left for England by boat. I went to see Bob to tell him that I would remain until he could find a substitute for me, and that I would work alongside the new man until he understood what was needed.

18
The wrong business

Back in London, I telephoned an old friend, Sam Heppner, who had been writing well of me in the papers just before I went to Africa. His immediate response was, 'Meet me at the Savoy for a drink at midday tomorrow.' Noting my hesitation, he added, 'Don't worry. It's all on expenses and won't cost either of us a penny.'

We met. He explained that, although he was primarily a journalist, he was also head of the public relations department (which he insisted on calling the 'pubic' relations department) of an advertising agency. Sam was a small man with a large appetite for humour. In his pocket he carried a moustache attached to a cigar, and he did a most professional impersonation of Groucho Marx, whizzing round the Grill Room, to the astonishment and delight of most of the diners.

The word 'agency' conjured up visions of dirty teacups as in Clarbour's Theatrical Agency. To me, all agents were scruffy and vaguely suspect people who lived like leeches, fixed on other people's work; from my short-sighted point of view, they were a necessary evil. There are a few beneficial theatrical ones who can and have done great things for talented people; but most of them did more harm than good and charged ten per cent for doing it. I remained politely, but not genuinely, curious.

He went on to tell me of a Mr Stanhope Shelton, who was the Creative Director of an agency situated right next door to the Savoy, and who wanted creative people, especially show people, since the Independent Television Bill was about to be debated in the House of Commons.

Still shy of the word 'agency', I listened and didn't see how it could apply to me, but Sam made me an appointment to see Stanhope Shelton in his office in Lancaster Place.

As I walked into the building, my ideas of an advertising agency were left on Waterloo Bridge. This was no hole-in-the-corner, ten per cent scrounging business, which lived parasitically on the efforts of others; they worked for their money and had done very well. They were called Mather and Crowther then, and have since become Ogilvy and Mather.

I met Stanhope ('Sherry') Shelton, the Creative Director whose job it was to pass, add to, alter or throw out the advertisements worked on by the agency, before they were offered to the advertisers. He sat at a light

Chippendale desk on which was a single piece of paper, a pencil, a telephone and a Georgian silver salt-cellar with a blue-glass lining, filled with sand, for use as an ashtray.

On one wall hung a water-colour of a Norwich scene by John Sell Cotman and a pencil sketch of some dogs by Edwin Landseer which, years later, he gave me. In a boozy moment of greed, I admired it and practically asked for it. In a boozy moment of generosity, he gave it to me, telling me that Landseer was a talented drunk who took many years beyond his contract to sculpt and cast the four lions for Trafalgar Square and who had made Nelson's Column too tall, so that the crane to carry the statue to the top had to be rebuilt.

He explained advertising briefly by saying that advertising agencies were seldom heard of by people outside their own world, but it was they who booked the space in papers and magazines and on hoardings for the advertisements of their clients, who might be Batchelors Peas, Kensitas Cigarettes, Shell Petrol, Pepsodent Toothpaste, etc.

These advertisers also had their campaigns thought up for them by the agency's creative department. After approval, the space would be bought, filled with the advertisement and billed to the agency. The owners of the space would then kick back fifteen per cent to the agency.

This was better than the old theatrical ten per cent, and in most cases was harder to earn, so it was no wonder that the offices looked so pleasing. They were filled with secretaries, some of whom later told me, 'Daddy thinks it a good idea if I do something useful for a while until I marry.' In spite of the impractical impression that last sentence gives, most of the secretaries would put other girls in other industries to shame by their efficiency, good manners and their ability to deal with awkward clients and write competent, properly constructed and spelled letters.

All this was far from the sleazy business I had imagined. Stanhope Shelton asked me outright how much I would want in salary if, after seeing other directors of the agency, I was offered a job there as a producer of commercials.

I named some miniature figure, based on my experiences of the BBC, which he asked me to repeat.

It was not repeated.

'No,' he said. 'You must treble that because if you don't charge more, they won't think you're any good.'

'Very well, Mr. Shelton, if that's the direction, I'll quadruple it. How's that?'

He laughed. 'Good. That's better.'

During the next fortnight I went to see other directors of the same company. Some of the interviews mere memorable.

I went into the office of the Media Director, the man whose department's job was to buy space on behalf of the client. As I entered, at ten in the morning, he was slowly closing a draw in his desk. (Others told me later that Tom always kept a glass of whisky and soda in there.)

He was a pleasant blunt Scot. 'Don't have any high hopes of this job you might be offered,' he said. 'You should know that there is no Act of Parliament yet; it is still only a Bill, to be debated. Even if it goes through, I don't think we'll ever sell "time", or whatever they're going to call it, to my clients. No one can even guess what it will cost or how we'll go about it. And who's going to make all the films?' And the interview went on in this negative mood.

Tom didn't like the idea of television, even when reminded that it was already selling goods in the USA. Of course, it is possible he felt threatened by it, since his whole life was spent selling space on hoardings, in magazines and in newspapers to clients, and this was something new that he could not get to grips with. He offered me a whisky, but it was too early for my unsophisticated tastes.

The Managing Director, Francis Ogilvy, was the next interviewer, about two or three days later. He wasn't particularly interested in television; all he had to say was that this was Stanhope Shelton's business and that he was allowed to carry on with it only because the idea had been passed at a board meeting by a board which seemed to know nothing about it. He began to open up a little when he told me that, in his younger days, he had always wanted to be an actor.

My last interview was with a big man of advertising, vice-chairman of the company, Gordon Boggon, who was the powerhouse behind the scenes. He was a man of immense charm, of whom Sherry Shelton later said, 'If he had told me to stand on my head on the parapet of Waterloo Bridge, I would have done it for him.' I think I would too.

Gordon was a large man with a craggy wide face, a great affection for alcohol, a limp due to losing a leg in the First World War, and a truly creative approach to getting new clients. One example: Mather and Crowther was a few minutes' walk from Covent Garden, at that time a jumble of wholesale fruit merchants. Gordon, with a couple of hours to spare one day, wandered knowingly but unknown into the market and picked out all the powerful fruit merchants available. He asked them to lunch with him at the Savoy a few days later. Once he had them all together, he suggested that he should represent them in advertising their wares collectively. He had a slogan for them. The Creative Department had worked on the idea for the campaign for weeks and had come up with the simple slogan: 'EAT MORE FRUIT'.

At the brandy stage of the lunch, Gordon got up to speak, outlined the idea and produced the huge slogan banner, which was hoisted and spread from one side of their private dining-room to the other.

It wasn't long before the whole of the UK was festooned with this simple banner; widely read newspapers also carried it, as did magazines. While he was at it, he picked up Fyffes Bananas and Outspan Oranges as clients. Fruit sales rose, as did the income for Mather and Crowther.

My handling of the Fyffes account later was fun, except that the Fyffes advertising manager insisted that every television commercial should include the words 'full fruit sugars fully matured'. I never managed to persuade him that while that was true, it was not the way the normal housewife would express the excellence of bananas. 'The consumer', wrote David Ogilvy, then head of a huge USA advertising agency, and Francis's brother, 'is not a moron. She is your wife.'

Gordon Boggon had done his homework on me. He remembered some of my shows at the BBC and mentioned them. He asked me no questions of any kind, except to find out whether I had any plans for lunch, because he would like me to join him.

Once you have been poisoned by an oyster, it can set up some sort of allergy, so that you can never eat one again. Before going to Africa I had been poisoned and as a result could not eat them.

Arriving at the restaurant, Gordon had his private room, and the table was already laid with oysters, champagne and Guinness. This was a place specialising in oysters. The effect of the poison had previously taken about three hours to show itself, I had to risk it. It was also possible that I was no longer allergic.

We tucked into two dozen oysters and half a bottle of champagne each, swilled down by a pint of Guinness. I was young and could take it. Gordon was old and could take it.

Over brandy, he said he knew enough to offer me the job of pulling together a television department if and when Independent Television ever got started. I would be sent to study commercials in the USA for a month. Meanwhile, I was to keep my eyes open for any boys or girls in London who might help run what would eventually become the television department.

New wealth was being thrown at me. However, after lunch I started to feel queasy. A taxi with all speed was now essential. I thanked Gordon for the excellent lunch. Years later, when we were having a laugh over the past, he admitted that he had noticed I was turning green and wondered what was causing it. The taxi arrived and sped up Regent Street, until I had to stop it in the middle of Oxford Circus in order to throw up. That bout lasted all night and into the first part of the next day. I have seldom felt so happy and miserable at the same time.

Before the end of March, Stanhope Shelton had seen to it that I had a good grounding in what at the time was the substance of advertising. He introduced me to newspaper printing, typesetting, type fonts, silkscreen printing, space buying, big-screen cinema advertising and so on.

As all I was doing depended on the Television Bill getting through, I spent as much time as possible up in the Stranger's Gallery at the House of Commons, listening to the debates on the topic. It was soon evident to me that both the Conservative and Labour Parties have their fair share of fools and wise men.

Having old friends at the BBC, it wasn't long before I heard that they would have to pay their staff more or lose their best men and women to the independent companies. For that reason, BBC staff were also hoping that the new television station would come into being. The good people could not lose.

There were one to two Jonahs who said that the BBC's staff had best be careful, as the whole commercial television idea was rickety, and their stations were more likely to go bankrupt than succeed. Anyone leaving for an independent company would be unlikely to get his job back if it failed. The same people also said that, if it did succeed, artistic talent would be spread so thin that TV would not be worth watching.

Independent Television started in 1955. There's no need to mention the month: it had to be (and it was) September. The first commercial ever shown in this country in public was for Gibbs SR Toothpaste. What a party we had that night! Gordon Boggon had it laid on for us at the Savoy. He had a phenomenal memory: everyone but me started with oysters. He had seen to it that I had smoked salmon.

He had also asked Enid and me to bring along a 'theatrical character'. We took Gerard Hoffnung, who behaved very well; he attacked Gordon Boggon twice, for believing in the commercialisation of television, which Gerard said would ruin and prostitute the real arts. But this was Gerard; any other behaviour would not have been in character. Everyone knew that, and they all loved him. After Gordon Boggon's speech, Gerard spoke, unasked, and we fell about as he lovably ridiculed what he called the disastrous monetary system that would surely destroy the finer instincts of the British people.

Advertising was not fun for me. I missed show business. Some people who are involved with television commercials mistakenly think they are in, or are at least on the edge of, show business; but show business and effective selling are completely different enterprises.

For me it was emotionally impossible to live without the former. Secretly I was writing shows for the comedian, Tommy Trinder, for most reasonable fees, so reasonable indeed that this gave us the deposit to put down on our present house in Hampstead Garden Suburb. I had also invented a game called 'The Brighter Sex', which ran successfully on Associated Rediffusion.

At the same time, 'One Minute, Please' was doing well on television, coast to coast, in the USA.

At the beginning of Independent Television, most of the distillers, Gordon's Gin, White Horse Whisky and so on, including the rum and vodka manufacturers, agreed to keep out of it. There was then no rule against it as there is now; it was just an agreement among the distillers. We had a client, Grant's Whisky, who felt they might benefit by at least seeing what a whisky commercial looked like.

We accordingly asked the celebrated author of *Whisky Galore*, Sir Compton Mackenzie, who had just been knighted, if he would appear in a commercial for Grant's. He agreed. He didn't care for having to arrive at the studio at 8 am, but he had said he'd be there. I sent a car for him and he kept his word. By nine o'clock he was made up and lit for a take.

The set was simple; it was panelled room with Scottish paintings on the wall and a small Sheraton table with a glass on it with a bottle of Grant's. Sir Compton's chair was close by. As he sat in it rewriting his script, I thought it better to warn him that the Grant's bottle was filled with cold tea because it was too early for scotch.

'And who says it's too early?'

'It's just nine o'clock,' I remarked.

'I know that! And it's so dammed early, I'd better have a stiff one to get me going.'

I changed the bottle of cold tea for the real article. (We had two crates of the stuff in the studio. Everyone was watching it like hawks.)

The commercial was to start with Sir Compton pouring out the equivalent of a treble, drinking it straight then putting the empty glass down by the bottle, so that the camera could follow it for a close-up of the label.

We wanted a rehearsal for the camera, so I suggested that, as it was not a 'take', there was no need to drink it.

'Why not? Why not, indeed? Of course I shall drink it. It's damned good stuff.' He gulped it down.

'No, no, Sir Compton. Please wait for the word, "Action". Say your lines while you pour your scotch. Drink the scotch. Put the glass down, and wait for the director to say "Cut".'

This time he waited for the word 'Action', poured out the drink, said his lines, drank it and put the glass down by the bottle.

'Perfect,' said the director. 'Let's go for a take.'

'You weren't filming that?'

'No,' I said. 'That was a rehearsal.'

'Very well.' He poured another.

'Wait,' said the director. 'Wait for me to say "Action".'

'Oh yes, so sorry.' I reached for his glass to pour it back into the bottle . . . Too late, he had drunk it.

We went for a 'take'. He spoke his lines beautifully as he poured the whisky out. He drank the measure and put the glass down. Unfortunately the glass was too far away from the bottle so that when the camera followed it down, it could not zoom in to the big close-up of the label.

We went for another take . . . and another. And by lunchtime he could not remember his lines. He was by no means drunk; his speech was clear and he walked steadily to lunch. Nevertheless we abandoned the commercial, and as no one was using the studio next morning we all agreed to meet again then. But it was expensive: the crew had to be paid again.

When you're sure all is going well, look out for the trip-wire – there is sure to be one. I didn't see it one very busy day, when I had to spend the first part of the afternoon at Sainsbury's head office near Blackfriars Bridge, discussing their next commercial.

At ten past three I left Stamford Street in a taxi, to be at Hesketh House, the Unilever offices in Portman Square, by three-thirty for a Unilever meeting on Pepsodent toothpaste. This taxi had to pass my office in Lancaster Place so I had already telephoned my secretary and asked her to be outside on the pavement with the storyboard which I was due to present at a Pepsodent toothpaste meeting at Hesketh House. (A storyboard is a series of still drawings or 'frames' on white cards shaped like TV screens, which have to be displayed one by one as the story, dialogue, jingle or whatever is read out. This is a rough but easy-to-follow representation of the final commercial as it will appear on the screen.)

As the taxi passed Brettenham House in Lancaster Place, I saw my sweet secretary, standing as requested on the pavement with the yellow-covered Pepsodent storyboard in her hand. I had already instructed the driver to slow down so that I could snatch the large folder as we went by.

Arriving at the Unilever building, I went up to the office reserved for the Pepsodent meeting. A ledge had been built against the wall of this room about four feet above the floor, designed for displaying various advertising gimmicks. It was ideal for displaying the storyboard: each 'frame' was clearly numbered on the back, so all I had to do was arrange them in numerical sequence facing the wall with their numbers rather than the pictures exposed.

The meeting started; the representatives of our client's board were all present, sitting along one side an impressive table so they would get a good view of the wall against which I had placed the dozen or so frames of the storyboard. They were all people I had met before, except for one, in whose shadow all apparently stood in awe.

Awe is catching.

'You'll wonder where the yellow went, when you brush your teeth with Pepsodent.' I said, and went on to emphasise that the theme of two teenagers on a motor-scooter would not be changed from the last ad. This met with general approval. However, the story *would* change and, after quoting the first line of the jingle, I turned over the first picture.

There, to my horror and chagrin, was a picture of footballer Billy Wright, holding a ballpoint pen with the slogan under it:

Wright on the ball!

It was the storyboard for the Biro ballpoint pens. This was a nasty moment, not helped by the total shocked silence of those lined up in front of me. However, Unilever employ very pleasant people; as soon as they had all seen that the awesome man was amused, they all laughed too, and the matter was straightened out before the end of the afternoon.

Not many months later I had another accident with Unilever at Hesketh House. I forget the name of the product. Anyway, at this stage it probably had a code name to prevent industrial spies gaining from it. All I knew for certain was that it was a pressurised can of shaving soap. I asked at the reception desk for the number of the room in which the meeting was to be held. This time there was no storyboard involved and groups of men and women were taking their places at the meeting table as I went in. My job was to listen, no more. I thought that once again I would be among friends: there would be a copywriter and an artist from Mather and Crowther, in addition to some Unilever people, the clients. I sat down and scribbled importantly on my pad of paper with the pencil supplied.

The meeting started with a Unilever representative outlining how good this would be for girls' hair. The speaker explained how it would make hair shiny, healthy and – what was he saying? He was talking about a shampoo. This was surely a shaving soap meeting.

I looked around the table at the faces – and did not recognise one. There was no one there from Mather and Crowther except me. Something was very wrong. It didn't take long to work out that I was in the wrong room and at someone else's secret meeting. Thinking it better to be discreet rather than brave, I spent the whole two hours at the meeting in silence and was never found out.

I left my good friend, Sherry, and his agency to go to another agency. Sherry had discreetly followed my progress – or lack of it – in my new job; he realised that I was just not cut out for advertising. The truth is that I had started to loathe it and, worse, I despised myself for being involved in it. Money often degrades. I was coming to the conclusion, probably wrongly, that advertising meetings seemed to be arenas where more skill and time were spent in scoring points off others round the table than in improving the client's business.

After just two years at this second agency, my chief fired me. I went home and had an attack of severe depression. It's common enough, and most people have had it to a greater or lesser degree at some time in their lives. With men, it often happens when they get to an age somewhere between forty and forty-five. I fell into this slough of self-criticism so deeply that I could not bring myself to watch television or read a book or a newspaper, or take any interest in anything. I had no wish to do anything: I could not or would not drive a car or even go out. I just sat all day and stared at the wall. It was totally destructive.

My own mother did not get in touch with us to find out what was going on. It was unpleasant, so she said it was not happening.

One day Sherry managed to shake me out of my lethargy by asking me to produce an advertising film for a client of his company. I stirred myself enough to do it and it was accepted by the client. He asked me to do another; that too was bought, and slowly Sherry coaxed me back into the land of the living.

Thanks entirely to him, we managed to keep the children at school and the larder full. I made another film for Sherry – and, while making it, like the magic sparkle in a cartoon film, inspiration struck. It was a godsend.

I invented a game. This was to be the beginning of my return to the people and the work I really love. It was to be the beginning of another long run in show business with people I understand and respect.

19

No more slips

THE WONDERFUL HAPPINESS OF RETURNING to show business was heralded by that game. The title I gave it was not changed by the BBC, which in those days was unusual, as the producer or Head of the Department always wanted to slip in his penn'orth. Changing the title was the easiest way to do this.

It was called 'Many A Slip'. The principle was that a chairman would read out short paragraphs, about five or six for each show, and in each paragraph there would be about ten errors of fact, grammar or consistency.

Two teams, two men versus two women, had to press buzzers when they spotted an error, and for that they could score a point. If the one who buzzes could also correct it, he or she would get a second point. If a trap has been laid, such as the correct use of a rare word – for example 'She was irritated by the dog's hylactism which was cunctatious' (. . . by the dog's barking which was prone to delay) – the other side would get a point for a word buzzed incorrectly, and a second point if the side which did not buzz could explain the word under suspicion.

Incorrect word-usage was fun and worked roughly as follows. A sentence full or errors would be read out: 'In between sneezes he thought his contribution adequate enough considering the past history of the days when the eight of them first began to help each other.' Corrected, this should read: 'Between sneezes he thought his contribution adequate considering the history of the days when the eight of them began to help one another.'

It was a fairly stout peg on which to hang laughs, so it was played before an invited audience. Its success depended on the light touch of the teams; had it been played by serious English scholars, it might well have been very dull.

The germ of the original idea came from a very old show, remembered from my early days at the BBC, 'Monday Night At Eight', produced by Harry S. Pepper and Ronnie Waldman. In one of their early shows they made a factual mistake. So that they would not blush among themselves too much, producer Ronnie Waldman had the idea of asking listeners the following Monday if anyone had spotted the deliberate mistake. Listeners wrote in their hundreds to claim they had. Harry Pepper and Ronnie Waldman had started a new idea by accident.

With this in mind, I telephoned Ronnie Waldman and asked him whether he would object to my extending his idea to half an hour of mistakes. After I had outlined the idea, he gave me his blessing, adding that it was so unlike anything on 'Monday Night At Eight' that he would never have guessed that the inspiration originated there. He was also kind enough to say that if I had any trouble selling it to Radio Four, he himself would go round and see the Head of Light Entertainment, Sound, Roy Rich, ' . . . and kick his backside, if necessary!'

Once the idea had gelled, I thought of as many tricks, traps and teasers as I could. It was time to set out with a full script to see Roy Rich; without wasting any time, he called in producer Charles ('Take It From Here') Maxwell. Together they made a first-class job of casting the show, so that it was in a fit state to be offered immediately to the planners of Radio Four. In it we hoped for Chairman Roy ('Desert Island Discs') Plomley, partly because he was a good showman and partly because, being an English scholar, I knew he could save my bacon if I made *un*deliberate mistakes.

The team we hoped to get would be Lady Isobel Barnett, from 'What's My Line?', and Eleanor Summerfield who had been in my first television play years before, versus comedian Richard Murdoch, ex-'Much-Binding-In-The-Marsh' and Arthur Askey's partner in 'Band Waggon', with tall, bald, avuncular magician, David Nixon.

To break the show up in the middle, we asked musicologist Steve Race to do five minutes of musical mistakes, which he did with great humour and skill; he has since told me that the wrong notes he played were contrary to his better instincts. He also gave wrong titles and, when they were the right ones, he would switch into the wrong middle melody, and so on. He was excellent; but, looking back on it, the show did not need breaking up. It was a light hearted entertainment habit in those days to put a little music in whenever there was much speech. Steve later confided to me that he hated having to sit on stage all through the show, just to do his few minutes. I felt embarrassed for him too, but the listeners were not aware that he was on stage until he spoke.

The people picked for the team were all available. A pilot was recorded. Thanks to Roy Plomley, Steve Race and the team, there was much laughter in the audience and we were booked for a trial six broadcasts to see if the listeners liked it. One Broadcasting House man of consequence said it was too erudite for Radio Four. The use of the word 'erudite' made me smile, as it is a word mainly used in fun. However, he was serious. I have avoided mentioning his name because a memorandum, shown to me be Roy Rich later, revealed that he needed the very advice that was given so freely in the show; in the note, he used the sentence: 'I would liked to have heard more of Eleanor Summerfield' and: 'Parts of it are so funny.'

I had made a few embarrassing mistakes too. Self-defence prevents me listing too many of them, but this one might amuse.

As I have always disliked interpolating foreign phrases into what would otherwise be an English sentence, on one occasion I wrote 'It is bad manners to speak French while speaking English.' Neither Roy Plomley, nor Charles Maxwell, nor I spotted how absurd that sentence was during our pre-recording chat. Richard Murdoch did. He pressed his buzzer and said, 'It's impossible!' This brought the house down and he scored three points.

'Many A Slip' became popular. It ran for fifteen years, during which time listeners were introduced to words such as tautology (saying the same thing twice, as in the phrase 'free gift'). We confused them with 'indexes' and 'indices', with 'centre' and 'middle', and so on. They were also told that if the result of not splitting the infinitive is a cumbersome sentence, it is better split.

There were so many letters on that vexing subject from those who had not read Fowler, Gowers, Partridge or Weseen, and who didn't know their Onions, that there was no way of guessing what was being taught in schools. They wrote 'to rudely correct us and to fiercely criticise the BBC who(m?), in the matter of the English language and the placing of prepositions, they had previously looked up to'. And those infinitives you have just read would be better mended, but to recast 'previously looked up to' might be considered pedantic.

There were also some letters saying that the show was pure snobbery. Several editions of the show had paragraphs in dialect, designed to illustrate, say, how difficult it is for a man from Glasgow to talk to a man from Cornwall. Curiously, this drew letters only from educated people, who claimed that dialects, local words and phrases were the salt and pepper of the language. These writers lacked the imagination to sense the discomfort and embarrassment a man suffers when away from his native area. Any true Cockney will say he feels ill at ease when talking to a 'toff': it's his speech and 'not his dirty face', as is so well underlined in *My Fair Lady*. Saying that the correct way of pronouncing 'ate' is not 'eight' but 'ett' (which it is) drew much flack. 'Decade' (meaning ten years) we pronounced 'deCAYED' (meaning rotted), and its proper pronunciation was quickly picked up as DECade. Many announcers and public speakers still get these and other words wrong.

By making the show humorous, we were soon hitting top ratings. As few people knew they were being taught English, they enjoyed it and unconsciously learned from it. One of the duties of the BBC is to educate. This show educated, and it had peak radio times, twice a week. One transmission was just before the one o'clock news, when women were usually in the kitchen cooking lunch, and the other was in the early evening, when people were listening on the car radio as they came back from work.

Usually we ran for thirteen weeks a year, but sometimes for twenty-six. The show was done on television a few times, to which it was quite unsuited because it had little or no movement. Schools were constantly writing for copies of old scripts: however, as not one school sent a stamped addressed envelope, this became a personal expense of increasing irritation, because all these requests were forwarded by the BBC to my home; I also had the cost of making photocopies. It would seem that schools taught appalling manners: not one ever wrote back to say thank you.

I was asked by an equerry if I would send a few scripts to him at the command of Her Majesty to play on the royal yacht while it was somewhere off Canada. I agreed, on condition that Her Majesty would contribute an amount at her discretion to any charity she would nominate. On repeating this conversation to the producer, Charles Maxwell, he jokingly said, 'Well, bang goes your knighthood for your contribution to radio!' Dr Barnado's Homes were made richer by £5.

It was the hardest £5 ever earned, as special paragraphs were written, getting facts wrong about the royal yacht, the crown jewels, the birthdays of the Royal Family, and many other subjects which few outside the Royal Family could correct. We had wonderful co-operation from Buckingham Palace press office.

All BBC overseas English-speaking stations carried 'Many A Slip', and a large number of non-English-speaking countries as far away as Peru could tune to it. We knew, partly because of the contracts and partly because we received letters from all over the world. Old boys of Winton House and Sherborne wrote to me from Australia, New Zealand, Canada and many other places. It was wonderful, being back in the swim again after so many years in the mental desert of advertising.

A couple of years after 'Many A Slip' had started, Anona Winn, ex-singer, ex-actress, ex-'Twenty Questions', called to ask for help with a programme she wanted to call 'The Ombudswomen'. Her original idea was that listeners would write in with their problems to her and she, acting as chairman before an invited studio audience, would get advice from a panel of four women.

I was still making occasional commercials for Sherry, and at one film studio, TVA, a series of commercials for the detergent, Flash, was being made, not by me, however, and not for Mather and Crowther. They were the commercials in which the earthy comedienne and star personality

Renée Houston showed the efficiency of Flash by mopping a black-and-white-chequered floor.

In her younger days she had been a great star with her sister, Billy, and on rare occasions with her youngest sister, Shirley. I remember as a schoolboy being taken to see *Babes In The Wood* by my father. The babes were Renée and Billy Houston. Father was not a monk and probably nursed secret desires for all three girls. They were all very pretty. When the Houston sisters played in variety bills at Wolverhampton, Birmingham or Dudley, Father always booked seats. Mother couldn't bear them.

It was at the TVA studios that I bumped into her. We knew each other only slightly, never having worked together. I knew she was capable of saying 'Bugger off!' if she wanted to, and she had few inhibitions. Being clever too, she was just the solid, earth, 'anchor woman' needed to help tame the ingenious Anona Winn. Anona's talent was great, but it needed to be matched by another sort of talent. Renée seemed just the one to do it. Anona was lady-like but talked too much. Renée was not lady-like and was quite capable of putting the brakes on Anona. The fact that they were both a little too talkative would naturally produce sparks between them. Renée also had compassion and could never help showing her feelings.

There was another reason for hoping to get her to do it. This would be a discussion show, and if any of the other women started getting too serious, Renée would quickly be able to take the 'curse' out of it and restore that vital contact with the listener. While still in the TVA studios, I outlined the show to her and said that, if she agreed, I would ask the producer to book her for the pilot recording. We had a long talk over a cup of coffee, which ended up in the pub and with a scotch each. She agreed.

Renée and Anona never hit it off; and this was yet another reason to engineer that they should be on the air together. It added an undercurrent which both were too professional to show on the surface. Each would confide in me now and again, 'Someone should get rid of that woman.' It is unlikely that Anona meant it; she had too much brain and could see that the real star of the show was Renée, who was lovable.

Anona and I thought that the three other panellists should be changed weekly. We picked on talented women and good speakers, such as Margaret Thatcher, Barbara Castle, Barbara Cartland (who told me to eat more honey), Marjorie Proops, Baroness Stocks, Beryl Reid, Katie Boyle, Teddy Beverley, Katharine Whitehorn and many others.

Politically, the BBC is careful to maintain balance. If someone of Margaret Thatcher's philosophy were on one week, the next week we would have someone of an opposing persuasion, such as Barbara Castle. We never quite knew what to do to get a balance with the Liberals.

I suggested to Anona that the programme should have a shape and not really be one giving advice. (One way to be unpopular is to give advice. To be even more unpopular, give good advice.) But that advice did not help me to be popular with Anona, although we saw eye to eye on most show business ideas.

For instance, in order to attract women listeners, the whole show should be slightly anti-man. This allowed us to drop the rather dull title of 'The Ombudswomen' and call it 'The Petticoat Line'. This was not what either of us wanted, because it was distinctly anti-feminist and, while we wanted entertainment first, we did not want to sound quite so trivial. We thought we might open with a humorous question, followed by a slightly more serious one. The middle question was to be one that would rouse passions, such as, 'Should we bring back hanging?' or, 'Is fox hunting cruel?' Follow that with a question that would bring very light-hearted advice from the team, and close with a slightly silly question, such as, 'Is it right that my husband likes to take a rubber duck into the bath with him?'

Anona and I took our time to make absolutely sure we were in total agreement on all aspects of the show. This took quite a lot of doing, as Anona could be as obstinate as I. Where I could talk for twenty minutes without a break, Anona could talk for over an hour. It was friendly, however, and it was fun. We went to see Roy Rich, who didn't take long to call in that talented producer, Bobby Jaye, who eventually became Head of Light Entertainment himself.

Between them, at the first 'Petticoat Line' meeting, Roy Rich and Bobby Jaye pulled the idea together and launched it into a fourteen-year run, with twenty-six shows a year at those same two peak times mentioned earlier.

Just before the pilot recording started in front of a packed Playhouse Theatre audience, Roy Rich, as Head of Light Entertainment, gave the team a pep talk, explaining that the four would be asked to answer letters sent in by listeners. I had written the pilot letters – I'd had to, because no one knew about the show. 'And,' he added, 'whatever else you do, ladies, don't talk over each other, don't interrupt, and,' he looked straight at Renée Houston, 'watch your language.'

'Yes, love,' she said. 'I'll be bloody careful.'

The red light came on. Our signature tune started from the control-room, relayed to the audience through the public address system. I felt sick. A green light cued the announcer to introduce Anona Winn, and with a round of applause we were away on our trial recording.

Renée interrupted, talked over other people, said 'bloody' a few times, and when the show was over she started to creep out of the theatre.

'Sorry, Ian, love,' she said, 'I've buggered it up for you.'

Roy, standing next to me, stopped her. 'No,' he said, 'I gave you the wrong steer. You were right: you're the joker, you're the wild card. Keep it that way. I think we've got a winner.

The studio audience thought so too; and, later, so did the listeners for many years. Eventually we had to ration Renée to three 'bloodies' in a show.

Renée was a Roman Catholic; in order to curb her bad language, I explained to her that 'bloody' is a corruption of 'by our Lady', referring to the Virgin Mary. She didn't believe me, so I went home to look it up in Eric Partridge's *Dictionary of Slang*, only to find that, according to him, she was right. And, according to a second reference book, she was still right. My cure was not going to work.

I said I was sorry; I told her that she was right and I was wrong. This made her worse – but is was easy to cut out the extra ones from the tape. (One enterprising engineer/editor saved a quantity of them in an envelope and edited them all together, using no other words except the occasional 'Oh!' and 'Er'. They made hilarious listening but were never broadcast.)

At the same time as doing this and 'Many A Slip', TV producer Kenneth Carter from the BBC was setting up a TV series on magic, starring David Nixon. David knew I was a magician (failed), capable of writing a gag or two and inventing a trick or two, so I was roped in to help.

David Nixon's TV magic series, 'The Nixon Line', was a huge success. In addition to his magic he had pulled in an endearing glove-puppet called Basil Brush, a fox with a passion for corny jokes: 'I respect men of letters, I always bow to the postman. Boom Boom!'

The script for David and Basil was beautifully written by an ex-performer from the Windmill Theatre, George Martin (not to be confused with the discs producer/engineer of the same name who made his name recording the Beatles and now records many of the top pop groups.) The show was always broadcast live, and George would be surrounded by the latest editions of the papers, writing topical gags up to the last minute. David had to have a remarkable brain to remember those jokes that were slipped in at the last second while someone was out front explaining the show to the audience.

I learned a great deal about comedy when I started to recognise 'topical' gags that had been used against one political party being used again with a name-change. Example: 'Mr X [fill in the name of Conservative, Liberal or Labour person in the news on that day] is a fine politician. He dodges issues in a simple straightforward way.'

Basil Brush's owner, voice and operator, Ivan Owen, was usually most uncomfortable during the show, since he had to be squeezed either into the back of a specially built, hollow sofa, inside a desk, under David's conjuring table or several other unlikely places. In there with him was a small light and TV monitor so that Ivan could see what was happening, which in turn allowed Basil to react correctly. The light and the small TV made working a very hot business for Ivan. The only advantage he had was that he could read from a script instead of having to learn it.

His attitude to Basil, and possibly the reason for Basil's popularity with the adults and children, was Ivan's total theatrical belief that Basil was in fact alive; he never allowed Basil to be seen motionless when, for instance, he took him off his hand and laid him on a chair. In Ivan's dressing-room there was never any evidence of Basil; he was always carefully concealed in a suitcase. During rehearsals, when Ivan was cramped up inside whatever container he had to suffer, Basil could be seen taking a lively interest in the activities on the stage, even when he was not participating. The sight of a shapely show-girl would send Basil into paroxysms of delight while his foxy eyes followed her across the stage.

The show went out from the Shepherd's Bush Empire, and each of the dressing-rooms was wired for sound so that we could hear all that went on from the stage. When David and I were trying to concentrate, this became very irritating. Neither of us could think against the band rehearsal or the singing rehearsal or the conversations between stagehands. The purpose of the sound reproduction in each dressing-room was to alert all performers as to what was going on, so that valuable time would not be lost. I found the chief engineer and asked if the speaker in David's room could be cut off because he was trying to work. The answer was 'No,' as they were all linked; to cut the sound at source would cut them all off.

David was driven to distraction, and he was also subject to blinding migraine attacks. Once, he was trying to sort a pack of cards and had to keep starting again because of the noise from the stage. I found a chair and climbed up to the speaker, which was over the door. It was easy enough to reach but, not having a screwdriver, there was no way of opening it and unscrewing it or cutting one of the wires.

'It's impossible to open, David. D'you happen to have a screwdriver?'

'Ace of Clubs, Nine of Diamonds, Queen of Hearts – a what? A screwdriver? No. Use a chair,' said David without looking up.

'A chair?'

'Yes. You're standing on one. Get off it.' I did so and without a word, David came over, picked up the chair and, using the wooden seat, hammered the amplifier into total, peaceful blissful silence. 'Oh dear. Look!' he said in mock horror. 'Someone's broken the loud speaker. That's a shame. It must have happened while we were at lunch. Now who could have done a thing like that? Seven of Hearts, Ace of Spades, Six of Spades, Four of Diamonds . . . '

When the broadcast was over, we had a quiet scotch together in his room while we held a post-mortem of that show. David also wrote a note to Anita Harris, whose show followed his the next day and who always used the star dressing-room. It read: 'Sorry about the amplifier, love. I think you'll like it better. David.' He left the note stuck to her mirror.

As we left the theatre he said to the stage doorkeeper, 'Someone must have busted the speaker in my room. From the look of it, it must have been vandalised I don't know what the world's coming to. I thought I ought to let someone know, as it will be needed for Anita Harris here tomorrow. Good night.'

David Nixon played chess almost to grandmaster standard. He called on Enid and me one evening after he had been working at Golders Green Hippodrome, to ask me for a game. We had played many times before and he always beat me inside the first twenty-five moves or so. He also loved my Staunton-design chessmen, made from Russian mammoth ivory and given to my father by the late Earl of Dudley. 'They make up for your lousy game.' he said.

Bringing out two decanters and glasses, I put one before him on the large chess table and one before myself, saying that these were Arabian habits; if he had his own bottle, he could help himself when he needed it and I didn't have to interrupt the game by offering him a drink.

We played. It was a long game. I won.

We met the next day for his magic show rehearsal at the Shepherd's Bush Empire.

He greeted me with, 'Ian, you bastard, you beat me. What the hell happened? You just don't play chess that well.'

'I cheated.'

'It's impossible to cheat at chess.'

'Remember, we each had our own decanter of brandy?'

'And very good it was too.'

'Mine was horrible. I had to beat you somehow, so I drank cold tea.'

That was the day he told me the story of being asked by Lord X to a hunt ball at which his hostess gushed to him and said, 'Oh, so you're David Nixon! I've heard that you're very famous for something or other.' David filled in with the appropriate self-depreciating noises, and his hostess resumed her mingling with her guests. Later that same evening she came back and said, 'Oh, Mr Nixon, I must apologise. I was joking just now, but someone has told me that you really are famous on television for something or other. We have a set – but it's only for the servants, who like that sort of thing.'

After we had finished one TV series, David went up north to work for a northern TV station, probably Granada. He rang and told me that, as he wasn't seen on TV in the south, everyone there thought he was out of work. Would I invent him a broadcastable game?

I told him that games are not just invented like that. They could not be ordered like pizzas. They would happen to me without any conscious effort. Once there, they could be worked on until they were just right.

He understood. 'But don't think I've forgiven you for beating me at chess,' he joked as he hung up.

I mentioned to Enid that David had rung to see if I could invent him a game. She said it should be possible if I thought about it. She listed many items that a conjurer uses in his act, from rabbits to dice, and added 'What about a game with playing cards with questions written on them?'

That was it. She had waved the magic wand, and the cartoon sparkle sprang out again . . . Playing cards with questions on them. An idea started to form. Suppose we had David in the chair and a team of three calling out cards in strict suit rotation: Spades, Hearts, Clubs, Diamonds. With three on the team, but with four suits, they would soon get muddled and forget which cards had gone. Let them lose points if they call for the same card twice. And so on.

A few days later, I wrote it all out and sent it to David under the title 'Fair Deal'. He loved it. We sold a series to the BBC in 1967; the team was astronomer Patrick Moore, comedian Willie Rushton and comedienne June Witfield. Many more series followed that first one. We still do a few shows every year on Radio Two even now, with magician Paul Daniels in the chair. The team is astronomer Patrick Moore and comedian Duggie Brown, with different girls from week to week in the middle. Willie Rushton gave me the title, 'Dealing With Daniels'. The producer is Richard Edis. The questions are crazy, but they have truthful answers, for example: 'Yes or no. Can cabbages get hernias?' Oddly enough, they can and do. 'Is it respectable to nictate in public?' Yes, it is. To 'nictate' is to wink.

Enid led me into that one, and she was to create the cartoon sparkle again. Because the BBC seemed to like what I was doing, she proposed that I should re-jig 'One Minute Please' and rechristen it with my old favourite name for it, 'Just A Minute,' which had been rejected by Michael Standing. That done, and having reduced the team from six to four and made other simplifications that had come to me in South Africa and New York, I went to see the Head of BBC Variety, Sound.

Roy Rich remembered the old show, liked the changes in the format and he understood how it had been streamlined; he immediately said 'Let's give it a go. Cast it, and we'll make a pilot.' He called in David Hatch to produce it.

David made a list of possible chairmen for the game from which we chose Jimmy Edwards. He also booked the studio, the old Playhouse Theatre, for a Sunday (when we knew we could get a full house. Laughter shows do not work so well in half-empty theatres). Apart from the sound of the audience, most performers like to experience the feedback, the reaction from the audience.

Jimmy Edwards always saved Sundays for his polo; he said he would love to do the show, but on any other day. David Hatch did not choose another day. The name of Nicholas Parsons was on the list because he had just won the title of 'Radio Personality of the Year'. David telephoned him. He was free. Also in the first show were Derek Nimmo, Clement Freud, Beryl Reid and an American girl, Wilma Ewart.

At the time, we were having an extension built on to our house. I told the builders when the pilot for 'Just A Minute' would be recorded and invited them to come to it with all their relations, because, if the show succeeded, they would be more likely to get paid. Masses of them came that Sunday, and the BBC Ticket Unit excelled itself. The place was packed.

Nicholas and the team were splendid, The audience fell about laughing. I went home after the show, feeling that we had winner. The producer, David Hatch, also went home knowing he had done a fine job. David let the show over-run by a few minutes to allow for any tightening up that might be needed. During the next day or two, he edited the tape to the correct length.

It had all gone so well I didn't see the trip-wire. I don't think David saw it either but it was there . . . There always is one when things go well.

20

A ludicrous precaution

THE TAPE OF 'JUST A MINUTE' had to be played to the Light Entertainment Department itself at its own programme board before it could be offered to the Radio Four planners.

Light Entertainment Department listened to it in puzzled silence and threw it out. They threw it out because so many rules in the game depended on the whim of the chairman. They said there were no hard, fast and proper guidelines.

David did two things. First he was kind not to ring to tell me we had been rejected. However, he had no intention of taking 'no' for an answer; his next step took great personal courage: in order not to fall down, he stepped over the trip-wire.

He wrote to the authorities to say that he earned his living by understanding entertainment. If they thought he could not distinguish between a good show and a dud show, he was taking his salary by false pretences. Therefore, either the show must go before the Radio Four planners, or he was in the wrong job and must act accordingly by resigning.

It was a very brave move for a young man with a wife, children and a mortgage.

It forced the Light Entertainment Department to play 'Just A Minute' to the Radio Four Planners. David's judgement has now been proved right by the length of the run of the show. It has enjoyed more than four hundred performances. It may still be running when you read this.

Better still, David was later promoted to Head of Light Entertainment. He was later promoted again to Controller, Radio Two; from there, he became Controller, Radio Four. After that, he became Director of Programmes and he is now as I write, Managing Director of Network Radio.

If you have heard 'Just A Minute' on Radio Four, you will remember its hilarious minutes, with Sir Clement Freud's dry sense of fun, Peter Jones's almost monosyllabic shafts of ridicule, the late Kenneth Williams's pointed attacks on the audience – 'They're all fools or they wouldn't come to a show like this!' – followed by his asking them, did they think Nicholas Parsons had been auditioned for the job or had he just slipped something to Messiter? Of his fellow competitors he would suggest disdainfully, 'They're just not as well read as I am.'

Derek Nimmo, one splendid evening, told us a limerick that might have got us off the air for ever:

> There was a young poof from Khartoum,
> Took a lesbian up to his room,
> They lay on the bed.
> Until one of them said,
> 'Who does what and with what and to whom?'

The audience fell about, and Nicholas Parsons was unable to speak, he was laughing so much. I had a job reading the stopwatch through my tears of hilarity, but we never had a single complaint. This was a long way from being carpeted after 'Twenty Questions' for having 'a fig leaf' followed by 'a sporran'.

Kenneth Williams was a constant source of wit on that programme. But the man was a different person from the actor: he was a kind and solitary individual who kept his own counsel. He did not like having people in his flat near Great Portland Street because as he said, 'Well, duckie, I just can't stand the idea of anyone using my lavatory.'

When I was having a few bones chopped about at Hampstead's Royal Free, he rang Enid every week to see how it was all going.

On one of his last shows I noticed that he looked very ill and thin, his skin was transparent and grey. He rang some days later, to say he did not feel like doing the next couple of shows. I wrote to him to say how sorry we all were that he had to take to his bed; I also passed on to him the information that producer Ted Taylor had told me: he would put out the shows from which Kenneth was absent in the middle of the series, so he would not be so badly missed. He replied by return post, to thank me for my letter. He was like that.

To gain any real knowledge of him was like trying to hold on to a handful of mercury; just when you thought you had grasped something about him was always the moment to find you were wrong; no one seemed to know much about him.

Before writing this book, I rang around people who I thought knew him well. Here are some of the questions I asked:

Q. Where did he go for his holidays?
A. I've no idea. I don't even know if he took holidays.
Q. If he took holidays, who do you think he would have gone with?
A. Probably his mother. They were very close. Please don't say who told you this because I might be quite wrong. Oh, there was an aunt

he was very fond of, but she died some years back. He had a sister, but she never seemed to be with him.

Q. What was his hobby?

A. Hobby? He never mentioned one to me. I know he liked classical music and he had a compact disc player. He read enormously. Mostly biographies.

Q. Was he interested in art galleries? Cinema? TV?

A. Don't know.

Q. Did he get on with his neighbours?

A. I shouldn't think he really knew them. His mother lived in the next flat to him and on the same floor.

It seems impossible to have known him for well over twenty years and yet to have known so little about him. He could talk as knowledgeably about classical composers as he could about the Beatles, the Who and modern composers. He could discuss the latest Archer novel as easily and fluently as he could discuss Publio Vergilius Maro (Vergil).

But he had friends. It is not generally known that he went with fellow *Carry On* star Barbara Windsor and her husband on their honeymoon. That is close friendship.

There were few biographies he had not read, which is why I would often give him great people to talk about on 'Just A Minute'.

Once, for devilment, understanding his love of biographies, however obscure, I gave him Heinrich Swartzberg. He took it up at once, telling us how this man was a famed Austrian psychiatrist who worked in Vienna and challenged Freud and other great names in that world. He completed the minute without interruption. What few listeners knew – and none of the team realised – was that I had invented the name 'Heinrich Swartzberg'. Kenneth guessed it at once.

He glanced fleetingly at Nicholas Parsons and me as he started. No one interrupted him, because they had no idea who this Swartzberg might be. After the show, he looked at me, raised his eyebrows, flared his nostrils and, in one of his deep professorial voices, said, 'Ian, you have to get up earlier than that to trap me. I know you made that name up!'

One of his catch-phrases was: 'I've not come all the way from Great Portland Street just to be insulted . . . ' He made it sound like a long way, because he always walked it. He walked everywhere he possibly could and would think nothing of walking a couple of miles to the theatre and back again after the show.

If he didn't like anyone, he could sting wickedly, but – and this is a big BUT – unlike the majority, who can be rude about people, he was never rude unless at the same time, it was immensely humorous, frequently accompanied by a clever and sharply accurate impersonation.

To read any of his books will show you that he was extremely observant of the most minute of human foibles.

Unlike some stars, he was never surrounded by hangers-on. He loathed them and would flick them off as a horse flicks flies away with his tail.

Who was Kenneth Williams? I am not sure he himself could have answered that one. He hid his real self under so many layers of comic, sad, weak, strong, domineering, incompetent, capable, literate, illiterate, erudite, ignorant characters, that perhaps there never was such a person. If there were, then possibly, not liking the man he found, he used his acting talent to buy books and records in order to get further away from himself in the works of others.

Other than books and music, he disliked possessions. He could have had a country mansion, a swimming pool and a bunch of sycophantic admirers. Few people saw inside his flat, but I heard that it was no more than a sitting-room, a bathroom, a bedroom or two, a kitchen and a broom cupboard.

One thing about Kenneth Williams is sure: while radio, television and cinema remain, he will never be really dead.

When he died, there were silly rumours about saying that he had committed suicide. I have no doubt that he died of an accidental overdose of the pills he took to kill the pain he was in. This is said with reason: one of the last things we talked about was a new contract for filming, a couple of months hence. He was excited about the idea and full of enthusiasm. A man in that mood does not take his own life.

Thanks to the solid team (and more recent additions, such as Wendy Richard and Paul Merton), it looks as though we will go on for some time having more fun on 'Just A Minute'.

But other things were going on in my life too. For instance at the beginning of July 1972 a very important-looking envelope appeared on the hall mat. It was a Royal Command to appear at Buckingham Palace to do some conjuring tricks. This happened in a most roundabout way.

Anona Winn knew I could conjure – I suppose I must have inflicted the cut-and-restored ropes on her or the red-and-black-card trick. Her charity work included organising entertainment for the 'Not Forgotten'; these are a group of men and women from the services who have given limbs and health for their country. Most of them are in wheelchairs.

Anona was sufficiently impressed by my nonsense to say that I should be one of three artists she had organised to appear at the Palace for the 'Not Forgotten'. The first artist was a very funny comic of great talent who is no longer in such great demand; next was the irrepressibly lovely Aimee MacDonald; last was the failed magician, who made ropes the theme of his act.

As Enid and I had not been to Buckingham Palace before, we were curious to know if we would really get the famous cucumber sandwiches for tea. (We did. They were rectangular, not triangular.)

During my performance, there was only one hitch in the ropes routine. One rope could be magically joined to another having a magnet craftily spliced into an end of each. When the ends of the two ropes were near – *click!* – the magnets seized each other and the join invisibly made. Disaster. As I picked up one rope from my table – *click!* – it grabbed my scissors. As I tried to laugh this off – *click!* – the other rope copied its twin and also stuck to the scissors. While I was trying to separate these three objects, the magnets found other things to stick to. The ropes became tangled and I felt like Tommy Cooper, only without the charm or the talent. The audience laughed and, having no idea what was supposed to happen, clapped like mad when I sorted it all out.

Shortly after this, two commercial radio stations were set up in the London area. More correctly, they were not 'commercial' radio at that time, but independent radio with advertisements. As with television, the advertisements were not allowed to relate to the programmes.

First on the air was Capital Radio. It was there because of the driving energies of Sir Richard Attenborough, John Witney and others. I was at their premises, Euston Tower, to see history being made at 5 am on 16 October 1973. Immediately before 5 am, carpets were still being laid, the smell of fresh paint pervaded everywhere, and people going about their business were careful not to let their clothes touch shiny surfaces just in case it was still wet paint . . . it usually was. Outside the studio and outside the competent organisation of the broadcasting area itself, all was chaos. Even climbing the stairs to the first floor where it was all happening was fraught with problems. There were paint tins, loose boards and all sorts of unlikely equipment left there for convenience and inconvenience.

What was going on in Sir Richard Attenborough's head was impossible to guess. He looked as calm and as authoritative as ever. Somehow he didn't look the sort of man whose stomach gets tied in knots.

The programme director, now well known as a competent TV cook, was Michael Barry. He was another with a calm exterior. He had rehearsed everything with great care and he knew what was meant to happen; but, inside, he must have been praying that everything would work.

I, with no real responsibilities on that scale, and with more radio experience than any of them, was tied in knots, possibly because I had been in so many foolproof broadcast situations which had managed to go wrong.

It was like watching a steaming pressure-cooker. In theory it could not explode . . . in practice it might. The second hand on the studio clock was nearing the moment of disaster or relief.

Sir Richard Attenborough had taken his seat before the microphone in the studio, ready to tell Londoners that Capital Radio was there for them.

Five seconds to go . . . four, three, two, one! Zero hour. Five o'clock.

A switch was touched. The National Anthem came out, loud and clear.

Sir Richard, still looking very calm, watched for the light that would be his cue to speak. He looked down at the piece of paper in front of him. He looked up again and smiled. His light came on. An engineer opened his microphone which fed it to live transmission.

'This.' said Sir Richard, 'for the very first time, is Capital Radio.'

And so with those words the United Kingdom had its first legal independent radio station. It was a major triumph in many ways: Capital Radio spent most of its airtime playing discs and, unlike the pirate radio stations, it was not stealing musicians' work. It was paying to play the discs, as did the BBC, and this in turn allowed the composers and musicians to receive the money they had earned.

Wavelengths had been chosen so as not to interfere with aircraft, police, shipping, the ambulance service and a dozen other essential services, which had (and still have) trouble with some of those pesky, anti-social, thieving radio pirates.

The BBC's radio monopoly had been legally broken for the first time.

The first disc Sir Richard played was 'Bridge Over Troubled Water'. The first radio commercial was for Bird's Eye Fish Fingers. The first quiz, skilfully conducted by Dave Cash, was devised and written by me.

With Nicholas Parsons we also devised the first Capital Radio soap-opera. It ran for a while, until Capital Radio realised that it was unsuitable for a mainly music station.

The rules of broadcasting were much the same as for Independent Television: programmes then were not to be related to commercials. This rule was waived for radio by the IBA in 1985, and Nescafé was the first client to take advantage of it.

The arrival of Independent Radio was a triumph.

In the spring of 1976, there were rumours coming from the BBC that all panel and quiz-games were about to be taken off the air. It is still a recurrent rumour, even with the various IBA stations. However, it was not true. Having heard it from two separate and normally reliable sources, it was natural for one to believe it; self-preservation suggested the wisdom of being prepared with something else. The precautions taken for self-preservation were ludicrous.

The horoscopes in the newspapers and magazines are fatuous. They vary, not with the position of the planets (usually wrongly called stars) but with the paper they are printed in, and yet they are still read. What is so strange about them is this: most of those who read them also think they are fatuous, yet they are read by millions. Mrs Bloggins likes to read her horoscope because it is all about the most important person in her life – herself.

Enid and I searched around for a way of juggling with the planets so that we could come up with some sort of apparatus which might give sensible advice.

The first hurdle was to think up something attractive to look at, followed by finding a reason for Mrs Bloggins wanting to own it. It seemed unavoidable that a book would have to accompany it, whatever it was. It was the book that worried us.

I have a publisher friend, who told me what hell it was going to bed and getting up each day, since his latest publication was stored in his sitting-room, in his dining-room, in the hall, up the stairs, and in the bedroom, both round and under the bed.

His wife left him.

He immediately said that the advantage of his wife's absence was that it allowed him to use her side of the bed and her wardrobe for storing more books. He couldn't keep books in the bathroom because of the steam, but they were stacked up against two walls in the lavatory, which became a very tricky room in which to manoeuvre. In addition, he was imminently expecting delivery of yet another of his publications from the printer. He was reduced to asking friends to help store it while he drove around to book shops with copies, trying to get sales. He is fortunate that he has friends. He makes sales and is moderately successful. But he said that, had he taken a warehouse, with the additional cost of warmth and burglar-proofing, he would be in the red.

Something that was cheap, small and easy to store had to be invented. The answer came out of the blue, like that old cartoon sparkle, as I lay in the sun during the summer of terrible drought in 1976. The answer was dice. Three dice, red, blue and yellow – each dice with six different symbols, such as Bat, Dagger, Snail and so on, would allow for eighteen symbols, which in turn allowed for two hundred and sixteen 'readings'. The system was as sensible as astrology.

There was no panic. The seven-day working weeks were already full because, in addition to doing the writing needed for my own shows, 'Many A Slip', 'Petticoat Line' and 'Just A Minute', there were other experimental programmes, including one-day shows, and guest appearances on various TV and radio stations.

Vast quantities of quiz questions had to be prepared for various stations worldwide run by the British Forces Network. There was a run of a quiz about the fairly recent past, asking who said what, to whom and under what circumstances. Getting myself talked into doing that was a mistake because of the tremendous research involved. Also the producer put me off by her opening words when we first met: 'Ian, when you work for me – ' That had been her mood. I stopped her and replied that I work *for* no one, that I would happily work *with* her. I was paying for her lunch at the time.

Perhaps one of the oddest programmes came about by my being asked to make contributions to a television series to be recorded in Bristol. After a few weeks' work on the script, it turned out that they wanted me to play a part in it. Driving back and forth to BBC TV in Bristol was a strain, but the fun there made up for it. The series was called 'The Adventure Game' and it starred the beautiful Moira Stuart before she became a regular newsreader. It was a sort of treasure hunt in which the players, stars from other shows, had to find their way to the magic diamond by following subtle clues. I was a cobwebbed old uncle who had the ability to turn into a huge dragon guarding the magic crystal. Being a dragon was difficult for a start: the costume was heavy and hot. I'm thankful they didn't ask me to breathe fire – although at times I was so hot it wouldn't have taken a great deal of effort to do so. At the point of change, the position of my feet was marked carefully so that the transformation into the dragon costume could be made optically.

I never quite found out what it was we were supposed to be doing, but children watching it on Saturdays liked it. My fan mail for the entire series amounted to two letters.

In the back of my mind remained the ghost of failure, floating on that unconfirmed rumour that quiz and panel games would be coming off the air. So I started to write the fortune-telling book in odd moments, and I searched around for a dice manufacturer who would copy on to dice the ideas sketched on three lumps of sugar.

We found a dice factory just off the City Road. Coincidentally it was September again. The man who ran it had a well-cared-for moustache which had been cut as carefully as his brown Savile Row suit. He rubbed his hands together while smiling permanently both at us and the factory girls as he gave us a tour.

He introduced us to a plump, aged foreman with a bulbous red nose and a bushy aimless moustache of such volume that he appeared able to talk without moving his lips. Over the clatter of machinery and the rattle of dice sliding down chutes, this man, a dice expert, told us about the trouble a good manufacturer goes to in order to avoid a die coming down too often with the same number uppermost. We really didn't want to know that.

He told of special dice with a blob of metal in them, they were thrown on to an electromagnetic table so that a double-six could be guaranteed every time the secret switch was pressed. I asked if he could make me one. No, he said, he couldn't.

The man in the smart suit said that this factory was the only one in the UK currently making dice; he said it so often, after he had discovered the problem we had had in finding him, that it made me feel he was making sure we would look no further, just in case we stumbled across a competitor of his.

After he had seen the eighteen drawings needed to decorate the three dice, he asked how many sets of three dice we would need.

It was impossible for us to say; this was our first experience of business. Pulling a figure out of the air, we said we would need two thousand sets of three and would he please put a quote in the post.

He produced three different-sized dice from his desk and, holding them in the palm of his hand as delicately as a ornithologist would have held three rare birds' eggs, he asked us to choose a size.

We asked for quotes for all three sizes.

On the way home Enid asked me. 'Why did you suggest two thousand sets?'

'How many would you have asked for?'

'Two thousand, I suppose.'

'That's why I thought it was the right figure.' We neither of us knew what we were talking about. We couldn't even guess how much storage space six thousand dice would take up.

After the quotes arrived two days later, I telephoned the book printers, Cox and Wyman, and explained to them that I wanted a small edition of a paperback printed.

About half an hour after telephoning the book printers, their representative was on the doorstep. He didn't have the sophistication of the dice man, but he made it clear that he thought I was quite nuts by explaining to me very slowly that a run of ten thousand books would not cost much more than one of two thousand. He then destroyed his own argument by saying, rather tactlessly, 'Yes, who do you think will buy this?'

The dice man had also shown his doubts concerning my sanity, but with more tact. It was his occasional raising of one eyebrow that had betrayed his opinion.

Within a few days I had quotes from the dice people and from the printers. It was all going to cost much more than we had thought . . . except that we had no idea what we had thought.

We knew then that we were going to start a business, so the next day Enid went to the bank because, as she told me, this business venture must be kept separate from broadcasting.

Her interview with the bank manager went something like this.

She told him that we needed to open a new account under the name 'Fortune Bones'.

'I'm sorry,' said the manager 'I don't think I heard you properly.'

'We want to start a business under the name of 'Fortune Bones.'

'Fortune – what?'

'Bones.'

'Bones?'

'Bones,' said Enid. 'Bones. I'll write it down for you.' She wrote 'Bones' on a piece of paper and handed it to him.

'Ah.' He said it as if seeing the planet Neptune in close up for the first time. 'Ah yes. Very interesting. Fortune Bones.'

'Yes.'

'Have you thought about this?'

'Of course.'

'Have you spoken to your husband about it?'

'Yes, but he doesn't understand money. He just has ideas.'

'How much capital will you need to borrow?'

'None. Please transfer four thousand pounds from our company account into an account I want called Fortune Bones.'

Silence from the staid bank manager.

Enid went on, 'I want to open an account under that name with my husband and me as joint proprietors.'

'Yes, but what are Fortune Bones?'

She told him. He looked exceptionally blank. She told him again.

He asked her if she would like some coffee. Enid thanked him but said she was in a hurry.

He thought for a minute, fiddled with some papers on his desk then said, 'Mrs Messiter, I think that's a very good idea. Don't you think it would be better if you went home, had a cup of coffee and discussed it with your husband again? You can't just start up a business called Fortune Bones – well, not one of this nature. To begin with, the business name has to be registered.'

'It is registered. We went to the place in the City Road. Here's the copy.' She showed him the necessary copy of the registration paper.

'Oh? Then you're serious?'

'Absolutely. I am serious. I never do anything with bank managers that isn't serious.'

He didn't smile.

On Monday 2 November, the books were delivered. On Thursday the 4th the dice arrived.

At that time we had a car that looked like biscuit tin on wheels; it was a VW Camper. We found we could pack up sets of dice and books in lots of one hundred, and pack a thousand into the back. It was a very big car, with its own gas stove so that we could make tea. There was also a gas fire in it to keep us warm and, as this was winter, we needed it.

The first three calls were to book shops, all of whom turned Fortune

Bones down. I felt a bit low, but that night I had to record a fresh 'Many A Slip'. I mentioned this let-down to Eleanor Summerfield, the actress, who was in the show. She suggested I call on actor Peter Bull, a friend of hers, who ran a 'psychic' shop near the Kensington High Street. I rang him the next morning and he asked me over. He bought fifty sets and offered me a cup of coffee. I told him about the book shops, and he suggested that I stop trying to interest them and go to the top shops, to sell the books as Christmas novelties.

My next call was to Harrods. We sold them a hundred sets. Next we went to Debenham's in Oxford Street and sold two hundred sets. Selling went on like that, with very few refusals. We sold various quantities to all the large London stores in a few days and, by getting up at five in the morning, we sold to stores as far afield as Reading. We were sitting up half the night packing them, three dice and a book in a plastic wallet, and then getting up early in the morning to sell them.

Remembering South Africa, where it was wise to call the client the day after his show to find out if he had any remarks, I called Harrods two days later to see how they were going. 'Glad you called,' said the buyer. 'How soon can you let me have another two hundred sets?' I told him he could have them that morning. 'That's good delivery,' he said. 'I have a slight complaint, however.'

'Oh, I'm so sorry. What's gone wrong?'

'I'm finding it difficult to get the sales girls to start work in the morning until they've read their "Bones" for the day!'

We sold out in a fortnight, then we made sales on the strength of samples, with the goods promised. Urgent calls went to Cox and Wyman and to the dice man. Thinking it a fluke, we only ordered another seven thousand books, which would require twenty-one thousand more dice. This relatively small order was because we were aiming at the Christmas period. I made an error of judgement in thinking that, when that was over, no more sales would be forthcoming.

By Christmas we were dog tired but we had got our money back. On paper we had made very much more than breaking even, in fact a surprising amount. There was, however, a drawback: the bigger the store, and the larger their order, the longer they took to pay. We had made a small cash profit on our outlay of £4000-odd. But the big profit was on paper only; Debenham's, for instance, did not pay for six months.

This gave us reason to think again: the stores liked a hundred per cent profit – in addition to paying as late as possible while they invested the money owed to us. To our surprise, our sales went on, unimpeded, long past Christmas. We had to find a way of cutting out the middle man. We found one: mail order. By advertising in the right magazines, people would write to us direct and send their money direct. Again Sherry

Shelton helped. He said that as Fortune Bones were totally original and not obtainable anywhere else, anyone who wanted a set would pay any reasonable amount We put the price up . . . They went on buying . . . Sherry Shelton was right.

To his surprise, the dice man realised that we were selling very well. Simultaneously, with his eyebrow raised, he told us that there was a shortage of the plastic from which he made the dice, so he would have to put the price up. Enid commented that to put the price up would kill the golden goose.

Panic! We had orders we could not deliver. We were lucky: we found a dice manufacturer in Hong Kong who would makes the things at one-tenth of the price of the London man. That solved all immediate problems, and our profits shot up. By now we were also selling across the US in major stores and we had discovered we were not seasonal.

There was a drawback again: panel-games and quizzes did not come off the air, as had been prophesied; they multiplied. There were now TV shows to be written. I had to go to Denmark, where a show of mine was topping the charts. Norway also wanted it, as did Sweden. I was helping in the writing of 'Celebrity Squares', chaired by Bob Monkhouse. Later, in addition to all the radio work, came 'Family Fortunes' and more recently, 'Bob's Full House'.

There were also regular weekly radio shows, guest appearances, including two on 'This Is Your Life', and supplying a regional independent radio station, Thames Valley Broadcasting, with a quiz run with humorous efficiency by Graham Ledger and, his charming wife, Renata. I made the format and Graham and Renata gave it the title 'Quickfire!'. It was and still is a lot of fun. Three publishers asked me to write on various subjects. No one was let down.

The day would start very early for us. The day's mail order had to be packed, addressed and stamped; Enid had to enter it up and look after the books. One of us had to post it. We had to make two visits a day to the Post Office, and all this had to be fitted in with the shows.

Enid flew to the USA and achieved good sales there. She learns faster than I do, and she wrote into our terms that payment must be made within thirty days of delivery. That did the trick.

Thames Television rang and asked me to appear with Fortune Bones, footballer Bobby Moore and Monty Modlyn at peak time one evening, so that Bobby could 'throw the Bones' on camera in the new pub he had just bought, redecorated and opened.

This we did. Bobby Moore threw his bones, looked up the 'reading' in the book – and was amazed. Call it luck if you like. The reading said 'Beware of fire.' He was as astonished as I was, because this new pub of his had been severely burned the previous evening. The fire damage was so bad that we were broadcasting from a small bar, not from the one intended. Neither Monty Modlyn nor I missed the chance to rub in the fact that this was a live show. Trickery was impossible because the camera had gone into tight close-up on the 'Bones' and then on the Book of Readings.

I don't believe in luck, except where health in concerned. There's nothing strange in noting how lucky hard workers are. This broadcast, at peak time and to a huge audience, brought in orders; that was nothing but luck. And it was luck again when, in a silly mood one Derby Day, Enid said, 'Lets get the Bones to choose a horse for us.'

I agreed, saying that if we lost the money we could set it against tax because we were testing the Bones. Enid, being an accountant, quite rightly said we couldn't . . . I still can't see why not.

She threw for first, second, third and fourth.

I said, 'Look, this is silly, these Bones are for people who haven't got all their marbles running the same way.'

Enid said, 'Well it's no more stupid than reading "form" and then having a bet as a result. If anyone knew anything about horses, all the bookies would be bankrupt.'

We don't gamble, except when we play poker with our grandchildren, but I went round to the local bookie and put a few pounds each way on those four horses.

They came in, first, second, third and fourth. We were over £500 better off. It was the only time I've bothered to watch horse racing on television.

It was odd. It was like Bobby Moore's pub all over again. Don't write either to the publisher of this book or to me for a set of Fortune Bones, because I have stopped selling them; they take up too much time. You may, with luck, find a set belonging to a friend. All the shops have now sold out. Sets of Fortune Bones are scattered all over the UK and the USA now. Don't blame me if you use the gambling instructions and bankrupt yourself. They only advise, they do not prophesy . . .

Or do they? It's a bit spooky.

Enid was working too hard, clearing up the paperwork, looking after the tax and the VAT, sending out the bills, looking after the house, the garden and all that the shows entailed. We were both working seven days a week. Our daily died and was in every way irreplaceable, because she had become a friend. Our gardener, whom we had known for over thirty years, had to give up because of age. Something had to stop: We were both tired.

We had promised each other we would retire at sixty in Enid's case and, being five years older, at sixty-five for me. It was ridiculous for us both to live in the same house, she in her study upstairs and I with my study downstairs, so that we met only for meals, before going back to our desks.

In the evenings, I would run off to some studio to see how the show was going.

Her father had been in the army, posted to India, and she had spent her childhood there. We promised each other to return for old times' sake. It was not to be. At least it is not to be just yet.

There was another irresistible show just round the corner.

21

'Children can always draw better than adults'

THE SHOW ROUND THE CORNER just happened. It wasn't intended. It wasn't planned. The idea came to me in September 1985.

One way to clear your thinking is to write things down; so it is written down. Writing it down would show up the flaws in it, and then it could be torn up and forgotten. But writing it down improved it. It was called 'Steal'.

Nothing was meant to be done about it, as both Enid and I wanted to retire. After writing it all out, our grandson, James Beaumont, the eldest of our four grandchildren and fourteen years old at the time, read it and said, 'Pomps,' (his nickname for me) 'no one's going to read all this. Can I put it on a computer so it can be seen in movement, colour and with sound?'

We had bought him a BBC-B computer, some months before. He now spent many weeks experimenting on how to lift the show off the dull paper and make it sparkle on the screen. As he tackled problem after problem, he would occasionally suggest an improvement to make the show more entertaining and get an extra laugh or two. He too could wave a magic wand and make cartoon sparkle come out of it. For every improvement he made, we gave him a percentage of however much some TV station would give me. He now owns a respectable slice of the format.

We agreed that there was a good TV show there, one which was different in so many ways from other game-shows: it did not depend on the inevitable question-and-answer format. It could also easily be turned into a children's computer game as well as a family board-game. When we were sure we knew what we were doing, I made an appointment with Jon Scoffield at Central Independent Television, the station most likely to be interested. My first visit was on my own. Grandson James had to go to school.

At Central Independent Television, I spread all the computer bits out on a table in a room near Jon Scoffield's office; when he came in with senior producer Tony Wolfe, he said, grinning, something like, 'I'm sure it will all explode when you switch it on, Ian, but I'll chance it.'

He was closer to the truth than he dreamed. What he didn't know was that, while I may have looked knowledgeable about computers, graphics and all those technical things, I really knew nothing about it; I stuck to James's instructions, which were, 'Pomps, switch it on, and for heaven's sake don't touch any buttons except the ones I have shown you, otherwise you may be left with a blank screen, a wasted journey and a lot of embarrassment.' James had also written simplified instructions on a little card which I had concealed in my left hand.

It all worked. Jon Scoffield and Tony Wolfe must have liked what they saw and realised that, properly mounted and with superior electronics, it could have possibilities.

Arriving home, I found James, his brother, Toby, and their grand-mother playing poker – the game which James shrewdly says is the only way some people can be certain of getting nothing for something.

As I came into the room he asked, 'Did they throw you out, Pomps?'

'Deal me in.'

'Yes, but what happened? Did you get thrown out?'

'No. They were very nice.'

'Great. They bought it.'

'No. But they were smiling when I left.'

'That could have been relief.'

'No, they seemed to like it. Obviously they must have discussed it after I'd gone.'

Some days later I had a call from Nottingham, asking me to demon-strate it again. We fixed a date. This time I was taking no chances; I asked our daughter, Susan, if she could get a day off for James so that he could accompany me. I wanted him to take the worry of working the computer off my shoulders and, as he is the co-inventor, he should have been there to answer questions and discuss any suggested alterations.

James went off to school to ask if he could have a day off; he got it; they were very understanding.

James thought, as I did, that we would be showing the demonstration to Jon Scoffield and Tony Wolfe, and no one else. He was nervous enough at the thought of just meeting them. On the way to Nottingham he ques-tioned me carefully about both of them. It was his first venture into the serious competitive world of show business and, as he later remarked, it had nothing to do with what he was learning at school.

As we were setting up the computer and keyboard in Central's building, a canteen lady came into the room with about ten cups and saucers and flasks of tea and coffee, and laid them all out carefully on the table so that she did not interfere with our complexity of wires.

'Pomps!' said James, with anxiety showing in his voice, 'I thought you said we were seeing only Mr Scoffield and Mr Wolfe.'

'Yes. However, it does seem as if a few more people might be coming to see it. Don't worry, they won't shoot us. Central have never had anyone shot yet. If they had, it would have been reported in the newspapers.' James didn't smile. 'The worst they can do is throw us out. They'll let us finish the coffee first.' To distract him, I added, 'The biscuits look very good.'

'I don't feel like one yet.' He looked scared, and I felt inadequate, overawed by Central's reputation for good shows. We had arrived an hour too early, in order to give us time to get it all ready before the meeting. This we managed to do very quickly, because James knew exactly what he was doing. We spent the rest of the time quaking in our shoes while we waited for people we hadn't bargained for to come to see our presentation.

The door opened and people started drifting in; the invasion was a little scary for us both. But all the newcomers did everything they could to put us at our ease. We even managed to control our nerves sufficiently to eat the biscuits without dropping crumbs on the floor and we drank our coffee without spilling a drop.

The upshot after a few days was that Central TV, after consultations with Enid through me, bought an option on the show. To those outside show business, it might appear that, once an option is sold, the next stage is a series. Unfortunately, in real life this is not so: many stations buy options, and many options are dropped after a few months.

There were many more meetings on the show. Central was now concentrating it into their Birmingham studio. There were alterations and there were suggestions. James and I had nervous moments when we thought the option would be dropped, but fortunately it was always renewed. If it had been dropped there was a German production house that wanted it. A Swedish TV station would also take it, and there was always the USA. However, although I think jingoism dangerous, I still wanted it to start in the UK. We were also both in the lucky position of being fully occupied with other things, so we did not suffer as we would have done if this had been our first and only idea.

As soon as I heard that the first twelve video recordings were to be made in September, I knew we would be all right. September is always all right.

Unless you have lived through the painful birth of a TV series, it is impossible to guess at the amount of work behind it. Most of the work is absorbed in the attention to minute detail, with the producer in the middle making sure that the various groups of specialists involved are aware of what others are doing. Added to that, the show which is the end product must look simple. People watch TV to relax, not to be bothered with wondering what the hell we are up to. Utter simplicity is essential, however complicated it may be to achieve. (The following description of how a TV game-show is mounted is of course simplified).

For the station involved, it is a most costly business and the producer has to answer to the Head of the Department. That makes him responsible for the cost of everything, from overtime down to the last paint brush. In practice these items are accounted for by the various departments he uses. But his is still the head on the block if the price goes over the top. He must also make sure that the various departments called upon – lighting, design and many others – all dovetail neatly together.

The producer must cast the presenter. If he makes a mistake here, the viewer will switch off. The producer has to find someone who will appeal to the viewer, look confident, make the game look easy, explain what he or she is doing without a lot of words, put the contestants at their ease without patronising them or making silly jokes, make the studio audience side with the contestants and present the show to the most important people, the viewers, as if the whole thing was being done just for them, which it is. The presenter has to glide smoothly from one section of the game to the next without a hitch, which means having an excellent memory.

The show is only as good as the people in it.

The presenter also has to know the whereabouts of each camera, and they move about. He must know which camera is on, in this he is aided by a light on top of the active camera – but even with this aid he must never for a second look into the wrong camera, or not know which camera is on him.

Unlike an actor, who has learnt his lines, knows where he must stand on the stage for each line, and who is playing with people whose lines and positions he also knows, the host of a game-show has only a rough idea as to the replies that will come from the competitors. He can never be absolutely certain what is coming next. Yet despite that constant uncertainty and inner tension, he must still look relaxed and be totally in control.

The only advantage he has is the dummy run, when he learns which camera is in what position at any given moment. The contestants also go through the dummy run to get an idea of the game. If it's a quiz show with questions, those questions will of course be different from the ones to be used in the broadcast show.

In 'Steal' the objects to be found are different and are in different places. And with 'Steal' there is the added complication of the computer element, designed originally by grandson James Beaumont on a small home computer, and then highly polished by a large Aberdeen Scot, Peter Henderson, on more powerful computers.

'Graphics' is the technical name for computer drawings, and Peter's graphics, which are reproductions of the originals, developed by Central's graphics department, are superb. They are beyond the capabilities of the little computer on which James originally worked it all out.

Come and take a look from behind the scenes and see the first show from the viewpoint of Peter Henderson.

'Steal,' says Peter Henderson, 'Is totally different from anything I have ever done before. Colin Ellis [Technical Co-ordinator] called it a "Programmer's Holiday" but there wasn't much time for donkey rides. There were so many problems to be addressed I was very busy from Day One.

'The main problem in the development of the game was that most of the hardware required was in almost continuous use in the studio, so we had to mount commando-style raids, bringing back as much as we thought we could get away with to our "HQ", where it could be hooked up for testing. This meant that all the game features could not be tested simultaneously. Of course, when we finally had everything set up in the studio for the first time to rehearse, the gremlins came out to play and had to be fixed.'

On the day of the first video recording, the four contestants were sometimes to be found sitting in the hospitality room, practising the little games that feature within the game on small computers, sometimes they were called to the stage to practise it on the set itself. It looked like a series of little sessions, so that the contestants could get accustomed to it all. But it was also valuable to the presenter and to the director, Jenny Dodd, who, although she had planned and plotted her camera positions in advance, could still find some extra camera positions and angles. The person in charge of lighting also gets a second chance to make sure that no unexpected shadow obscures something.

Whenever possible – as there are no real breaks, just moments that are not quite so hectic as others – the patient stills photographer would grab someone to be photographed for a later press release.

The contestants themselves do not just arrive by chance. There are many victims offering themselves for public torture on television every day. These are then auditioned. The boys and girls who audition them in the first instance are looking for a combination of looks and quick reflexes. The would-be contestants who thinks he or she is the comedian of the year and comes back with 'funny remarks' is almost always rejected because there is something phoney about a non-professional trying to be funny. It may not show in his or her home, but the camera and studio conditions make that person an embarrassment to him or herself, to the studio and to the viewer. Many a rejected contestant should be grateful that he or she was never allowed to appear.

By the time you read this, the first twelve 'Steal' shows, produced by Dennis Liddington, will have been transmitted.

If you've seen it, you will know that it is the show in which contestants have to remember the contents of sixteen squares which are rotated after they've been memorised. It ends up with a spoof bank-robbery, during which the final contestant has to be careful not to step on a policeman.

While I was up in Birmingham for Central Independent Television, I went back to Dudley, eight miles away, on Tuesday, 13 September 1989 to see again the house where I was born. I should have telephoned first to ask if I might visit: I didn't know the phone number. I should have written: I could have done, as it is an address I will never forget, but I knew that a letter would commit me to going there, and I was frightened of my emotions. At the last minute, courage could fail me and the visit would be out of the question.

It was an odd feeling, remembering that I had left the industrial Midlands forty-seven years earlier to seek the 'glamour' of show business in London. Yet here I was, only a few minutes from the studio of Central Independent Television, where I had started probably the last series of my life. I had gone full circle.

The country lane which ran past the house is now a wide road leading to the Birmingham–Wolverhampton main road. Buses ply back and forth. Half of Mrs Over-the-road's monstrous Victorian mansion and much of her garden have been shaved away to make room for the lane, now widened to a large road. Our draughty old Georgian house, built by my great-grandfather, now has double yellow lines outside it.

The stables are still there; it was interesting to see that the huge stable-doors leading from the road to the stable-yard, are still too heavy for their hinges, making them drag on the ground. As I passed them, I wondered what went on inside; there would certainly not be any horses. The three rooms there are probably garages. And up in the loft above there could not be a trace of the sweets Hugh and I hid after we had found a ten shilling note and bought all the forbidden sweets we could.

I left the car and walked from the stables to stand on the steps outside the front door. I was just about to ring the bell when I was joined by a lady, Mrs Burn, who was coming back from her lunch. I explained my mission; she understood at once and asked me in. This was very kind of her as, whatever the business conducted in the house, I could tell they were very occupied, and she, I realised, was a partner. No, they were not accountants, as I had heard. They are solicitors.

Inside the house where I was born, the lovely rooms have been turned into neat offices. Strip-lighting hangs from the ceilings on chains. The old pantry seems full of word processors. The bedroom I was born in is not recognisable at all. It is filled with administrative equipment, calculators and more word processors.

Curiously, the old bell-pull handles are still in the walls of most of the rooms. They no longer work, the wires having rotted away; and the bells themselves, which hung in a row high up on the kitchen wall with the name of the appropriate room under each one in gold leaf on red glass, have long since been removed.

I was not supposed to go into the kitchen as a child, but we ordered the *Daily Mirror* for the maids, and I liked it better than *The Times*. It had to be read every day because of the strip cartoon with its dog, Pip, its penguin, Squeak and Wilfred, the rabbit.

But now even the kitchen has gone. That large stone-floored room with its enormous and impossible black-leaded range is also an office. There was therefore no permanently steaming one-gallon black kettle sitting on the hob, and no kitchen clock ticking comfortingly over the high mantel-piece. There is no kitchen now, except for a bit of a place upstairs in the corner of one of the maid's bedrooms, where a snack meal can be prepared or cups of tea made.

It brought a lump to my throat to imagine dog Sago running around. A reception desk is at the far end of the hall, close to where the huge cupboard once stood, in which Sago's lead was kept. He always got excited if anyone even touched that cupboard, because he thought it a prelude to a walk.

My playroom, also full of office equipment, still has the mantelpiece made from polished stone, locally quarried, known as Dudley Locust because it is packed with the fossils of trilobites, one of which still looks like a face with a beard. The scratches I made with a nail to make it look like Father Christmas are still there today; it looks just the same. I can see the eyes and mouth where I inflicted them with that nail in 1926. They don't look nearly as good as they did when I was six. But, as Picasso said, children can always draw better than adults.

I imagined I heard the echo of Nanny Bags' voice as it came back over the years. I could picture her again in her blue uniform with its heavily starched white breast-plate, like a galleon in full sail, and I could almost smell the disinfectant and peppermints as I remembered her telling Father what I had done. I imagined them down in the hall, and I, listening in terror over the balustrades, frighteningly high above that stone floor. Father came slowly up the long stairs to look at what I had done to the mantelpiece. I was frightened, so it was a relief to see him smile as he turned and said. 'Don't do it again!' That time I was not whipped.

Only the top of the garden has been turned into a car-park. A few apple trees may still exist beyond the tarmac. They grew only cookers, so in season we had apple pie every day; this continued for weeks into the winter as Tonks, the gardener, in his greasy flat, brown cap, took seemingly endless days picking and wrapping the fruit in newspapers, to lay carefully on the shelves in a small windowless room known as the store cupboard. Mother always held the keys; she said this was only fair, as it prevented the servants being tempted to steal.

Tonks, with his gnarled brown hands, dirty finger-nails, torn clothes and an upside-down walnut pipe in his mouth, would make bows and arrows from string and garden cane for my sister and me. I wonder now why he did this, when we had so much and he had so little. His pipe seemed to grow from his face; it was as much a part of him as were his ears, and it never left his mouth, except when one of the maids came down the garden with a chipped white-enamel mug of tea for him. Father frequently complained that he spent all day smoking in the greenhouse instead of getting on with his work.

The dark windowless room where the apples were stored in the winter held other mysteries, such as eggs 'put down' in large brown ceramic vessels, filled with isinglass to preserve them. Later they would come out for our cook, Gladys, to bake into fruit cakes, which were always soggy in the middle and so hard on the outside that there was a danger of breaking any tooth that bit on a solid, jet-black, pebble-like currant. I could almost hear Mother's voice again, saying, 'But you must finish your cake. It's home-made.'

Outside the store room, in the passage that ran past what had once been the kitchen, I looked up to see the half-dozen meat hooks, hanging to this day like stalactites from the ceiling. In the old days, someone would climb the steps and hang game on them; it was usually pheasant or grouse, but occasionally venison, a dry and tough meat if not properly hung and marinated.

The stone scullery, with the deep well and the bake oven for bread, was not sealed off.

The far end of the garden had been allowed to run wild, so Sago's grave is still undisturbed. It would have been morbid of me to go down and look. I didn't have the courage; but I know exactly where he is. I was afraid Mrs Burn might sense the sadness of my nostalgia. You can close your eyes to reality but not to emotions.

I love that house, and I agree with Jane Austen, who wrote that one does not love a place the less for having suffered in it.

Seeing it all again made me look back and wonder, given the same start and knowing what I know today, what would be changed. Probably nothing.

Cambridge might have offered more wisdom or usefulness. Inventing a few game-shows is probably not as useful as designing a bridge, digging a drain or healing the sick; but it might be . . . Making people laugh is good for them, and it is possible that more laughter would make the world a happier place. So the answer to the question depends on what is meant by 'useful'. Perhaps further education would have answered that one.

Socrates said that the unexamined life is not worth living. Perhaps that was just his way of letting us know he had examined his life and found it had been useful.

Father's words came back over the decades as I went, for the first time in many years, into his consulting-room, now with its battery of office machinery. He had said that the nine o'clock news was read by actors and as actors can't be trusted, it would be better to wait to see what *The Times* would say tomorrow. So, from, his point of view, I was associating with untrustworthy people. He was wrong. They are my friends.

Pleasure is not something we can go out and buy, beg or steal. Pleasure can be found only by giving it. That is what marriage is for. That is what children, grandchildren and friends are for. That is what my 'inventions' have been for.

There's just a hint of more cartoon sparkle glittering about and a possibility of at least one more show. There's a chance that the viewers will be entertained by it if . . .